MORAVIAN WOMEN'S MEMOIRS

Women and Gender in North American Religions

Amanda Porterfield and Mary Farrell Bednarowski, Series Editors

Other titles in the Women and Gender in North American Religions series:

Moon Sisters, Krishna Mothers, Rajneesh Lovers: Women's Roles in New Religions.
 Susan J. Palmer
A Still Small Voice: Women, Ordination, and the Church. Frederick W. Schmidt, Jr.

MORAVIAN WOMEN'S MEMOIRS

Their Related Lives, 1750–1820

Translated and with an Introduction by

Katherine M. Faull

Syracuse University Press

First Edition 1997
09   10   11   12   13   8   7   6   5   4

Some material in this book appeared previously in articles by Katherine Faull in "The American *Lebenslauf:* Women's Autobiography in Eighteenth-Century Moravian Bethlehem," *Yearbook of German-American Studies* 27 (1992): 23–48; and in "Faith and Imagination: Nikolaus Ludwig von Zinzendorf's Anti-Enlightenment Philosophy of Self," *Bucknell Review* 38, no. 2: 23–56. Use with permission by the Society for German-American Studies and *Bucknell Review,* respectively.

The paper used in this publication meets the minimum requirements of American National Standard for Information Sciences—Permanence of Paper for Printed Library Materials, ANSI Z39.48-1984. ∞™

Library of Congress Cataloging-in-Publication Data

Moravian women's memoirs : their related lives, 1750–1820 / [edited
by] Katherine M. Faull.
p.   cm.—(Women and gender in North American religions)
Includes bibliographical references and index.
ISBN 0-8156-2689-4 (alk. paper).—ISBN 0-8156-0397-5 (pbk. :
alk. paper)
1. Moravian women—Pennsylvania—Bethlehem—Biography.
2. Moravians—Pennsylvania—Bethlehem—Biography.   3. Spiritual
biography.   4. Bethlehem (Pa.)—History—18th century.   I. Faull,
Katherine M.   II. Series.
BX8591.M67   1996
284'.6'092274827—dc20
[B]   96-21261

To my parents, Peter and Inge Faull

KATHERINE M. FAULL is associate professor of German at Bucknell University, Lewisburg, Pennsylvania. She is the editor of *Anthropology and the German Enlightenment: Perspectives on Humanity*.

CONTENTS

ILLUSTRATIONS

Following page 64

PREFACE

In 1727, just before Anna Fenstermacher departed for North America, her mother took her to one side and told her not to concern herself with gaining great wealth in the New World but rather to look after her children and to watch out for snakes. She then added: "I have heard for a long time that a congregation of God is to be founded over the ocean, just as it was in the Apostles' time, and when you hear about it . . . join with them. They think much of the sufferings of Christ; they move from place to place, but when only three are gathered together, remain with them, for it must be again as it was in the beginning." With these words she bade farewell to her daughter.

This book is about that "congregation of God," known today in the English-speaking world as the Moravian Church and, in Germany, as the *Brüdergemeine, Brüder-Unität,* or *Herrnhuter.* Claiming its prereformation origins in the present-day Czech republic, the Moravian Church was "renewed" in the early eighteenth century by Count Nicolaus Ludwig von Zinzendorf. Groups of peasants, artisans, and craftsmen, mostly Protestant, flocked to the Moravian settlements in Germany, seeking a different kind of spiritual life. In the major Moravian settlements of Herrnhut and Herrnhaag, they found freedom to practice their religion in a community designed to foster individual spirituality and communal faith. As these settlements grew, mission congregations were set up in the Caribbean, Greenland, South Africa, North America and elsewhere. One of the consequences of this world-wide Moravian mission was that a simple woman, like Anna Fenstermacher, could find herself transported from rural Germany to the forests of Pennsylvania within the space of only a few years.

This volume is made up of the autobiographical writings of thirty of the women who lived in the major North American Moravian settlement of Bethlehem, Pennsylvania, at varying points in the eighteenth century. What follows are their memoirs, fascinating documents that contain insights into the lives of the women and men who lived in the Moravian communities in North America. They are kept in the Moravian Archives in Bethlehem,

Pennsylvania, and, until now, have been available only to scholars who can read the archaic German script in which they were written over two centuries ago.

For the last five years, I have transcribed and translated these memoirs, convinced of their great value both to the general reading public and to specialists in a variety of fields—social history, history of religion, women's studies, and literature. For these Moravian memoirs provide not only some of the earliest examples of women's autobiography in North America but their authors are also from a far more diverse social and ethnic background than the contemporary Colonial Quaker or Puritan journals. The extraordinary Moravian custom, which required that each member of the community should write a memoir, ensured, for example, that nearly all women, whether slave or duchess, whether German or African, wrote or dictated a memoir. The authors represented in this collection are predominantly either German or Colonial American, but memoirs are also included by women from Africa (1), Moravia (2), Antigua (1), France (2), and Great Britain (1). None of the authors in the volume come from the nobility but are rather from peasant or artisan families. And all of these women left behind them a memoir *(Lebenslauf)*.

I have decided to translate and publish only women's memoirs for several reasons. Personal documents by members of any intentional community, whether religious or secular, are particularly hard to find, especially in large enough numbers for the researcher to be able to gain any insight into its internalized world. It is also especially difficult to find such memoirs from the eighteenth century. When such memoirs do exist in the public sphere, they are invariably those written by men, and then they are invariably by the founders and leaders of that community. To date few memoirs by women from a religious community, such as the Moravians, have been published. However, it is invariably a woman's experience that acts as a litmus test for the emancipatory claims of the founders of these alternatives to mainstream society. The record of a woman's experience can expose the nexus of forces that meet in her everyday life, that is, the ideological forces that shape the limits of her existence, the actual, physical reality of her work, her place within the family and social structure.

These Moravian women's memoirs reveal the intersection of the private and the public spheres of their lives. They are records of their spiritual paths in a world that in most cases challenged the bounds of knowledge inherited from their parents. However, whatever private insights these memoirs afforded the writers they were written to be shared with the congregation as a public relation of the author's spiritual and secular path through life. These memoirs formed part of the discourse of faith within the Moravian church. The memoir was a form with which all Moravians were familiar, either because they had already related their lives or else because they had heard the lives of many others related to them. Although the Moravian memoir later became a highly stylized form, these earlier documents reveal what the writer thought about herself, what she chose to include in her account of her life, which events she considered to be significant, and which she chose to omit.

Each memoir is an individual's story. The experiences each woman describes are shaped by the external circumstances of her life: life in Colonial America, or a quasi-feudal German state, or eighteenth-century London. In addition, the description of her spiritual life, her relationship to Christ, her understanding of her individual place in God's order, also was molded by the theological concepts of the founder of the Moravian Church, Count Nicholas von Zinzendorf. It was Zinzendorf's Christocentric version of Lutheranism, which stressed salvation through personal faith, that attracted these women to the Moravian *Gemeine* or congregation. The experience of God within a Moravian congregation in the eighteenth century, presented in the form of hymns, poetry, liturgies, homilies, and speeches, was one that personalized the relationship to the Holy Trinity, God the Father, Holy Spirit the Mother, and Christ the Child. Again and again we find the authors of these memoirs employing their own versions of Zinzendorf's vocabulary of faith. In these autobiographical texts, we find women talking about themselves and their lives in a dialogue with Christ (their "best friend") in a way that expands the concepts of both female subjectivity and spiritual autobiography in the eighteenth century.

Although scholars have maintained that it is only men's, and not women's, spiritual autobiographies within the Pietist tradition that include accounts of professional careers and adventures in the outside world, these Moravians memoirs also describe the extraordinary professional freedom afforded the women within the Moravian church in the eighteenth century.[1] These memoirs open up a whole new panorama of experiences of how one particular set of women lived in Colonial America. As we will see, it was not only Bethlehem's communal structure between 1742–62 that affected the shape women's lives could take but also the implementation of Zinzendorf's theology of a gender- and age-specific spirituality that necessitated women assuming spiritual leadership within the church.

Technical Information about This Edition

Through the transcription and translation process, I have developed the following editorial principles. Included in this volume are only the narratives of women who lived in Bethlehem at some point during the "General Economy" (1742–62). This decision is based, as stated above, on the need for primary source material by women from the eighteenth century and, second, on the unique structure of the Bethlehem community during that period. This does not mean, however, that the narratives themselves were written during this period but rather that the authors were all present in Bethlehem during the "General Economy." I have also decided to transcribe and translate the version of the memoir which is written in the first-person-singular, as it is this form which corresponds most closely to the author's own memoir before editorial emendation.

I have decided to group the memoirs by "choir." This is in keeping with Zinzendorf's theory that religious experience differs according to age, gender, and marital status. This means that memoirs by married women are in one section, those by single women in another, and those by widows in another. Where the author has referred to specific people and places that are not referred to by other authors, these references are explained either in the prefatory comments which introduce each individual memoir or else in an explanatory footnote. Thus, each memoir within each section is introduced by a brief explanation of historical detail specific to that particular memoir. This introduction is designed to reduce the amount of annotations to the individual memoirs, thereby increasing the ease of reading. Within each section the memoirs are grouped alphabetically.

My translation of each document is into modern English. Where, however, the terminology used is specific to the practices of the Moravian Church, I have used the appropriate corresponding term as found in eighteenth-century English narratives. I also attach a German-English glossary of recurrent terms. Terminology and practices peculiar to the Moravian Church in the eighteenth century as well as frequently cited Moravian settlements and dates are explained there.

Most of these memoirs are framed by the scribe's comments. I have included these comments in the translation as they provide, for example, important information about the dating of the actual memoir. For example, in the scribe's comments the reader learns that Martha Büninger's memoir was composed in 1752, and yet she did not die until 1812. These framework comments also include information about the author of the memoir that she would or could not include herself. On one occasion I have also translated the service during which the memoir was read out to the rest of the congregation.

For the convenience of the reader, an index is provided and a select bibliography of works cited is also to be found at the end of the book.

• • •

The completion of this volume would not have been possible without the assistance of many people in both North America and Europe. I would like to thank the National Endowment for the Humanities for its generous financial support of this project and also Bucknell University for both financial and institutional help. For his invaluable assistance in this project and others I remain indebted to Reverend Vernon Nelson of the Moravian Archives in Bethlehem, Pennsylvania. His gentle encouragement and wise counsel have helped this work towards its completion. I should also like to thank Janet Halton of Moravian Church House, London, and Ingeborg Baldauf of the Archiv der Brüder-Unität, Herrnhut, Germany, for their help and guidance. Much in the initial stages of this project was moved along by my capable research assistants, Bettina Jaeger, Claudia Knödler, and Dora Czike, who listened diligently to hours of Moravian German and typed my dictation into intelligible text. I also owe a great debt to Dr. Colin Podmore of London for his invaluable suggestions, both editorial and linguistic, without which the present work would, to a great extent, lack historical authority and verbal polish. For their meticulous reading of the final manuscript I thank Peter Vogt and Dr. Ruth Drucilla Richardson. For my initial tutoring in deciphering German script I thank Reverend Nelson and Dr. Lothar Madeheim of the Moravian Archives in Bethlehem, Pennsylvania, and my mother, Ingeborg Faull. To my mother and my father, Peter Faull, I owe thanks and love for instilling in me from an early age a passion for stories and language and for promoting my facility to create both. Finally, I thank my friend Gloria without whose love and assistance I could never have finished this volume.

The preparation of this work was made possible in part by a grant from the National Endowment for the Humanities, an independent federal agency.

Lewisburg, Pennsylvania   Katherine M. Faull
January 1996

INTRODUCTION
The Moravians

In 1740, Moravian settlers arrived at the forks of the Delaware River in Northampton County, Pennsylvania, to found a religious community in North America. For more than the next hundred years, this community was open only to members of the Moravian Church, and, furthermore, for the first twenty-one years, it was run on communal principles.

The Ancient Unity of Brethren

The Moravian Church claims its origins in the Unity of the Brethren or Unitas Fratrum, a Protestant church founded in 1457 by followers of Jan Hus (1373–1415), the Czech religious reformer.[1] Almost one hundred years before Martin Luther led the Protestant revolt in Germany, Jan Hus was executed in Constance for his protests against the authority of Rome. In his work, *De Ecclesia*, Hus had argued for the institution of Christ as the only true head of the church and against the need for cardinals and the Pope. After his execution, Hus's followers back in Prague divided themselves into two groups: the Utraquists, who were more inclined towards compromise with the Roman church, especially in matters concerning communion, and the Taborites, so named after the mountain near Prague, who were separatists. The Utraquists joined with the Catholics and succeeded in suppressing the Taborite movement. The Brethren, however, joined neither group. They wanted neither allegiance with the Catholic Church nor did they wish to take up arms for their faith. Rather they existed both within and without the Utraquists and the Taborites.

In 1457, the Unitas Fratrum, or Jednota Bratrska, was founded and settled the village of Kunwald in Eastern Bohemia. Here these early Protestants lived a life modeled after that of the early Christians, living in poverty, with patience, and loving their enemies. These Brethren took as the governing principles of their settlement the following: the authority of the

Bible as the only source of Christian doctrine, public worship in accordance with Scriptural teaching and modeled after the apostolic church, the celebration of Holy Communion in faith without an attempt to explain it in authoritative human terms, and a godly life understood as an essential part of a saving faith. Unfortunately, their peace lasted only a few years as the nobleman, George Podiebrad, on whose estate they had settled, now had ambitions to become Emperor of the Holy Roman Empire. The presence of these heretics on his estate greatly lessened his chances of election and so, in 1461, the persecutions against the Brethren began again and continued almost to their extinction in the Thirty Years War.

In the last quarter of the sixteenth century, there was a brief respite in the repression of the Brethren. It has been claimed that when Rudolph II ascended to the throne of the Holy Roman Empire in 1576, over two-thirds of Bohemia had gone over to Protestantism. Rudolph II recognized the strength of the Brethren's movement and, although heavily influenced by the Jesuits (the sworn enemies of the Brethren), he signed a letter of majesty granting liberty to the Protestants throughout Bohemia. For the next twenty five years, Brethren schools flourished, the Bible was translated into Czech (the Kralice Bible) and sold at a price that ordinary people could afford, and the Brethren's hymnbooks were repeatedly published in cheap editions.

This period of unrestricted activity did not last long however. In 1602, the Jesuits persuaded the Emperor to ban the Brethren once again, to have their ministers imprisoned and their books burned. The Protestant noblemen of Bohemia rebelled and demanded that the Emperor hold to the Confession of 1575 by which he was bound to guarantee religious freedom in Bohemia. After years of prevarication on the part of the Emperor and threats of war from the Protestant nobleman, Rudolph finally agreed to assure the Brethren religious liberty. It seemed as though the days of persecution were over. However, with the death of Rudolph in 1612, the political situation changed once again. His successor, Ferdinand, archduke of Styria, was a fanatical Catholic and determined to rid Bohemia of Protestants. Thus began the Thirty Years War.

The Brethren fled to Poland and established their headquarters at Lissa, the birthplace of one of the most famous theologians of the Ancient Brethren, Jan Comenius (1592–1670), who had written some of the most influential works of the Brethren on education and faith. The Polish welcomed the Protestants and once again a period of relative freedom began. However, with the close of the war, two events occurred that threatened the safety of the Brethren. First, the Catholic Bishop of Lissa demanded the return of the Brethrens buildings to the Catholic Church. And then the King of Sweden failed in his attempt to overtake Poland for the Protestant church, leading to a vicious backlash on the part of the Catholics. The Brethren were once again persecuted and hounded out of Lissa. The closing years of the seventeenth century and the beginning of the eighteenth found the Brethren almost completely decimated. Small pockets of secret communities existed in Poland, Moravia, and Bohemia, but they seemed to be on the brink of extinction. It was at this point that Count Nicholas Ludwig von Zinzendorf (1700–1760) entered the history of the Church of the United Brethren.

During the years of persecution one of the ways in which the Brethren had maintained their faith was through itinerant preachers, the most famous of whom was Christian David (1690–1751). It was he who, concerned with the plight of the Moravians in Bohemia and Moravia, pleaded with Count Zinzendorf to provide the Brethren with safe refuge on his estate in Berthelsdorf in Upper Saxony. Zinzendorf, who had been raised a Pietist, did not object. In 1722, Moravians arrived in Berthelsdorf and immediately began to fell trees in the nearby forest to build houses and thus founded their new community, Herrnhut.

Count Nicholas Ludwig von Zinzendorf (1700–1760)

Count Nicholas Ludwig von Zinzendorf was born in Dresden, capital of Saxony, in 1700 (illus. 2). He was a descendent of Protestant Austrian nobility and was raised by his grandmother, Henriette Catharine von Gersdorf, after his father's death and his mother's remarriage. The influence of his grandmother on his religious awakening and subsequent treatment of women often has been cited.[2] His grandmother, an educated and talented woman, exercised great influence on the politics and pietism of the day. Philipp Jakob Spener, August Hermann Francke, Karl Hildebrand Canstein, and Paul Anton, the major proponents of the Halle school of Pietism, were all welcome guests at her castle of Großhennersdorf.[3] Zinzendorf was educated at Francke's school in Halle, where he defended himself against the harsh treatment by teachers and other pupils by retreating into prayer. At the age of fifteen, he and another young count, Frederick de Watteville, organized a society called "The Order of the Grain of Mustard Seed," in which members swore an oath of allegiance to Christ and vowed to live honest, upright lives. Zinzendorf's interest in mission work was also awakened at Francke's school in Halle. It was there he first came into contact with mission work through the reports of two missionaries, Ziegenbalg and Plütschau, whom the Halle Pietist educator Augustus Hermann Francke had sent to Tranquebar.[4]

In 1716, Zinzendorf was sent to Wittenberg, the bastion of Lutheran Orthodoxy, to study law, although his interests and passion grew more and more to be the study of theology. It was especially on the customary "grand tour," taken after he had finished his studies, that spiritual questions became paramount. During this time, around 1720, he met with various Church leaders of different denominations, including Cardinal Noailles in Paris and the Archbishop of Canterbury, in his attempt to develop an ecumenical vision of the Christian church. Even though Zinzendorf was forced as a nobleman to take a position as counselor at Court in Dresden, he desired to implement some of his early ideas on faith and religious community.

The Establishment of Herrnhut

It was shortly after his return from his European tour that Zinzendorf received Christian David's request for asylum for the Brethren. Although initially merely interested in the lives of these settlers, Zinzendorf quickly recognized the opportunity the Brethren offered him to put some of his ideas on faith into practice. As word of the sanctuary spread back to the Brethren's hidden communities in Moravia and Bohemia, where some of them were in danger of being imprisoned (see, for example, the memoir of Rosina Stoll) or actually already in prison, more and more of the Brethren asked for permission to move to Herrnhut. In addition to the members of the "Ancient" church, as it was now beginning to be called, other Protestants who were facing poverty, persecution, or spiritual crisis also applied to join (see, for example, the memoir of Susanne Nixdorf) and came to Herrnhut. Clearly, the Brethren's original intention to build their own exclusive community in a safe place was not viable. Quickly, disagreements broke out as to the shape Herrnhut was to assume. Was it to be a community after the fashion of the Brethren's settlements in Kunwald and Lissa or a new kind of settlement, whose shape would be determined not only by the Ancient Brethren but also by the newcomers? In 1727, Zinzendorf heard of the disagreements taking place on his estate and returned from court. Upon his return he drew up a document, *Manorial Injunctions and Prohibitions* (May 12, 1727), which was designed to regulate civil life in Herrnhut. All the residents were asked to sign and then, soon after, he drew up the *Brotherly Agreement*, which regulated the religious practices of the inhabitants of Herrnhut.[5] That August, the inhabitants of Herrnhut and Berthelsdorf joined together for a communion service at the parish church of Berthelsdorf. It is said that such a presence of the spirit was felt that all who were there shed tears and felt themselves united in love and faith. Until this very day, August 13 has been celebrated as the birthday of the Renewed Church (called in America the Moravian Church).

It was also in the summer of 1727 that Zinzendorf actually sat down and read Jan Comenius's *Ratio Disciplinae,* a work that described the history and principles of the Church to which the Brethren who had come to live on his estate belonged. Zinzendorf suddenly saw the parallels between his own thought on community and church order and that of the Brethren, and he began his active leadership of the religious community at Herrnhut.

Zinzendorf's Theology

By the mid-1740s, Zinzendorf and the "Renewed Unitas Fratrum" had become a well-known and influential group in eighteenth-century Germany, Great Britain, and Pennsylvania. Called one of the most "fertile" German theologians between Martin Luther and Friedrich Schleiermacher, Zinzendorf was to challenge and redefine many of the theological concepts of his time.[6]

Zinzendorf was not a formal theologian by any means. He did not write systematic works of theology. Rather he delivered his ideas on religion in the form of sermons and speeches to the Moravian communities throughout Europe and North America. However, in his early pre-Moravian writings, Zinzendorf did attempt to situate his thought within the context of the early Enlightenment. His major endeavor was to enrich and inform the Enlightenment with an understanding of the true nature of religion. In his view, in contrast to the natural theology of the Enlightenment, religion is not associated with reason but answers to the anthropological need pertaining to the well-being and happiness of the human being.

From his earliest days, Zinzendorf conceived of religion not as a matter of reason but rather as a matter of the heart, a *Herzensreligion.* Accordingly, knowledge of God cannot be attained through the exercise of reason but rather through an exercise of feeling and the will. For Zinzendorf, religion was a living "impression" *(Eindruck)* made on the heart and soul *(Gemüt)* of the individual. Zinzendorf did not, however, propose a simple opposition of "feeling" and "reason"; rather, he recognized the power of reason and also its limits. For him, reason belongs to the realm of the practical, it should be implemented to unravel the mechanisms of nature and history. In the realm of religion, it is the heart and soul *(Gemüt)* that act as the organs that distinguish what the human being needs and does not need. Conflicts between feeling and reason only arise when one faculty attempts to exercise its power over the realm of the other, e.g., when reason claims to be able to posit the soul *(anima)* of God.[7] Such knowledge of God can come only through the knowledge of Christ.

One of the most striking features of Zinzendorf's theology is his Christocentrism. Zinzendorf considered Christ to be the total revelation of God to humanity. What humanity can know of God is presented through Christ. In the memoirs this Christocentric understanding of God is evident in the exclusive references to Jesus as Saviour and the remarkable lack of references to God the Father. It is only through Jesus that the Moravian men and women come to a consciousness of their own sense of religion.[8]

Both before and after his contact with the Brethren, Zinzendorf's theology was informed by three major influences: Pietism, Orthodox Lutheranism, and the Enlightenment. Church historians have long argued that the core of Zinzendorf's theology is Luther's teaching of justification by faith, the *Rechtfertigungslehre*[9] (as is evidenced by his argument with John Wesley that led to the split between the Moravian and Methodist churches). As proof of his Lutheran beliefs, Zinzendorf was successfully examined by the theological faculty in Tübingen in 1733 to gain recognition as a Lutheran minister. Indeed, he has been called the renewer not only of the Unity of the Brethren but also of Lutheranism itself.[10]

Zinzendorf owes much also to the traditions of German mysticism and Pietism. Reacting against the danger of sterility or *Zuchttrockenheit* that reigned in Wittenberg's orthodox Lutheranism, Zinzendorf turned to the nonverbal, visual emphasis of mysticism in the work of figures such as Gottfried Arnold (1663–1705), Paul Gerhardt (1607–1676), Franz Buddaeus (1667–1729), Madame Guyon (1648–1717), and Fénélon (1651–1715).[11] He also owed much to the theology and practice of the Pietist thinkers Phillip Jakob Spener (1635–1705) and August Hermann Francke (1663–1727), in particular their emphasis on the personal relationship with Christ. Zinzendorf rejected a complete adherence to either Pietism or mysticism for, although both traditions were indebted to a religion of feeling, Zinzendorf saw the danger that this could result in merely blind enthusiasm *(Schwärmerei)* and thus becoming overly subjective and also inconstant.

Zinzendorf also rejected many of the early Enlightenment notions of ethics. For him, the English moral philosophers (David Hume and John Locke) sought to improve humanity through the imposition of a heathen ethic.[12] Ethical behavior, Zinzendorf argues, comes not from the consideration of an abstract *a priori* principle but rather from the contemplation of the suffering of Christ.[13] Ethical behavior is not an unattainable philosophical ideal of human potentiation but rather the reattainment of true humanity was made possible by the incarnation of God in Christ.[14] The understanding of human needs and behavior is not achieved through the study of humanity apart from Christ, as was the case with most Enlightenment thinkers, but rather through the examination of Christ as human.

This reliance on the contemplation of Christ's suffering is evident in the memoirs where the women speak of seeing the stigmata, or the Side-Wound, of the crucified Christ. For example, when faced with a crisis of faith, Eva Lanius describes Christ as walking towards her and allowing her "to cast a believing glance at His meritorious sufferings."[15] Margarethe Edmonds closes her memoir with the words, "I hope that my dear Savior will keep me in Him and in His wounds and in His dear Congregation, and always wash me in His costly blood until I receive the grace to see Him face to face and to kiss His pierced feet."[16]

The authors of the memoirs also stress the representations of Christ as friend and bridegroom. Benigna Zahm writes of First Communion as an experience of "the indescribably great grace of enjoying, for the first time in Holy Communion, the body and blood of my Friend who was tormented for me."[17] Once she has joined the Girls' Choir she spends hours in the company of "my invisible but inwardly near Friend."[18] Johanetta Ettwein describes how even when her faith was weak, "my best friend did not leave me."[19] Zinzendorf argued that seeing Christ as "best friend" or "eternal husband" allows men and women to be presented with the model of God in Man: "In a word, as soon as we regard the Saviour, everything which we seek in morality is found in his humanity."[20] The fact of Christ's own "natural" human state shows humanity that it is possible to live a holy life in this mortal, corporeal world[21] (illus. 3).

The "Choir" System

Zinzendorf argued that the Congregation or *Gemeine,* the Moravian system of living together in community, best supported the need of men and women to experience God's grace. The form this took in the Moravian communities was that of the "Choir" system. In his *Berliner Reden* (1738), Zinzendorf stated quite clearly that "the difference in class, temperament, life, age all make an immediate difference to the way in which the individual serves the Savior."[22] And these differences were reflected in the Moravian custom of living in Choirs. Choirs were groups of Moravians who lived

together in units based not on their degree of piety but rather according
to their gender, age, and marital status. The Choir structure recognized
that Creation, redeemed by Christ, is blessed and to maintain the natural
order is the way best suited for the mutual development of religious consciousness. Accordingly, the community was divided into bands of people
of like age, marital status, and sex. The choir system emerged in February
1728 when a group of unmarried men moved to their own dormitory in
Herrnhut. Here the residents lived, worshipped, and ate together. In 1730,
the unmarried women made the same move and founded the first Single
Sisters' House. Eventually, there existed choirs of boys, girls, single men,
single women, married men, and married women, widows, and widowers.
This abundance of distinct groups of the faithful gave rise to a multiplicity
of religious services as each group celebrated its own communion and
also instituted more informal forms of worship, such as the *pedelavium*
(footwashing), lovefeast, singing hour, the *Chorviertelstunde* (Choir quarter
hour), and cup of covenant. The musical and liturgical culture of Moravian
Herrnhut began to flourish.

    News of the success of Herrnhut as a religious community soon spread
throughout Germany and the rest of Europe. Moravian "Diaspora" workers
could be found in Great Britain, Russia, Poland, Holland, Sweden, the
Baltic states, and Switzerland. These lay persons, whose task it was to go
forth and preach the Gospel, were given specific instructions not to evangelize only for the Moravian church but rather to awaken souls that were in
need of Christ's salvation.[23] Diaspora workers succeeded in attracting many
people to the Moravian church (see, for example, Maria Reitzenbach's
memoir in which Br. Michael Graf visits her after soldiers have brought
Moravian texts to her home town of Lauffen). The success of the Diaspora
was followed up by the establishment of more Moravian communities
throughout Europe, some in the form of exclusive communities (such as
Herrnhaag and Herrndyk) and some as congregations within a city (such
as in London and Berlin). Those women who joined the Moravian church
in the 1740s were able to move from one community to another, if their
"Plan" so allowed, granting them a mobility quite unique for the eighteenth century (see, for example, the memoirs of Anna Piesch, Anna
Hasse, and Christiana Detmers).

The Establishment of Bethlehem

Work in the mission field had been a central component of the Moravian
Church from its very renewal. From almost the very outset of his involve-

ment with Pietism and the Moravian Brethren, Zinzendorf had been especially interested in the work of missions and the conversion of the
"heathen." It could be said that both the impetus to begin the first Moravian mission on St. Thomas and the stance to be adopted toward the slaves
there came from the same source. In 1731, while on a visit to the court in
Copenhagen, Count Zinzendorf had met Anton, the slave of the director
of the West Indian-Guinea Company, Count von Danneskjold-Laurvig. During this visit, Anton apparently recounted to Zinzendorf the story of his
enslaved sister, who was still living on St. Thomas. He expressed the hope
that if his sister were to hear the Gospel, as she desired, she and many
other slaves there would convert to Christianity.[24]

Listening to Anton's words, Zinzendorf saw how his own desire to start
a mission might be realized. In July 1731, Anton returned to Herrnhut
with Zinzendorf, presented his story to the assembled Moravian congregation there, and suggested some of the problems inherent in such a mission
program. After a year of deliberations in Herrnhut, delays caused by the
Elders' skepticism about the scheme, Martin Dober and another single
brother David Nitschmann (who had met Anton in Copenhagen) were
dispatched to St. Thomas.

The missions in the Caribbean were extremely difficult to maintain, not
least because of the large distances involved between the West Indies and
Germany. Thus, when in 1734, the Trustees of Georgia suggested that
the Moravians secure land for themselves in that colony, the Moravians
responded positively. Not only could they set up a mission center from
which they could supply workers to the West Indies far more quickly
but they could also initiate their mission work among the Creek and Chero-
kee peoples. In 1735, ten men left Gravesend, England, for Savannah,
Georgia, one of whom was Peter Rose, the father of Anna Boehler. However, the settlement did not succeed. Illness and the call to arms against
the Spanish forced the remaining Moravians to leave Georgia and head
for Pennsylvania.

In 1740, the Moravians came to Pennsylvania. The great evangelical
preacher George Whitefield had purchased five thousand acres of land in
the "Forks of the Delaware" where he planned to establish a school for
Black children. He invited the Moravians to come to supervize the building
of the school and they accepted. However, a doctrinal disagreement between Whitefield and the Moravian preacher Peter Boehler caused the
former to order the Moravians to leave his land. After negotiations with
William Allen, the Moravians (who had since been joined by a party from
Europe) purchased five hundred acres of land where the Monocacy Creek

flowed into the Lehigh river. In the early spring of 1741, the first log cabin was erected on the site and that December, during Zinzendorf's visit to America, he named the settlement Bethlehem (illus. 4).

For the next twenty years, during the period known as the "General Economy" (1742–62), Bethlehem was run on communal principles.[25] Unlike Herrnhut, there was no private property; all land, houses, and businesses were communally owned. However, as in Herrnhut, women and men, even when married, were strictly segregated, living in their "choir houses." Children were removed from their parents as soon as they were weaned and then placed in the "Nurserie." However, the communal principles of the "General Economy" were abandoned in 1762 as an economic crisis threatened the Moravian Church in Germany. Families then lived together, and the choir houses remained only for the unmarried and widowed men and women.

This communal structure was implemented during the period of the General Economy for both theological and economic reasons. Bethlehem was founded both as a mission center, consisting of a *(Pilgergemeine)* and also a permanent settlement *(Hausgemeine)*. For the inhabitants of Bethlehem, missionary and spiritual work was of primary importance: their sole purpose for being in Bethelehem was to evangelize in North America and also to act as a base for missionaries to the native North American tribes and the slaves in the West Indies (for example, Anna Hasse is sent with her husband to run the Moravian mission in Carmel, Jamaica). August Gottlieb Spangenberg (1704–1792), one of the most important leaders of the Moravian Church in the eighteenth century, laid out the plan with the following:

1. In America there should be both a Pilgrim Congregation and a Place Congregation; and we should create as many little congregations as is necessary and possible.

2. The Pilgrim Congregation ordinarily meets in Bethlehem but moves around like a cloud of grace wherever the wind of the Lord blows it and makes everything fertile.

3. But in Bethlehem there should also be a House Congregation, to develop the Economy there to serve the Pilgrim congregation and its intentions and to stay on location when the latter is moving around for a while.[26]

Thus the brothers and sisters who stayed in Bethlehem were to sustain those, like Margarethe and Johann Jungmann and Maria and Johannes Rothe, who worked as missionaries to the Delaware Indians. The communal structure of choirs enabled the individual brothers and sisters to devote all their energies to the formation of a steady religious and economic base (the House or Place Congregation) from which satellite mission communities (the Pilgrim Congregations) both in North America and the Caribbean could be supported. All members of the community were fed, clothed, and housed according to their needs and the ability of the General Economy to support them.

The Bethelehem Moravians supported the communal economic system and when asked in the 1750s whether they wanted to set up their own private households there came the resounding reply "No!" As one of the Single Sisters, Marie Minier, answered:

> For 12 years now I have enjoyed the care [of the Economy] and eaten from one bread and been clothed, all of which to this hour has been great and of importance to me. I have given myself once and for all to the Savior with body and soul, possessions and blood and greatly desire to do what I can and accept things the way the Brethren do things, for it is a wonder to me daily that He has maintained so large a community, and we cannot say that we have ever gone without but believed that He would bring us through. I cannot thank the Savior enough that I may enjoy unspeakable grace and happiness that He bestows upon his congregation. This often makes me bend down before him in the dust, red with shame, and I do not wish for anything greater in this world than to pass my life thus in the Congregation until I also as one of the happy souls may pale into death in his arms and bosom.[27]

Marie Minier desired to stay in the choir system because of the relative freedom, security, and independence it afforded single women who otherwise, in the eighteenth century, would have been significantly socially and economically disenfranchised.

Zinzendorf and Women

Zinzendorf's theology had a lasting effect on both the possibilities afforded women in the Moravian communities and also on the forms their sprituality could assume. For example, Zinzendorf considered women to be more receptive vessels for the kind of feeling that constituted his notion of religion. Women, he writes, are more delicate than men because they have been formed not from clay (like Adam) but from flesh and blood.[28] Women are also stronger than men in that they are more faithful, more responsive, and more watchful; these qualities also make them into better nurses or "sickwaiters" than men.[29] However, Zinzendorf argues that this delicate nature also prevents women from being natural leaders and thinkers. Women cannot think as deeply, or broadly, or in such a sustained fashion as men. Rather, Zinzendorf argues, their faithful, simple, childlike side is that which makes it likely that Jesus, when he comes again, will appear first to a woman.[30] These qualities should be encouraged whereas wit, super intelligence, and reasoning should not. A "sister" should have an unaffected, playful, and sensitive nature; she should be like a virgin. In fact, the ideal Moravian woman should reflect the image of both Jesus and Mary in her eyes; she should keep the picture of Jesus always before her as a reminder of his suffering for her, and also a picture of Mary to be reminded of the virgin birth. *Keuschheit* or chastity is of paramount importance throughout the whole of a sister's life. Not only when she is unmarried should she keep herself chaste for Jesus but also after she had married she should maintain the stance of chastity.

If this is the ideal stance of a Moravian sister, what actual roles were open to her in the Moravian communities? According to Otto Uttendörfer, women were fully employed by the Moravian congregations.[31] As can be seen from the memoirs that follow, married and single sisters in Bethlehem worked as nurses, teachers, seamstresses, laundresses, cooks, maids, gardeners, and took care of the livestock.

Women, however, filled not only practical positions. Despite Zinzendorf's claim that women were not natural leaders, they also held positions of spiritual leadership. For example, during the period of the General Economy in Bethlehem, the effects of the choir system were far more drastic on women than on men.[32] Generally, Zinzendorf held that the differing nature of women to men, both physical and spiritual, made it impossible for women's spiritual and pastoral needs to be met by a man.[33] Therefore, each spiritual position within the community had to be filled twice[34] (see illus. 5). This meant that women could attain positions of great authority within the community. Women were to preside over the temporal and spiritual lives of each other from birth to death. Thus, women should be ministered to by women, girls should be taught by women, women should pass the host to women during communion, and women should receive their final blessing before death from a woman. The offices held by women were those of Eldress *(Ältestin)*, Choir Helper *(Chorpflegerin)*, Deaconess *(Diakonin)*, Choir Labouress *(Chorarbeiterin)*, Acolyte *(Acolutha)*, and Servant *(Dienerin)*. Zinzendorf himself described the Eldresses as "the ideal religious personalities, people of God, whom the Saviour chooses."[35] The Helpers (or Labouresses) were those within a Choir to whom the spiritual life of the Choir was entrusted. It was with them that the members of the Choir held their "speakings," conversations about their spiritual state. Zinzendorf described the post of acolyte as being the preparatory step towards spiritual service (the first women were ordained as acolytes in 1745). The role of Deaconess was to be a helper to the priest. At Communion, for example, the Deaconess would hold the bread basket for the Presbyter or minister.

On May 12, 1758, during the ordination ceremony of Nathaniel Seidel (the husband of Anna Seidel, see below) Zinzendorf also ordained three women as priests: Elisabeth Lairiz, Benigna Zinzendorf (illus. 6), and Lenel Vieroth. Zinzendorf says:

> My brethren and sisters, today we have a new phenomenon after 12 years, although it is not new in the Church of God and in our hearts and souls. At first we tried it with two sisters, then with eleven (about whom you will receive more information at a Congregation Day [*Gemeintag*]) who, however, are all involved with such important business that a public account of this honor would not be seemly. Now after 12 years, we are again beginning publicly to ordain women before the Congregation into this state.
>
> The sisters, like the brethren, also have a right to the priesthood; they have among themselves and in their capacity the first three ranks of the congregation's offices. The rank of Elder in the congregation is an honor, which is bestowed according to one's years, but the priesthood is motivated by a certain necessity of religious office. It is supposed thereby that no-one receives this honor for whom it would not be suitable among her people.[36]

In 1758, fourteen women in all were ordained.[37] After Zinzendorf's death in 1760 the practice was not repeated.

One of those women who had probably been ordained a priest in 1746 was Nathaniel Seidel's wife, Anna Johanna Seidel (1726–1788). Her life provides an excellent example of the extent of professional freedom afforded single and married women. Before she married, Anna accompanied Count Zinzendorf on his travels to the Moravian communities in Europe and North America. At the age of nineteen she formed the Single Sisters' choir in London (and learned English), and at the age of twenty-one she was made the General Eldress of all Single Sisters' choirs. In 1752, she traveled to North America and visited the various missions and congregations. After a year, she returned to England and then Germany. In 1760, upon the death of Zinzendorf and his second wife, Anna Nitschman, Anna Seidel's life changed completely. She writes: "After the going home of these two dear people, I now thought to dedicate my life completely to my dear Single Sisters' Choirs and to apply double faithfulness and hard work to them. But the Saviour had arranged things quite differently and gave me a quite different field to plough."[38] Anna is instructed to go to North America and assist with the transformation of the General Economy in Bethlehem. In order to accomplish this, however, the lot has decided that she is to marry Bishop Nathaniel Seidel.

Like everything else within the Moravian church in the eighteenth century, marriage was entered into not because of personal preference but according to the needs of the community. If a Single Sister or Brother wished to be considered for marriage, their names would be put forward to the Elders by the Helpers of their respective choirs. Couples from within the Moravian Church were then selected by means of the Lot. The Lot was asked whether the Saviour felt that Brother X should marry Sister Y. Prior to the Lot being asked, the Sister was also asked whether she was willing to marry. She did retain the right to refuse the suggested Brother.

In response to the decision of the lot, Anna Seidel writes: "I was happy to go to America, but to enter into marriage! That cost me dear and there was much bitter pain until I was able to give up my will to the intention of the Saviour."[39] At the age of thirty-four, having held the highest position of authority over the Single Sisters on all continents, Anna agrees to marry and, with her husband, take over the administration of the Bethlehem community. As one of the strongest proponents of the Choir system, especially with its positive emancipatory effects for single women, Anna is disappointed to see the effect of the changes on the Single Sisters.

In 1762, the first task was the turn around of the communal economy, which was a difficult job that caused my dear husband and me many a sleepless night. But the Saviour stood by us with His grace even under these difficult circumstances.

For the first few years I stood in true heartfelt trust with my dear Single Sisters' Choir here. My being married did not disturb either them or me, and through all of this I would gladly have stayed with them with all my heart. But the change in their Labouresses also caused a change in this, which pained me greatly, but with time I learned to fit in with this also through the support of the dear Saviour.[40]

Anna sadly recognizes that women's previous economic equality cannot be maintained within the new nuclear household structure.

Although the possibility of women's spiritual leadership within the Con-

gregation might seem to indicate that Zinzendorf was an early advocate of
women's equal rights with men, it was far more a by-product of Zinzendorf's strict segregation of the sexes and the notion that each sex, race,
and age-group had its own particular form of spirituality that was best
encouraged and understood by others of a like status. The actual relationship between men and women was determined by the Biblical ideal of the
wife being the helpmeet of her husband. How exactly this was to be realized depended on the individuals within the marriage. However, the ideal
dynamic between husband and wife was parallel to that between a daughter
and her father, a prime minister to the king, or the Church to Christ as
the Eternal Bridegroom.[41] It is this ideal that we must keep in mind as we
read the women's memoirs.

The Shape and History of the Moravian Memoir

The genre of the Moravian memoir, although familiar to the scholar of
German Pietism, has remained virtually untouched by the scholar of North
American spiritual autobiography.[42] Fortunately, a few individual memoirs
from Bethlehem have been published in collections, providing what Rosemary Radford Ruether and Catherine Prelinger have termed "an invaluable source of insight into the nature of Moravian personality and
experience."[43] Although they have included two Moravian memoirs written
in English in their volume, enabling readers to witness what they describe
as the Moravians' "socio-economic egalitarianism,"[44] Ruether and Prelinger give only a brief description of these predominantly German immigrants to America and the shortest amount of information about the genre,
history, and significance of the Moravian memoir.

The memoirs in this volume provide a vivid portrait of the life, practices,
and theological beliefs of the women in the Moravian community in Bethlehem. The reader can determine how the community was run and what
expectations were put upon the individual members all in the common
service of God. However, the Moravian memoirs also describe the living
faith of these Moravian women. The texts reveal how these women per-
ceived their relationship to Christ and what effect that relationship had on
their lives.

Although scholars working with the Quaker journals and Puritan narratives have encountered problems when they have attempted to read the
spiritual narratives as documents expressing personal emotions and experiences, the Moravian memoirs are rich in personal detail interwoven with
secular experiences.[45] Some German scholars, discussing German memoirs

in the Pietist tradition, have considered them to be rather formulaic, that is to say, they repeat to an extent certain phrases, usually from the Bible, in their descriptions. However, this is not to say that such documents lack valuable information about the individuals who wrote them.[46]

The Moravian memoirs are also certainly written according to a standard exemplary life (that of Christ). They depict the spiritual growth of the individual and thus many follow a common pattern: they describe the innocence of childhood; a troubled adolescence; acquaintance with the Brethren; the journey to Bethlehem; acceptance into the community; confirmation and first communion; employment when single; marriage; employment when married; and final illness.[47] However, throughout all stages of life, the consciousness of individual sinfulness or unworthiness and the desire for redemption permeate all action. As each individual's experience of faith is different and is a response to quite different life events, so each memoir is also a highly personal and frank autobiography.

Zinzendorf introduced this practice of writing memoirs for two reasons. First, he felt that the deceased individual should have a chance to say goodbye to the rest of the community, just as the members who heard these words would be able to say their farewells also. On 22 June 1747, at Herrnhaag, Zinzendorf bemoaned the fact that nothing remained of the departed brother or sister but his or her earthly vessel, or *Hütte*. He decided that, from now on, the memoir of the departed person should be read at the service of song, or *Singstunde,* on the day he or she was buried in order that one could wish "vale to their soul, just as when as a final gesture one gives a handshake and says farewell." [48] Frequently, the memoir is composed in old age, when its author has the opportunity to look back on life, bearing in mind that its words will only be heard when he or she has died or "gone home." Because of the dangers associated with childbirth, a woman frequently composed her memoir before she married.

Second, Zinzendorf also saw these documents as an important part of the history of the Moravian church. Zinzendorf considered religion to center on the individual's *Vergegenwärtigung,* or re-presentation, of Christ's life and death. Through this process, which in the women's memoirs exists frequently in the form of a dialogue with Christ, the individual is made highly conscious of Christ's presence in her life, thus making of the *Heiland* or Savior a tangible partner. Repeatedly, the authors refer to their personal conversations with their "invisible friend," relate the revelations of his love for them, and make almost tangible their "bridegroom."

Zinzendorf, coming from the Pietist tradition, continually stressed the personal experience of Christ's passion and death, which is related through the *ita sentio*, or "it seems to me that," of religious consciousness. By feeling the Savior or Heiland, it appears that a knowledge of Christ can be made almost immediate through the power of the imagination, through the words of the memoir and the particularly active role of the creator of that memoir. Thus, every time a member of the church writes about her relationship to Christ it constitutes a personal and individual consciousness of him. This proximity to Christ provides not only a *unio mystica* for the sentient subject but also makes of the Savior an active and present force in one's life. For example, Sarah Grube (1727–1793) writes the following passage in her memoir during her final illness:

> In 1748, when I became severely ill, the Saviour appeared before my heart, and it seemed to me as though He were standing right in front of me in person and was showing me His hands with the marks of the nails, and said, "Look, into these hands I have inscribed you," and He assured me that everything He had done and suffered was also done for me. O, with what sweet feeling was I able to lay my head down on His head that was crowned with thorns for me: I heard in my heart the words, "It is finished!" [John 19:30] Yes, I often felt as though the Saviour were looking at me and saying, "You are truly beautiful and pure." The answer of my heart was, "Dear Saviour, it is with your righteousness that you have clothed me; now I can believe that you are my God and Saviour." [49]

Here we can see the implications of Zinzendorf's notion of *ita sentio*. Sarah Grube maintains a personal relationship with the Savior that is different from that of anyone else in the community. Each memoir, as the narration of that relationship, adds another unique piece to the overall picture of the community. [50]

However, it is not only the personal relationship to the Savior that constitutes the unique nature of each memoir but also the awareness that this relationship is being related, or told, to the rest of the writer's choir or congregation. Sarah Grube knows that when she is writing about her encounter with Christ she is also describing her spirituality to her church. Thus the tropes and vocabulary she will use to describe that personal and individual moment will be those that are current in that community.

Zinzendorf's own theory of language, as most extremely expressed in his "Sifting Period" vocabulary, allowed women to express in what might today appear to be shockingly realistic language their dependence on and love for the Heiland. However, during the eighteenth century, the idiosyncratic terminology used by the Moravians during what they later termed the "sifting period" (that lasted in Europe from 1743–50 and in America from 1743–51) was actually a means by which to describe the *"innigste Verbindung"* or innermost connection with Christ in terms familiar to one's audience. During this period a particular devotional vocabulary and practice was developed, most notably at the community at Herrnhaag in the Wetterau, which centered on the ultrarealistic depiction of Christ's wounds. For example, Martha Büninger (1723–1752) expresses her heartfelt wish that the Lamb keep her in His bleeding wounds: "May the Lamb keep us in His bloody wounds, that no harm come to us until we can see Him and kiss the wounds in His hands and feet. Until the kiss of His side wound."[51] This Sifting Period vocabulary is highly sensual and, at times, almost repugnant in its realism. Indeed, not all eighteenth-century women found it attractive. Rahel Edmonds, for example, writes: "[Brother Rogers] spoke at length about our Saviour and his blood and wounds, which seemed foolish to me because I had never heard of these teachings before."[52] German scholars, such as Oskar Pfister, have pointed to its obviously sexual overtones and have even accused Zinzendorf of promulgating a "theology of sexuality."[53] One certainly can interpret the enthusiasm of the Single Sisters' choir for the five wounds of Jesus as a projection of sexual desire. However, according to Zinzendorf, the function of such vocabulary was to arouse in the reader a consciousness of the suffering of Christ and subsequent gratitude for being saved.[54]

Although Zinzendorf forbade the more extreme instances of the blood-and-wounds symbolism after 1750, many of the Moravian brothers and sisters continued to use such vocabulary. In these memoirs, the women frequently claim that they are unable to find the words with which to describe the proximity of the Saviour either at their first communion or at their spiritual awakening *(Erweckung)*, yet they often express their desire to taste the blood and feel the body of Christ. Thus although the official language of the personal narrative had been "cleaned" of this vocabulary, it continued to appear in the memoirs. For many women, this language served as the only vehicle through which they could express fully their personal relationship with the Savior.

In addition to this "blood and wounds" vocabulary, the women's relationship with Christ is most visible in their frequent description of him as their "bridegroom." The Single Sisters clearly felt that Jesus was very close to them. They depict him as their friend, they speak of their faith and their ability to endure hardship through his love for them. Marie Minier (1732–1769) describes her awakened feelings towards Jesus during a communion service. When she writes her memoir, Marie is unmarried, in her mid-twenties, and living in the Single Sisters' Choir. She describes her relationship with Christ as one of utter dependence; she has ecstatic visions and feels his presence with an almost embarrassing sensuality. The vocabulary she uses is typical of the period; Christ is her "friend" and "bleeding Savior," and she feverishly describes Holy Communion as a kind of wedding night, anticipating the time when she will meet her "bridegroom" in heaven.[55]

> With body and soul I could give myself up just as I was and want nothing else in this world than to depend on him: for this grace could be felt so strongly in my heart that I thought, "there is nothing more for me here"; and it was just as though the tormented body of the Bloody Saviour were hanging there right before my eyes. Now, because it was Communion day, I could hardly wait until I got to enjoy his Body and Blood in the Sacrament, and as I was actually enjoying it I could hardly remember whether I was still here or already in the marriage hall. That was a great day of grace for me which I shall never forget.[56]

At this point the text breaks off and further biographical information is added by a narrator (probably the minister).

The model of self-consciousness operating within Marie Minier's description of her relationship to Christ is recognizable as that identified by feminist scholarship on the autobiographical genre as an intersubjective "conversation" with an Other or others (in the case of the spiritual narrative, with Christ; and, in a communal society, with others in that communal structure).[57] One scholar of eighteenth-century women's autobiographical writings, Mary Mason, has argued that the original model for women's writing can be found in such spiritual autobiographies as Marie Minier's, where the recognition of female self-identity through the consciousness of a partner in dialogue enables women to "write openly about themselves."[58] Certainly, the Moravian memoir contains a pattern of self-relation that fundamentally questions the dominant Enlightenment notion of the self as autonomous. Moravian women's (and men's) memoirs reveal the development of a model of self-knowledge and ethical behavior in which self-awareness springs from the act of communion with Christ and communication with the congregation rather than autonomous reason.

Although the custom of composing a spiritual autobiography is not peculiar to the Moravian Church, the particular form and function of the memoir within the religious community warrant special examination and comparison with contemporaneous spiritual narratives on the North Amer-

ican continent. As a Pietist, Zinzendorf knew the tradition of writing a
memoir as it had been revived by August Hermann Francke (1663–1727).
Francke's own memoir narrates his trials of conversion *(Bußkampf)* and the
sudden awakening that accompanied his successful penance. However, as
Reichel points out, such a time of trial followed by a sudden conversion was
something that Zinzendorf himself never claimed to have experienced.[59]
Zinzendorf, rather than thinking that an awakening could follow a set
pattern of introspection and enlightenment, believed that each person's
faith is attained and maintained in a different way for each individual. The
notion of the individual was of great importance to Zinzendorf, as he
maintained that each person is an original and cannot be shaped to fit a
foreign mold. In a speech to the Synod in 1756, Zinzendorf states: "In the
congregation each person should remain in their original form and no-one
should shape themselves according to another."[60] This stress on the individual and unrepeatable nature of each person is reflected in the Moravian
memoir.

The Moravian memoir is unique as a theological and literary genre in
that both the reason for writing the narrative and the point in the author's
life at which this was done distinguish these Moravian texts both from
contemporary German Pietist versions and from North American Quaker
journals and Puritan spiritual narratives.

As can be seen from the following memoirs, Moravian memoirs do not
always contain a single pattern of spiritual conversion that is to be followed;
rather, they usually depict the truth, whether good or bad, about the individual's life.[61] Moravian memoirs often include dreams and visions only as
indications of either a troubled soul or imminent grace and not as moments of possible revelation of the Truth. Furthermore, the attempted
subordination of individuality in the Quaker journal is certainly not found
in the Moravian texts. The Puritan narratives were required of the appli-
cant for admission into the community "to convince the elders that the
presence of grace was evident in their experience."[62] In contrast, the Moravian memoir can span an individual's entire lifetime as it intermeshes with
and illumines the life of the Moravian community. In almost all the memoirs both inner and outer lives are described: the personal relationship
with Christ, feelings at first communion, the atmosphere in the early, almost experimental, community, parents' reactions (not always positive) to
their child's decision to join the Moravian Brethren. They also are full
of information about life in Colonial America. They tell of Indian raids,
captures, kidnappings, the setting up of the schools, farms, and Indian
missions.

There are potentially three versions of any one memoir. There is the original memoir, which was either written by the individual (which is rare) or else dictated to the minister or family member during her or his final illness. The final moments of the person's life were then added by the scribe. From this "original" version a report was made which appeared in the Bethlehem Diary, the official diary of the community that recorded all comings and goings, religious services, births, deaths, and marriages. There could then also be a version included in the *Gemeinnachrichten,* the handwritten "newsletter" that was circulated to all the Moravian communities around the globe.

There can be real differences between the three versions. Comparing the two or three versions that exist, it becomes clear that overtly personal, or what might be seen as superfluous, detail is omitted in the later versions; particulars which might contradict the accepted picture of the community are deleted; style is improved; and the whole story is sometimes completely rewritten. In this collection, the first version of the memoir is included.

The Place of the Moravian Memoir

These Moravian memoirs are self-narrations; they are recountings of women's lives that are inextricably tied to a theology that defined each individual as unique. They were written with a constant eye on the changing conditions of mind and heart *(Gemütsvorgänge)* that accompanied the women's worldly existence. This self-scrutiny reflects a radical shift of perspective in the spiritual autobiography in the late seventeenth-and early eighteenth-century in Europe when the object of interpretation in the early modern period changes from the traditional one, the Scriptures, to become the scrutiny and interpretation of the self. Samuel Preus writes "that all-embracing biblical framework is becoming too narrow to account for what people are coming to know about space (geographical and cosmic) and time (chronology). The known world is bursting its scriptural containment. The overarching biblical narrative is being eclipsed in favor of new competing narratives." [63] And what is taking the place of interpretation of the biblical "mega-narrative"? It is the divination of the individual life whose new hermeneutic "requires us not to ascend to the realm of spirit to read the significance of earthly matters, but rather to descend into the minutest trivia of daily life to show their spiritual meaning." [64] What lends meaning to life is the interpretation of the everyday, how one comprehends the causality and significance of events such as a boat sinking (see Anna Seidel's memoir), or a river being too swollen to ford (see

Margarethe Jungmann's memoir), or the accidental fall down the cellar steps (see Christiana Detmers' memoir). In the Moravian memoirs these secular details become embued with a meaning that transcends the everyday.

As Ian Watt has claimed, the individual act of self-scrutiny with the aim of enlightenment transforms a religious process into a secular narrative: the individual believer positions him- or herself outside a text (his or her life) and reads, rather than writes, its process of signification.[65] The spiritual narrative is based upon this move from the predominantly Protestant religious act of the individual's divination of God's word from the Bible as text to the divination of God's will from the events within an individual's life. The hermeneutic that had previously applied to reading the Scripture as sacred text is now applied to interpreting the significance of life of the individual. In this way, all lives are significant, as all are instances of God's will and grace.

One who accepts Preus's description of the "bursting" of the scripture through the expansion of knowledge of the world in seventeeth- and early eighteenth-century England can only imagine the challenge that North America posed to the mega-narrative of the Bible. As a transition between the intensely personal confessional of, for example, St. Augustine and the secularized autobiography of the nineteenth century, the Moravian memoirs display a fascinating balance between the introspective contemplation of the relationship between the author and God and a detailed descriptions of life-in-the-world, the "New World."

Accompanying this movement toward self-scrutiny there also occurs a significant shift in the narrative voice in the Moravian memoir over the course of the eighteenth century. As Günter Niggl has pointed out in his study of the memoirs written by members of the Herrnhut congregation, a definite change from third- to first-person narration occurs in the first twenty years of the practice, a change that transforms the text from a simple list of dates into an introspective confession.[66] Fortunately, however, the form of the Pietist autobiography itself requires inclusion of detail of one's secular life in order to demonstrate the action of God's will and grace.[67]

Not only did the form of the memoir require the inclusion of secular detail and introspection, thereby ensuring the twentieth-century scholar a fuller picture of the lives of women in the eighteenth century. The secular world outside Bethlehem also plays a major role within the account of women's spiritual growth.[68] The memoirs contain accounts of Indian raids (Marianne Höht), travels through the wilds of Pennsylvania (Margarethe

Jungmann), indeed across the world (Anna Seidel, Anna Anders) and detail women's administrative responsibilities in the community of Bethlehem and elsewhere. This integration of secular detail into women's spiritual narratives constitutes a significant departure from the accepted pattern for women's autobiographies in the eighteenth century. Margarethe Jungmann's experience of the Savior is very different from that of Marie Minier. Whereas Margarethe led a life about which one could almost claim that the gender of the personal pronoun is irrelevant,[69] Marie describes a model of consciousness that is clearly gendered. In this context, it is interesting to note that Margarethe Jungmann's memoir is composed at least twenty years after Marie Minier's and yet displays very little of the later notions of gender. Similarly, Marianne Höht's memoir is composed in the late 1760s and combines Sifting Period vocabulary with an adventure narrative.

These significant differences point to the central importance of the individual's different experiences of lived faith in the act of writing the Moravian memoir. Rather than generalizing about how all women might have written at one particular point in time, the modern reader should recognize the significance of divergence from accepted patterns.

The memoirs in this volume demonstrate clearly the variety and richness of experience that women enjoyed in their lives in colonial Pennsylvania. In contrast to the spiritual narratives that have caused some German scholars to claim that these texts are purely formalistic, lacking any personal comment by their authors, we see a fascinating interweaving of spiritual introspection and secular experience.

The Moravian *Lebensläufe* are written to depict the spiritual growth of the individual. However, as the texts themselves reveal, this growth is not described only in terms of introspection or the slavish adherence to the imposed patriarchal form of the memoir. The combination of the Pietist concept of the individual's close relationship to Christ, the particular social structure of the Bethelehem community in the 1700s, and the challenges of living and proselytizing in Pennsylvania makes these women's spiritual narratives unique in the eighteenth century. Whereas it was usually men who wrote professional or adventure biographies and women spiritual narratives, in these Moravian memoirs we find a rare mixture of all types of autobiography. For example, Marie Minier's narrative is highly personal and introspective; Anna Johanna Seidel's is about her career; Marianne Höht's and Susanne Partsch's resemble more the adventure narratives. However, in all Moravian women's texts, as in all Moravian lives, Christ is represented as a friend, a companion in times of trouble, a bridegroom, or a *Gesprächspartner.* Despite the seeming passivity, or selflessness, that this relationship with the Saviour might invoke, the female self is experienced as recognizing an absence and a presence of God, a recognition that constantly awakens a consciousness of unworthiness and a need for redemption and also, by necessity, a consciousness of female selfhood.

As the subtitle of this collection, "Related Lives," suggests, these women write about their lives in relation to Christ and the church; they relate their lives to each other, aware that their words will be heard only after they have "gone home" to their Saviour, and are also aware that their memoirs will join the already present web of related lives in which they have lived in the Moravian congregation. The interconnections between the Sisters who follow are myriad; they are connected by work, by place, by choir, and by faith. When read together, these related lives bring to life Zinzendorf's claim that it is the individual members of the congregation who in comuunity make up the Church.

As one moves on in intellectual history to the gender theories of the German Romantics and the theory of Ideal Womanhood in North America, it is important to bear in mind that some women did lead full and varied lives at one point in the eighteenth century. Although in a secular age it might be hard to accept the notion that a religious group enabled women to live relatively independent lives, it is clear from these Moravian Lebensläufe that the Moravian church, for a short period of time during the General Economy, did precisely that. Not only did these women live remarkable lives but they also wrote about them in a way that is unmatched by their contemporaries.

Memoirs of the Single Sisters

THE SINGLE SISTERS
An Introduction

Organized in June 1742, the Single Sisters' Choir in Bethlehem originally consisted of twelve women, led by Anna Nitschmann, Zinzendorf's travel companion and later wife, and his daughter, Benigna. Among the number were the three daughters of Philadelphia Quaker and philanthropist, Anthony Benezet, Judith, Molly, and Susanna, and also "a Negress" Magdalene (not Magdalene Beulah Brockden whose memoir appears in this volume).

The Single Sisters' Choir was initially situated in Bethlehem until a house could be built for them in nearby Nazareth. While they lived in Bethlehem, strict segregation from the male members of the community was enforced to such an extent that even the Single Sisters' walks were to be taken in the opposite direction to that of the Single Brethren. In 1748, the Single Sisters' Choir moved into what is still today called the Sisters' House on Church Street.

Young women usually entered the Single Sisters' Choir at the age of seventeen or eighteen, if they were already members of the Moravian congregation. In the Single Sisters' choir the women ate and slept in a large communal room; they worked at spinning wheels or embroidered and held frequent religious services, such as the *Singstunde* (service of song), *Chorviertelstunde* (quarter of an hour prayer service) and *Liebesmahl* (lovefeast). The latter ceremony was based on a form of the early Christian agape meal in which the participants shared food and drink, and sometimes sang and made music. During the lovefeasts, as well as other services, religious feeling could run high as the members of the choir prostrated themselves before their friend, Jesus Christ, or exchanged the kiss of peace (see illus. 7). In the Diary of the Single Sisters' Choir (taken from the late 1740s), which was kept by the Elder, Anna Rosina Anders (see her memoir below), we read:

> In the afternoon we had our choir's Lovefeast in our hall, during which we
> also had a few good prayers. Brother Johann had us sing the cantata from

3

1747. It was a most dear precious Lovefeast. Our choir was dressed all in white and the hall was preciously decorated in green and a few pretty verses. It looked very dear. In the evening, the dear heart Johan held for us an exceptionally beautiful quarter of hour's prayer service for all communicant sisters. And then we also performed the footwashing, and we all felt good in our hearts during this. After all the services we celebrated quite a happy and contented communion with all the communicant sisters. I cannot describe our feelings during this. Our eternal husband was unspeakably close to our choir. He especially allowed us to feel His proximity to us, His embrace, and His feet. We all felt very happy inside, and so the day was passed happily and quite preciously.[1]

The Single Sisters' great attachment to this *modus vivendi* is attested to by their all-too-frequent reluctance, like that of Anna Johanna Seidel (see under "Widows"), to follow the recommendations of the lot in marriage.

Despite the emphasis given to a Single Sister's chastity, Zinzendorf considered marriage to be the true calling of the Single Sisters.[2] However, it is clear from the Instructions to the Helpers in the Married and Single Choirs that men and women were not expected to have any "knowledge" of the other sex before they married. Marriage was to be ordered according to Zinzendorf's concept of the *Streiterehe* (the marriage militant), and theologically reinterpreted. As part of this process, women who were to be married in Bethlehem in the 1700s were prepared for this change of state by the Choir Helper. The Single Sister who was to be married was told quite explicitly that she was the bride of Christ and that everything in marriage happened according to the service of Christ.

The Single Sisters' Choir was always in financial need, and this situation only worsened after the dissolution of the General Economy in the 1760s. The Single Sisters continued to work until illness or old age prevented them from carrying out their responsibilities for the Choir. For example, Margareth Seidner worked in the Choir's vegetable garden and tended their livestock until 1786, when, at the age of seventy-two, she suffered from a stroke. She recovered partially from that and "helped where she could" until another stroke rendered her incapable. As mentioned in the introduction, many of the Single Sisters worked as teachers in the Children's Home; however, with the abandonment of the communal system and the growth of families with households, their services were not needed there either.

Anna Rosina Anders (Anna Rosel)
1727–1803

Anna Rosina Anders, the Single Sisters' Labouress from 1748 until 1764, led the Single Sisters' Choir through the early years of the settlement, the French-Indian War, and the break up of the communal household (illus 8). She figures prominently in the Diary of the Single Sisters' Choir during these years and is frequently referred to in the memoirs of the Single Sisters. As she died in Fulneck, Yorkshire, her own memoir was located in the Moravian Archives of the British Province and was written in English. It is here reproduced in its entirety, although the spelling and punctuation have been modernized. Anna Rosel's memoir is a fascinating example of the English vernacular of the Moravian Church in the eighteenth century. It also provides the reader with a representative portrayal of a leader of the single women in the Moravian Church in the eighteenth century. It makes for an interesting comparison with the memoir of Anna Johanna Piesch Seidel (see under "Widows").

Our dear happily departed Sister Anna Rosina Anders has left the following account of herself:

I was born the 9th of Aug 1727 at Berthelsdorf. My parents belonging to the Congregation endeavour'd to bring me up in the same connection with the Congregation and sent me from my earliest years every Sunday to Herrnhut to the Children's meeting, which the late Count Zinzendorf kept. He asked me many questions, and though I did not always understand him, yet it made an impression on my heart and I felt a desire to be happy. When I was in my seventh year my Father departed happily to our Saviour, after which the late Count took care of my Mother and her Children, she came to live in the widows house at Herrnhut and her Children in the Orphan House, but I for my part had no inclination for it but chose to stay with my Grandfather in Berthelsdorf. After a few years my Uncle in Lobenstein desired me to come and live with him, which I was very glad of. I was there above a year but did not find it so agreeable as I thought, and I prayed many times with tears to the Lord to help me away again, which He graciously did. For it happened at this time that the late Count came to Ebersdorf, and my Uncle had an opportunity to see him and told him that I was very unhappy here; on hearing this he took me under his care and sent me to Marienborn to the Orphan house. I prayed to the

Lord to preserve me here and make me happy and that I never might come to any other place except among the Brethren, because I was sometimes enticed by my Uncle to go back with him to his home. At that time during a severe sickness which I got, I learnt to pray earnestly for my happiness. I found many friends here who wish'd me well and to see me prosper for our Saviour; particularly one Sister will always be remembered by me, who, when I had recovered, took me with her into the garden, and kneeling down with me, put up a fervent prayer in my behalf to our Saviour, which I shall never forget. But it was not sufficient to make me happy; because I must feel my Saviour's comfort and forgiveness for my own heart, and this happened in a very particular manner. Being quite alone in a place I fell down at His feet and implored His mercy and forgiveness for all my sins through His precious blood. At that time I felt something, which I cannot express, His comfort to my troubled soul and His mercy shown to me, melted my heart in thousand tears. In 1740, I was after the then usual manner received into the Children's Congregation, which proved a great blessing to me. I devoted my heart to our Saviour to live to Him and serve Him; however afterwards, I must own, I had many things to experience, by which I learnt better to know myself, but our Saviour was faithful and helped me through, I always felt freedom to speak my mind openheartedly to my Labouress, which was a great help to me. In the year 1741, I was received into the Great Girls' Choir, and in the same year I enjoyed the holy Communion for the first time, which was an unspeakable blessing to my heart. At that time there was a company of Great Girls, which the late Count took particular care of, he kept our Choirmeetings and instructed us how to become useful in our Saviour's service. I was appointed to keep the Children's and Great Girls' bands and enjoyed many blessings from our Saviour, when we spoke together of his great love and mercy. Soon after I had the Office of an Assistant among the Children conferred upon me and moved in the same year with this Oeconomy to Herrnhaag. All these appointments taught me to come into closer connection with our Saviour and showed me that I could do nothing of myself. His mercy and love shown to me bowed me in the dust before Him; I had the confidence to cleave to Him as a poor sinner and believed He would help me through. 1743, I was accepted an Acolyte with a large company, which encouraged me anew to live to Him and serve Him as a poor Child that has nothing to plead but his mercy from day to day.—

　　1744, I was received into the Single Sisters Choir and 1747 blessed for a Deaconess. 1748, I received a Call to be Single Sisters' Labouress at Bethlehem in America. In London, February the 10th, I was blessed for my Office and set out in June. September the 20th, I arrived in Bethlehem after a troublesome voyage. I cannot but take notice that this year the 13th of November was celebrated the first time in America, which brought the first impression of that in Herrnhaag 1741 very fresh to my mind, but I was sorry I could not enjoy it in such a manner as I wished to do. I had to struggle, particularly in the beginning with many difficulties, being young and unexperienced, and had nobody to whom I could open my heart and consult with so as I wished, which made it sometimes very heavy to me. But my dear Saviour helped me through whenever I turned to Him in my distress. I visited frequently in the most of the Country Congregation which lay very distant from each other. In the year 1755 a war broke out between the French and English, and as the Indians generally took share and joined one or the other party, we had very difficult times at Bethlehem and Nazareth. First the Settlement of the Brethren at the Mahony about twenty-seven miles from Bethlehem was destroyed by the Indians, where eleven brothers and sisters lost their lives; after which many murders were committed much nearer, till at last within six miles of Bethlehem. We knew that we were closely watched by the Indians, who would gladly have destroyed the place, which at that time was the only one capable of making any resistance to their incursion. The reports of their cruelties at other places kept us in continual alarm and apprehension, particularly as Indians were sometimes observed to lurk about and in the place at nights. However the strict watch kept by the brothers and sisters in many parts and particularly about our house, but above all the protection of our good Lord, always frustrated their designs. During all these heavy times our dear Saviour was our only comfort, and his peace was very sensibly felt among us.

In the year 1762, Brother Nathanael Seidel arrived here from Europe, who had lately been married to Sister Anna Johanna Piesch an old acquaintance of mine; from whose conversation and support I received much comfort. In the year 1764, I received a Call to return to Europe, Sister Susanna de Gersdorf arrived early in that year to supply my place, and I left Bethlehem in company with Brother and Sister Boehler and some other Brothers and Sisters in the beginning of May. We had a very quick passge, arrived in London the 24th of June, and at Marienborn where the Synod was assembled on the 4th of July. After the Synod was closed I went to Herrnhut and in the year 1765 received a Call to serve the Single Sisters' Choirs in England. I first went to Fulneck, where I stayed about a year, then got a Call to Bedford, where I served the single Sisters until the year 1772 when I return'd again to Fulneck. To go any further in relating my course I don't think needful.—

Our Saviour's passion and death and that He has redeemed me poor Sinner with His own precious blood is to me above every thing in time and in eternity. He has helped me through this vale of tears and given me grace to place my confidence in Him in which I never have been part to shame. When I have the favour to see Him face to face I shall kiss His feet with Sinner-tears for all His mercy bestowed upon me.

Thus far has this faithful handmaid of Jesus left us an account of herself and of that what the Lord has done for her Soul. There would be much to say of all the proofs of grace, wherewith He has crowned her endeavors and blessed her services to so many souls, in advising, comforting, and showing them the way to true happiness; but we shall content ourselves with rendering unto Him, who is the giver of all good gifts, our humble thanks and praises for all the mercies bestowed upon her, during her pilgrimage here below. Her character and the blessing which attended her Labour is known and acknowleged with thankfulness, and we heartily wish and pray that we may follow her footsteps. In the year 1772, when she the second time arrived in Fulneck, the Single Sisters' Choir and Oeconomies in Yorkshire were in a very hopeful state, and she was received by them with much love and affection. In this vineyard of the Lord she labored with the utmost alacrity both of body and mind, deeming it her highest privilege to win souls for Christ. The weakest of the flock were always objects of her peculiar care and concern, and she spared no pains whatever in tending and bearing them in love; and in such instances when all means proved ineffectual, it was evident to all around her how she always bemoaned their loss. On the other hand, our Saviour gave her the satisfaction to see many faithful handmaids, whom she had trained up for the Lord, enter into the different services of his house, which she always looked upon as the greatest favour conferred on herself. As the Choir here in Fulneck considerably increased, it was in the year 1780 taken into consideration to build a Single Sisters' house in Wyke, and the proposal having been approved of, our late Sister had the pleasure to assist in laying the foundation stone, which was a blessed solemnity. When it was finished and inhabited by sisters from Fulneck, she used to visit them frequently with great faithfulness and took particular share in their weal and woe; as also in the welfare of the Sisters Oeconomies at Gummersall, Mirfield, and Littlemore; when several years ago the latter was given up, it was a great concern to her mind. Of late years she grew weak and could not be so active in her Office as she wished, nevertheless, her mind was continually employed for the welfare of her Choir. Great as her delight had been in the beginning, to see her Choir in such an increasing and flourishing way, so great was her concern of late years to see it gradually declining in number and but few new ones coming in. So much the more might truly value their lot of grace and enjoy the blessings and privileges, which were so precious to herself. For as to her own person she regretted exceedingly, that in her latter days old age and weakness prevended [*sic*] her attending every opportunity for edification and encouragement as much as she wished to do. May the 1st 1802 she was seized with a paralytic stroke, but recovered so far again that she on the 4th of May could attend the meetings in our house. During this winter, her weakness increased, and she was much confined to her room. Feb. 15th [1803] she had another stroke, which quite took away the use of her right side, and the next day she had strong convulsions so that we all expected her dissolution. She had often expressed a wish for Brother Benate to pray with her at her departure which was now done, and after the prayer the blessing of the Lord was pronounced over her. The feeling of the peace of God on this occasion will leave a deep impression on the minds of all them who were present. After the first paroxysm she fell asleep and slumbered for the most part, but when she between times awoke she seemed to be sensible, though her speech was so far gone, that she could only say "yes" or "no" to the questions asked. The 18th some Sisters assembled in her room to sing some Verses expressing our foretaste of that happy lot to be at home with the Lord; she seemed quite delighted with it and kept awake the whole time. The 19th in the afternoon she appeared more recollected than before and could speak several words, and when the girls came to see her, she gave them all the hand and said, "The Lord bless you!" Afterwards she slumbered again till about evening, had a very restless night, and the 20th in the morning about 7 o'clock her redeemed and through the blood of Jesus sanctified soul went gently and happy over into the arms of her beloved Bridegroom, during the singing of that verse: "When in the arms of Jesus, thy lips shall pallid grow" etc. Her age was 75 years, 6 months.

Maria Barbara Horn
1729–1797

In her memoir, Maria Horn describes how the Protestant spiritual awakening in Franconia in the 1740s caused her to run away to nearby Herrnhaag at the age of twenty. When Herrnhaag was disbanded in the early 1750s she, like all other members there, was relocated and, again like many of the other Single Sisters, she went to the congregation in Zeyst, Holland. Here she stayed for thirteen years before finally going to America in 1763, as the Bethlehem Economy was being reorganized. (illus. 9)

In 1791, our late Sister, Maria Barbara Horn, dictated the following short account of her life:

I was born on February 5th, 1729, near Werthheim, in the village of Eichel. My father was Johann Heinrich Horn and my mother Anna Catharina, née Diemern. My mother, who was a very God-fearing woman, was very concerned about bringing her children up in the name of our dear Lord. She often told us that, if we did not love the Saviour and give ourselves up to him completely, we would be lost. This often confused me and caused me to pray to the Saviour[3] as well as I knew how.

In my 13th year, I went to Holy Communion for the first time, at which I felt an inner contentment. I promised the Saviour that from now on I would lead a life pleasing to Him. But, all too soon, both this resolution and the feeling that I had from Him were lost again, and I began to love the world. When my mother noticed this, she sent me to a God-fearing woman in the town,[4] who accepted me as her own child and attempted to keep me safe from the world. She often fell with me to her knees and begged the Saviour to bring me to a knowledge of my lost state. This prayer was heard. I began to become aware of my unhappy state and feel painfully my deep sorrow and my corruption, which disconcerted me greatly, and yet at the same time I wanted to appear better than I was. The faithful Saviour soon made me recognize that I had no strength in my self to be good through my own efforts. He made me into a true poor sinner, and I laid myself at His feet as lost and as damned as I felt myself to be. I begged Him for the sight of His grace and for the forgiveness of all my sins, which He granted me by His grace. I will never forget the feeling that I had then, and the Saviour, through His grace, has preserved this for me until now.

Soon after this, I heard of the Congregation in Herrnhaag, and it seemed to me as though I belonged to them. I went to my parents, told them of my intention, and that I had a longing to go to the Congregation. They were very pleased about this and gave me their parental blessing to do so. When I told my cousin,[5] she was very unwilling to allow me to leave her (because she had no children) and promised me that if I stayed with her, she would leave me an ample fortune so that I would never be in need. However, I thought, I would rather have nothing temporal in this world if only I can achieve my eternal salvation. Therefore, I put together just a small bundle because I had to go most of the way on foot, and I arrived in Herrnhaag on March 31, 1749, where I asked for and, to my joy also, received permission to stay. Although I did not have it as good here in material things as I was used to, I soon became accustomed to my surroundings and was childlikely content in my poverty. In 1749, on August 3rd, to my great shame I was received into the Congregation and, in 1751, on May 12th, I was allowed to go to Holy Communion with the Congregation. With each act of grace that the Saviour allowed me to experience, I felt myself ashamed and thankful, and I asked Him to keep me with Him by His grace.

When the Herrnhaag dispersed I came to[6] Zeyst, where the dear Saviour allowed me to recognize my sorrow and corruption more thoroughly but also granted me a childlike heart towards Him and a trust in my Labouress, so that I never had to remain long in that state.

In 1763, I received a call to America, along with several other Single Sisters, and I arrived in Bethlehem on November 4th of the same year. This change was somewhat hard for me but, because I had once given myself up to the dear Saviour completely, to want nothing but what is His will, He also helped me there. In addition, He wanted to direct all my actions and endeavours to His honour.

She served loyally in our kitchen here for some years; ten years ago, she started to become sickly, which weakened her memory greatly, so that one occasionally had to bear with her with patience. When one spoke with her about her heart, however, one saw clearly that she had a tender love for the Saviour. Finally, tuberculosis set in and she had to suffer a great deal in the final days with shortness of breath. On the last day,[7] she was especially cheerful and very desirous that the dear Saviour bring an end to her suffering. And[8] in the afternoon at 4 o'clock the blessed moment came, when she went over into the arms of her Redeemer softly and happily with the blessing of the Congregation and her Choir, amidst a truly blessed feeling. She achieved an age of 68 years, 2 months, and 11 days.

Eva Lanius
1743–1801

Eva Lanius was born in York, Pennsylvania. Her parents were Juliana and Jacob Lanius, the first members to be received directly into the Moravian congregation there. Eva, herself, was received into the Congregation only after many trials. She visited Bethlehem, wanted to join the Moravians, but her application was denied.

After this disappointment she became distracted by the ways of the world and was brought back to her original intention only through talking with Sister Schlegel, wife of the Moravian minister in York at that time, John Friedrich Schlegel. Once she was received into the Congregation, she worked all her life as a nurse.

The verses that are attached to the memoir follow a common pattern. The first stanza is a common Moravian funeral ode, which was sung at the burial of the departed, and what follows is improvised on the theme of the first stanza and tailored to suit the life of the departed (in the Bethelehem Diary *version, only the first verse is reproduced,* Bethelehem Diary, *vol. 40, 120–26).*

The memoir of our Sister Eva Lanius, who died peacefully here on October 7, 1801. She has left the following short account of her walk through this life:

I was born on May 1, 1743, near Yorktown in Pennsylvania and baptized in the Reformed Church. It was very important to my parents to raise their children for the dear Saviour, and I must admit that in my childhood I felt Him touching my heart more than once. As my parents had been acquainted with the Brethren for some time and finally became members of the Congregation themselves, in 1757 I visited the congregation here in Bethlehem. Everything I saw and heard here pleased me unspeakably. Especially during this visit my heart was touched anew by the love of the Saviour, and I immediately asked for permission to stay here because it was my parents' ardent wish that their four youngest children, of whom I was one, should move to the congregation in Bethlehem. But at that time I did not receive permission and to my great pain had to go home again. Gradually, however, the feeling for the Saviour disappeared in me as did also the longing to join the Congregation and, on the contrary, I began to like the world. In September of the same year, a Synod or conference of the Labourers from the Country congregations was held in Yorktown. At this meeting Sr. Schlegel, then the Labouress in the congregation in Yorktown, spoke with me in a most motherly and deep way about my condition and pointed me to the Saviour as the most faithful and only true friend of all poor sinners. But she also asked me about what had happened to my longing to join the Congregation and added that I should remember that it was the earnest wish and longing of my parents. Finally, she advised me to write a letter to Brother Joseph and to ask once again for permission to go to Bethlehem, which I then, therefore, did. However, when my request was actually granted, I must admit that I was not happy about it at all. I accepted it to please my parents for the meantime and acted as though I were quite happy and pleased about it. I did this so as not to sadden them because I had often heard my mother especially pray to the dear Saviour at night in bed that he should bring me and her three other youngest children to the Congregation, which also came to pass.

The following October 14, I arrived in Bethlehem and soon settled in. On May 28 of the following year, I was received into the Congregation. But afterwards I entered into an indifferent frame of mind and remained so for about two years. In the meantime, when one of my comrades progressed further in the grace of the Congregation and I had to remain behind, this served me as an opportunity to examine the condition of my heart thoroughly before the Saviour. After this I spoke openly about everything with my Choir Labouress, who led me in a truly motherly way to the dear Saviour's infinite grace, faithfulness, and mercy. And because I followed her advice I also experienced, as never before, the way He accepts sinners and saves them. That moment will remain important to me for the rest of my life. On August 28, 1760, I had the great grace to partake of Holy Communion with the Congregation for the first time. The enjoyment was something quite indescribable (and I must say that my dear Saviour has renewed for me every time by His grace). And I must admit that, since I have been found worthy of partaking of it, Holy Communion has been and remains something so great and important to me that I will not be able to thank the dear Saviour enough in all eternity. But after the first celebration of this high blessing, the dear Saviour took me into a new school in which He clearly showed me my lack of faith in Him. O, what went on inside me then! That I should not believe in Him, after He had been so good to me! But yes, it was so. I saw and felt that I had no strength to so do and was in quite a miserable state. At night I would often get up out of bed and throw myself down upon my face and cried to be granted faith. Now my faithful Saviour showed me mercy. I felt as though He were stepping towards me, saying, "I will help you!" He allowed me to cast a believing glance at His meritorious sufferings. Then, with thanks and deep humility, I understood that I could neither believe in Jesus Christ my Lord and His efficacious atoning sacrifice for redemption nor continue in faith by my own reason or strength, but only through His grace. I then asked Him imploringly never again to let me feel what unbelief is but rather to give me the grace to lean on Him and stand by Him and His holy merits faithfully like a child in all circumstances and occurrences of my life; this request He mercifully granted me. And I hope and pray and trust in Him that He will preserve for me that precious jewel of walking with Him in trust and embracing Him in all His power and constantly cleaving to Him until I see Him.

I was now often employed in the care of the sick, until the office of sick-nursing in our Choir House here was given to me in 1785. I accepted this office willingly and with trust in the help of the dear Saviour. I had the grace to take care of thirty-two Sisters until their going home to eternity. The effort and work, which was not to be avoided in the care of the sick, was richly rewarded through the unspeakably blessed enjoyment of the nearness and the faithful help of my dear Saviour, and every loss was rewarded in the most perfect way. Now I too am His sick one and am taken care of and am truly happy to be in His care for He is a compassionate, good doctor. He is good to me. I glorify and praise Him for the innumerable good deeds that He has done for me during my life; and I am humbled and ashamed before Him for everything in which I was not a joy to Him. More than I can describe, I look forward with pleasure to the unspeakably happy and blessed moment when He will fetch me—for I long for and desire with all my heart to finish my earthly life and to be with Him, when I will kiss His pierced hands and feet as my election by grace.

Thus far our departed Sister's own words.

Even a long time ago her health suffered with bad chills, and she was afflicted with rheumatic as well as asthmatic attacks for a number of years. Through all this, she carried out her duties with great faithfulness and care and spared herself no pains; indeed, she often forgot her own weakness, as she had a special gift for caring for the sick. A year and a half ago, she had to withstand a bad illness and appeared at that time to be near her end. She recovered again, but her body was much weakened by this, and the rheumatic attacks that now greatly increased meant that she was rendered incapable of dedicating herself to her tasks according to her wishes and her custom. But she did not cease to serve with her advice and labour as much as she could; especially helping the sister, whom she was given first as an assistant and later as her successor, to whom, as to others, she was also very grateful for everything that was done for her. She bore her long, painful illness with indescribable patience, and whenever one pitied her that she had so much to bear, she expressed herself thus: "The Saviour is good to me, why should I complain? He bore so much for me. If He burdens you heavily then He also helps you to carry that burden. Her joy in faith, the unwaivering happiness of her disposition and heart, her strong desire to greet Him personally the sooner the better, Him who had bled to death for her. And at the same time her childlike submission to His will and great patience through her pains were an edification and joy to all who visited her. On September 25, a great change came to pass so that it seemed that the Saviour were hurrying her to her end; but it went on for quite a while. After that, she spent most of her days and nights in what seemed to be a gentle slumber, and whenever a strong paroxysm would overcome her, she would say, when she awoke once it was over, "Well, a difficult hour has again passed! The Saviour helped and He will continue to help. Whenever liturgies were held by her bed, she would often start to sing the following verse: "I will see Him, the friend so beautiful, who has already taken my heart, and then I shall never leave His side." And, "the suffering of this life is never worth the glory that the children of God will experience when that which they await comes; that is, when Christ will reveal Himself." At the beginning of this week, she asked whether this were not Communion week? And when she was answered with "yes," she replied, "Oh, what an important week this always was for me, and Holy Communion is something so great for me! But this time I do not wish to enjoy it down here."

On the 7th of this month, after she had spent the whole day in a gentle slumber, she had a strong paroxysm in the evening at around 7 o'clock. One could only guess that the hour of her long desired blessed end would soon be there; for this reason various Sisters had gathered in a larger room and were singing gently for her and keeping watch, of which she seemed to be fully aware. She then received the blessing for her Going Home, at which she folded her weak hands and repeatedly held them high until the blessed moment occurred at 9.30 P.M. when the Friend of her soul took her home gently and peacefully and thus mercifully fulfilled her greatest and much repeated wish and request, after a pilgrimage down here of 58 years, 5 months, and 6 days.

> So rest then in the arms of your Saviour
> Enjoy the happiness for which you longed
> For which your eyes so often shed tears
> Here your element was His mercy only
> His death and Suffering the pasture of your heart
> Now refresh yourself with it in eternal joy.
> Now you may praise the Friend undisturbed
> The beautiful Friend, who took your heart
> Who came to your aid in times of distress.
> And made the hardest tests easy
> You, Sister, eternally did you shed tears
> And eternally you see Him now who has redeemed you.
> How must you feel now, gazing at the holy Wounds
> In which you have seen your happiness and election to grace

As a comfort and joy in the Vale of Tears
Especially in the hard times of pain
When you enjoy the great glory
Which rewards you handsomely for suffering of this Life.
You are lucky, You are close to the Highest
To whom you often looked full of faith
To whom you sent not a few little tears
To the Friend, who saw your misery full of compassion
And as soon as His blessed hour struck
Carried you home to His chamber in Joy.
Live well there at home, where many of His sick ones
Whom you have cared for have gone before you
For every act of faithfulness, which you have shown here
You will receive the reward from Him Himself
A look of Grace from God's own Son
Is surely for you a too great reward.

Margareth Barbara Seidner
1714–1796

Born in the southwestern corner of the Holy Roman Empire, Margareth Seidner, like Maria Horn, experienced first hand the Protestant spiritual awakening in Franconia. Like thousands of other Protestants before and after her, she read Johannes Arndt's 1605 volume True Christianity. *One of the most popular Protestant devotional books of the seventeenth and eighteenth centuries, Arndt's* True Christianity *belongs to the baroque tradition of employing emblematic symbolism in the development and maintainance of individual faith. The book, which went through many reprints both in Germany and in North America, is illustrated with woodcuts, representing various stages of faith, which are then elucidated in both symbolic interpretation and biblical exegesis.*

Margareth Seidner's path to full membership in the Moravian Church is not straightforward. Once received into the congregation in Herrnhaag, she was not automatically admitted to Holy Communion. Rather, she had to wait for three years before she was able to join the other members of the congregation in what was considered to be the pinnacle of the communal experience. From her experience it can be seen that first communion did not automatically follow reception into the Congregation but rather that it might be delayed for some time. Prior to Holy Communion, candidates would be interviewed by Choir Helpers to determine whether or not they were ready to participate. If the Choir Helper, by means of the lot, deemed that the condition of their soul and heart was not prepared for Communion, they would be asked to wait for the next Communion, when they would be interviewed again. Once the individual was admitted to Holy Communion, it was assumed that an interview [Sprechen] was only necessary if there appeared to be a good reason for it.

Our departed sister Margareth Barbara Seidner has left us the following about her course through life:

I was born on April 9, 1714, in Grünwerth in Franconia, about an hour from Wertheim. It happened to be Maundy Thursday, and I was baptized on Good Friday. My late father, Georg Seidner, who was a wine grower and farmer, and my mother Anna Margretha, raised me according to their knowledge in the fear of God. Already in my tender youth, the Holy Spirit was at work in my heart, but at that time I did not rightly understand this fact, until I was older and came to love the world and things that belonged to it. But I could never pursue sin and the things of this world without feeling the greatest unease in my heart. In my 26th year I was brought to reflection through reading Arndt's *True Christianity,* and the Holy Spirit made me recognize that I could not be saved in the condition in which I was. For some time I continued in great distress about my unblessed state, until I happened to become acquainted with Br. and Sr. Lutz, who had two daughters in Herrnhaag. When they noticed that I was worried about my salvation they advised me to make a visit to Herrnhaag with them. This I gladly accepted. Thus, in February 1742, I travelled there with them. Straight away I got the strong impression that these were truly a people of God. I immediately applied for permission to remain with the Congregation, which, to my joy, I received. After some time my parents required that I should come home to give assistance to my mother, who was sickly. In the meantime my heart remained full of longing and desire to return soon to the Congregation. Finally, my father went for a visit to Herrnhaag himself to see what kind of people these might be to whom I so dearly wished to go. When he arrived there he received such a strong impression that these really were a people of God that he was not only helpful to me in returning to the Congregation but he also said, "If I were still single, I would go there myself to live."

After some pressure and mockery that I had to endure not only from my mother but also from my friends, I returned with the help of my dear father on December 28, 1743, to dear Herrnhaag where I soon settled in.

On February 29, 1744, I was received into the Congregation, at which point I gave myself up anew to the dear Saviour as His own in eternity. At the same time I asked Him not to allow me to be admitted to Holy Communion before I had got to know myself thoroughly, who I am and what He means to me, so that I would not have to go one time and then remain behind the next—which I was afraid of, and He also heard me in this my request. On April 21, 1747, I enjoyed Holy Communion with the Congregation for the first time. What I felt and enjoyed then no words can express. And thus the dear Saviour kept me (in our dear Herrnhaag) in all my poverty and with my many faults and wants until, in 1750, I along with a company of single sisters left as exiles for Zeyst, where we stayed for nine months. During the last month before our departure for America, we had a truly blessed choir Holy Communion in the dear Disciple's House.

Thus far her own words.

In 1762, our late sister took over the care of the vegetable garden and the livestock for our choir's Economy, tasks she performed very faithfully for twenty-four years. She enjoyed good health thereby, for which she thanked the dear Saviour very often. In July 1786, she was affected by a stroke so that she was completely crippled, but through the application of medicines she recovered enough that she was able to walk again. She had a tender love for the Saviour, and she appreciated the good fortune of being in a congregation of Jesus. And so for the last eight years she spent her time quite happily and helped where she could, as much as her weakness permitted her to, until, in July 1794, she had another stroke and had to move into the sickroom completely. The dear Saviour had to comfort her often, especially when the time before she could go to Him sometimes seemed too long and her desire for this became stronger and stronger. Two weeks ago the attack came again and she was completely paralyzed on one side, so that she now had to be cared for like a child. This continued until on the 27th in the evening at a quarter past nine, the blessed moment arrived when she was released from her pain, and her soul went over into the arms of her Redeemer with the blessing of the Congregation and of her choir at the age of 81 years, 10 months, and a few days.

Benigna Zahm
1748–1804

Like Eva Lanius, Benigna Zahm was born in Pennsylvania in the 1740s. However,
unlike Eva, Benigna was actually born into the Moravian Congregation in Bethle-
hem during the time of the General Economy. As her memoir reveals, the communal
structure of the congregation at that time meant that she was not raised by her
parents but rather in the Nursery. From the Nursery she went on to the Greater Girls'
Choir and then the Single Sisters where she became a teacher to the children. Be-
nigna's memoir provides the reader with an excellent example of a life shaped from
cradle to grave by the Moravian Church. Both her vocabulary and the expression of
her faith in terms of her complete reliance on Christ, coupled with her humility, reflect
Moravian piety of the eighteenth century. Of additional interest is her description of
the effect of the breakup of the General Economy on the schools and thus also on the
employment of the Single Sisters.

Our dear late Sister Benigna Zahm has left the following short account
of her course through this life.

I was born on October 18, 1748, in Bethlehem and moved that same
year with my dear parents to Nazareth and on April 5, 1750, entered the
Nursery. In 1752, I returned to Bethlehem to the Children's Home. I loved
the children and soon felt Jesus' torment and death in my heart. If I erred
somehow, I could not be at peace and be content until I received complete
forgiveness for this from the Saviour and my superiors. I often found cause
to cry in solitude over my mistakes before my best Saviour, and He never
left me without comfort. On February 26, 1760, when the watchword read,
"If we confess our sins, He forgives us according to His faithful heart and
in His holiness He frees us from all that is not right. On the day of judg-
ment, in the light of His light it will be revealed how the spattering of
blood keeps our garments clean!" Br. Peter Böhler[9] gave a memorable
address on this verse and an especial visitation of grace came upon the
older children. The Holy Spirit showed us that some of the things that
happened among us did not accord with the mind and heart of the Saviour.
We became greatly troubled at this, confessed our errors to the Saviour,
and also spoke openly to our Labouress. She recommended us in all our
misery to the Saviour, and He was so merciful and granted us complete

forgiveness and absolution. I shall never forget this event and the impression of it and what it accomplished for my heart and my future life. Now I could really make use of the last year that I had to spend in the Children's Choir. I entered into a tender relationship with the dear Saviour. In the evening, when I went to bed, I was in a favorite little place where I could talk things through with the best friend of children quite undisturbed. Oh how happy I was! How sweetly close He was to my heart! The children's meetings were great and important to me and offered a true blessing to my poor heart. At that time I also made use of the Holy Communion days, especially when the Congregation was together in the Hall. I liked then to walk in quiet to talk to the dear Saviour, and often during such conversations with Him, I would receive the most blessed glimpse of Him. During just such a conversation with my Friend and Lover, my good fortune at being born and raised in a congregation of Jesus became all at once so great and important to me that I thanked my Saviour with a thousand tears.

On March 25, 1761, I was received into the Great Girls' Choir. On this occasion I committed myself to the dear Saviour anew and asked Him to assist me especially in this Choir. It soon became my desire to be received into the Congregation, and I cried quite a few tears to my best Friend on His faithful heart about this. He was soon moved by my entreaties for, in that same year on December 6, He granted my wish. My heart dissolved in shame and humility at my Saviour's feet. But I found that my longing had not been quite stilled. A new desire was aroused in me; namely, my longing soon to become a partaker of the body and blood of my Saviour in the Holy Communion. At the same time it was still my chief request that He should reveal Himself and His whole meritorious suffering and death to me, so that I could receive a quite strong impression of this. He would surely allow me to partake of the Congregation of grace at the right time. And so it was; I did not have to wait long, for on May 8 I experienced the indescribably great grace of enjoying, for the first time in Holy Communion, the body and blood of my Friend who was tormented for me, during which I was heavenly happy. Later, I often remembered this first enjoyment of Holy Communion and the last year that I spent happily in the Children's Choir. Also, I will never forget the first two years in the Girls' Choir and what my heart enjoyed then in quiet company with my invisible but inwardly near Friend. But the older I grew, the more that which was not good inside me awoke. To my pain I also noticed that my heart was no longer in such a continual conversation with my Saviour and also that I no longer had honesty of heart. This often drove me to hot tears and moved me to plead passionately with the Saviour. But even in this He was moved by my entreaties; He gave me courage and joy to reveal myself to my Choir Labouress just as I was; in all my misery she guided me to Jesus' feet and, thus comforted, I dared to go to my favourite place and cried myself quite dry and stammered out my misery to Him as well as I could. I did not leave that place uncomforted; no, I experienced grace and mercy. From then on, it became clear to me that honesty of heart was an essential thing to walk happily and contentedly in His footsteps.

In August 1766, I was sent to the children. For the first few years I had quite a time of trial; I often therefore wished to be relieved of this post, which was really difficult for me, but when I had to spend eight weeks in the sickroom—I had burnt my foot with boiling water and it became very nasty—I wondered earnestly whether the dear Saviour did not want to tell me something with this. I cried out many things to Him and asked Him that, if it were His merciful wish that I should be of some use in the service of the children, He should make this service a grace to me. He did this too, for on the day on which I could once again leave the sickroom the Saviour filled my heart with comfort and joy, and I could confidently hope that He would help me through all hardships.

On May 4, 1767, I was received into the Single Sisters' Choir. I gave myself anew to the Bridegroom of my soul and made the covenant with Him to become and remain His faithful handmaiden. I felt His gracious presence the whole day long in the most blessed fashion, especially during the enjoyment of Holy Communion, which we had at the close of this happy festival day I cannot describe how I felt then, especially as I prostrated myself and enjoyed His body. I felt something that I had never felt before during any Holy Communion. I wanted to remain prostrate before Him and cry myself away to Him. From then on the Choir Holy Communion remained especially dear to me. In this Choir that was so dear to me I also got to know myself better and better with the schooling of the Holy Spirit. I often recognized that I am a poor sinner that cannot come to rights without the Saviour.

On March 11, 1770, in a Congregation Hour that the late Br. Thrane[10] held on the watchword "I gave my back to the smiters. The scourges and the fetters, and what you endured, that has paid the price of my soul,"[11] it was as though all the sins that I had committed throughout my life were standing there in front of my eyes, with which I had often tortured my Saviour again and anew. And at first a fear came over me that made me tremble. But finally I burst into heavy tears. I implored the dear Saviour to forgive me everything, which He also did. From now on sin, yes, everything toward which until now I had felt inclined, became abhorrent to me, and I wished to have nothing more to do with it. If, however, from time to time some of that was aroused in me again I complained of it to the dear Saviour with many tears and whispered to Him to His heart and ear, "You know that I want to have nothing more to do with this, so free me from it completely," and He heard me, for I truly felt that the power of His merits and suffering killed the sin in me more and more. At that time the Holy Spirit made the whole passion of my dear Saviour quite clear and apparent to me, and I received a deep impression of this that remained with me. I could think with an honest heart—"The scourges and the fetters, and what He endured, that has paid the price of my soul." Yes, when I considered His tortured beauty and entered into a conversation with Him about it, each time it seemed to me as it is expressed in the verse "My heart becomes alive, when I see the heavy blows to His back, how they lacerated Him, the pure body, the chaste one, oh, thus He pleases my soul!"

On October 26, 1772, when the Hourly Intercessions were implemented anew, I experienced the grace of becoming a member of the same without having any notion of it; what my poor heart enjoyed there when I could speak so confidentially and alone with my unseen but very close Friend, and lay to His heart my own needs, the affairs of my Choir, which was so dear to me, and of every individual person, the joys and woes of the whole Moravian Church, of the missions among the heathen, the educational institutions, yes, everything that concerned His Congregation and its classes. And what a rich blessing I harvested from this. About this I do not have the words to express myself as I would like to. So, in this same year on Christmas Eve, I received a deep and lasting impression of my dear Saviour becoming incarnate so that my heart was drowned in many tears. And the following day, that is on Christmas Day, during our Choir worship, I was able to make the merits of His holy incarnation quite especially my own, and I thanked Him especially for the fact that He had assumed our mortal frame in the body of a young virgin, and I was happy that I too am able to enjoy and benefit in body and soul from all the blessings that lie in His holy incarnation. At the end of the 1775th year, I became distressed that I could not follow in all parts the example that His holy pilgrimage on earth provided. Yes, I found myself to be far behind. I could not yet think, speak and act like my Jesus, how He had thought, spoken and acted on earth. I prayed fervently to Him, to make me ever more like His pattern, yes, to form me into it quite utterly. At this I felt His blessed nearness in the strongest fashion and received from Him the assurance in my heart that He would keep His dear promise that I should still become His whole joy.

Thus far her own words.

On September 4, 1779, she was released from her thirteen years of service in the Children's Home after the Home here had become smaller and smaller and the then Children's Labouress, the late Sister Esther Wappler, who had until then lived in the Children's Home, moved into the Sisters' House. The faithful assistance that she gave the above mentioned Sister most willingly during her service in the Home and then for many years in the Choir House until the late Sister's death has justified her among us. But her humble and lowly spirit has not permitted her to say much about her service in the Home and in the raising of the children. Also she left word both by mouth and in writing that not much should be said about her after her going home, for, she said, she had nothing but poverty and misery to show and everything that was good about her was only the undeserved grace and mercy of her faithful and good Saviour. In spite of this, those who enjoyed her good and loyal instruction and education cannot be completely silent. In any case only this much should be said: that she was tirelessly faithful and watchful day and night and took care of the school instruction in the best and most punctual fashion. But what was the closest to her heart above anything else was the welfare of the children who had been placed in her care. She used every opportunity to show them the love of the Saviour towards them and to awaken their love for Him, to have them learn verses that were about this and to sing them often with them. Her service is and will always remain a blessed and pleasant memory to all those who enjoyed it.

In the above mentioned year she was accepted as an acolyte along with several other sisters. She now spent her time quite happily in a sister's room in quiet conversation with the Friend of her soul, until in the year 1790 she allowed herself to be found willing to serve as the Eldress of the Great Girls, in the service of whom she remained until this her final illness and until five weeks before her end. Their welfare was close to her heart, and she cried many a sigh and quiet tear on their behalf at Jesus' feet, and He who forgets neither a little sigh nor misses a little tear will, as we hope, let us see rich fruits from this.

As far as her actual character is concerned, her choir associates say in unison that she was truly a poor one of the Lord. Her superior gift and patience in dealing with the young, her willingness to serve others without thinking of herself, her tender relationship with the Friend of her soul shone forth from her whole general behaviour; her happy, cheerful and blessed nature, her ability to sing extremely beautifully with which she was a daily edification to her choir and often also to the whole congregation, her taste for the choir and congregation meetings, taught us to treasure her like a jewel and her all too early loss is mourned by our whole choir. But let us be silent—it is the Lord's doing. To us she was dear and worthy, but she was too dear to Him to leave her longer with us.

Her final illness was a consumption, which was probably the result of a high bilious fever that overcame her last year in the month of March, but from which she recovered against all expectations, until the beginning of this year the cough that her last illness had left her with became ever heavier and more painful. But during this she remained happy and content. She also took care of her affairs as much as possible, until she was overcome by a great weakness last February 25 and had to move into the sickroom. But neither she nor we believed that she was so near her end. On March 29, Maundy Thursday, early in the morning, a great constriction of the chest befell her, and it could soon be seen that the lover of her soul was hurrying with her completion. When she was told that it seemed as though the dear Saviour would soon bring her home to Himself, she smiled and said, "I am not worthy that He does this with me so beautifully! But He never comes to me too soon, the sooner the better!" It was remarkable to us that her day of going home fell according to her wish; she had often said, even in her days of health, that she could think of nothing more beautiful than if Good Friday could be her day of going home. And so it happened, for on March 30, quite early in the morning, she fell asleep quite gently with the blessing of the congregation and her choir. She had reached an age of 55 years, 5 months, and 12 days.

> Dear Child of Grace
> Soft and quick
> You went into eternal joy.
> There unknowing of care, fear and suffering
> Close to Jesus' breast
> Your soul now
> Drinks only the oil of joy
> The eternal sun now gives you
> Only happiness and bliss
> Which with its beam
>
> Brightened for you this earth
> Through the dark valley
> Until you reached
> Your place in the eternal tabernacles

Where the Lamb is enthroned in the midst,
The Lamb that was slain for us
And who carried you through

Carried you beautifully through
And made you quite happy
Were bliss, peace and joy
To you in all hours, Life and blessedness.

You wanted to be His
Completely and alone,
Were that too—to Jesus' praise,
Whether loud or soft.
You clearly showed
What had happened to you.

Gentleness, humility
Poverty, sincerity
A deep and beautiful submission
Were yours, excellently.
Loyalty, punctuality
Were always

Your decoration here.
With loyalty and pains
You raised the young,
Taught them to flee evil.
A few little tears
Flowed into His heart.

For their welfare
For their salvation
That they would always cling to His stem
As good vines
And only in Him
Be found.

For that reason they call out
"Thank God for her trouble
Give her for our sakes

For this an eternal blessing
May not a single sigh
Be forgotten."

So now recommend the reward of loyal maids
To the bored-through feet
Which you will kiss a thousand times
For your lot of grace
Which is truly great.

All grant you your happiness.
We who remain here
Will hope for that moment in faith
When also for us
Jesus' arms and lap will open.
Oh what a lovely lot! (See illus. 10)

Memoirs of the Married Sisters

THE MARRIED SISTERS

An Introduction

Unlike other religious communities in both Germany and North America in the eighteenth century, the Moravian church did not advocate celibacy but rather encouraged marriage. Zinzendorf did not consider the Married Choir to be in any way a lesser order in the Moravian Church than the Single Sisters and Single Brethren (in contrast, for example, to the House-holders in the Ephrata Cloister).[1] On the contrary, Zinzendorf understood marriage to be a service to the church and Christ and, therefore, defined marriage as a positive (and also necessary) step in a women's life. His notion of the "marriage militant," or *Streiterehe* meant that married women gave up their children to the nursery as soon as they were weaned in order to devote all their energies to working with their husband for the church as missionaries or on farms or in trades for the community. The Elders decided where the married couple should fulfill their "Plan" and some-times moved the couple from congregation to congregation as they saw fit (see, for example, the memoir of Anna Worbass).

When Bethlehem was first organized into choirs in June 1742, the married people were the cornerstone of both the House Congregation (eleven couples) and the Pilgrim Congregation (four couples) (see illus. 11). However, married men and women did not live together in Bethlehem in the early years of the settlement but rather they formed their separate choirs. Attempts were made to ensure that the married couples were able to meet in private once a week. With the dissolution of the General Economy, the married couples lived together in their own households.

Married women fulfilled a variety of roles within the Moravian church. Married women, working alongside their husbands, were storekeepers (Edmonds), financial managers (Grube), missionaries (Jungmann), and stewards, who took care of the temporal affairs of a congregation or choir.

Some of the women who entered the Moravian Church did so without their husbands (see Johanna Parsons and Marianna Hoeht), some married after they had entered the congregation, and some came into the congregation with their husbands. Especially in the latter case, it was the task of the Married Choir Helper to define Moravian marriage as a part of one's service to God and as a relationship in which both partners must love God more than they love each other. Occasionally, a married couple would consider that marital relations were contrary to God's wishes and would opt for celibacy. In such cases the Helper had to make it quite clear that marriage was a good *Gottesdienst* or service to God.

Zinzendorf considered that everything that took place within marriage should be understood as a *Gottesdienst,* including marital relations. "The human being is the noblest creature especially in the moment of conception," he claimed.[2] The Instructions to the Helper of the Single Sisters in Bethlehem state quite clearly that "everything that married people do who are the children of God in word or deed happens in the name of Jesus Christ and in His presence so that in the married state as little as in the single state they may serve the pleasures of the flesh but rather must take care of their souls through the Holy Spirit and make their bodies a sacrifice to God."[3] Marital union or *Vereinigung* was blessed by the Creator, and thus the conception of children was a respectable activity. But marital relations were not only blessed because of the conception of children. Zinzendorf emphasized the fact that marital relations were in and of themselves a pure act if performed with the innocence of Adam and Eve before the Fall. The reproductive organs *(Zeugungs-Glieder)* existed not only to procreate but also to achieve the innermost connection *(innigste Verbindung)* with each other and the church: "the whole way of marriage must be an image of Christ and His Church, even in this matter,"[4] the instructions to the Single Sisters said. Marital relations were considered to be a liturgical action.

The married women's memoirs do not contain much detail about husbands or children. A husband, as in the case of Margareth Jungmann, was a partner in God's work. Primary importance was given to the nature of the women's relationship to their eternal bridegroom, Christ, rather than to an account of their earthly marriage.

Martha Büninger, née Marriner
1723–1773

Martha Büninger's memoir is the earliest in this collection, dated 1752. It is presented here with the comments of her husband, Abraham.

Having gone to serve the mission at Gnadenhütten on Mahony Creek, northwest of Bethlehem (a task not without dangers — on November 23, 1755, the mission was burned down and most of the missionaries killed by Indians; see below passim), both Abraham and Martha were requested to write something about their lives. Martha did not know her exact date of birth, nor did she ever know her father. She became an indentured servant at the age of seven. She was awakened during the Bible classes given by Thomas Noble, a merchant in New York, who was a friend of the Moravian Church and with whom Zinzendorf stayed when he first arrived in America in 1741. Here she met many other Moravians, among others Elizabeth Boehler, wife of Peter Boehler, the leader of the Moravians in New York at that time. Martha joined the Single Sisters' Choir in Bethlehem in 1746 where she lived with the other Single Sisters under the guidance of Eldress Anna Rosina Anders. Shortly after entering the congregation Martha was asked to marry Abraham Büninger, who had joined the Brethren in Georgia in the late 1730s and followed the Moravians to Bethlehem in 1742. A native of Switzerland, Abraham was ordained in 1756. He and Martha worked with the Indians (as we can see from this memoir) and then also in the West Indies. As stewards of the congregation at Gnadenhütten, Abraham and Martha were in charge of its temporal affairs, although they may also have had religious duties. Abraham died in Salem, New York, in 1811, a year before his wife. Penciled onto the original memoir is the information "D. 1812, Salem NY."

On January 2, 1752, I arrived with my dear Martha in Gnadenhütten, I as teacher and steward of the small congregation, and Martha as steward and cook. The following is by my dear Martha:

I was born in Rhode Island. My father's name was John Marriner, my mother's Elisabeth, born in New England, my father however in Old England; I never knew my father. I was baptized by a Presbyterian minister. When I was a small child, I went with my mother to Jamaica in the West Indies. My mother went there in the hope of seeing my father but could learn nothing about him. He is probably buried at sea. When I was 7½ years old, my mother indentured me until the age of eighteen to a Quaker, Augustus Hix, on Long Island. I was with him on Long Island for four years; when he moved to New York I stayed with him until my time was up. He is a good master and looked after me like his own child. When I was released from him, I stayed in New York for a while, after which I went to Brunswick. Here I came upon the awakened people and was awakened by them and stayed with them for three months. The first feeling that I had of the Saviour and His bloody wound and that He had died for me too was in a Bible class, which Brother Noble held in New York. At that time I received an inclination to the brothers and sisters and soon became acquainted with Sister Boehler. When the Act[5] against the Brethren came out in New York, I went immediately to Philadelphia. There I lived with my old master Augustus Hix for five months, also a time with Mr. Evans.

I came to the congregation in Bethlehem on March 26, 1745. I stayed there until the Single Sisters went to Nazareth.[6] In Nazareth, many things happened to me, such that I wanted to leave several times. The dear Saviour, however, made it so that I received a blessed and contented heart with the Single Sisters. On September 28, 1746 (old style), I was received into the Congregation by the dear mother Maria Spangenberg.[7] My heart was thereby very blessed.

On October 1 o. s., the dear mother Spangenberg spoke and proposed my marriage to my dear husband. I immediately gave myself up to the will of the dear Saviour. On October 5/16 I was married. On October 11 (old style) I went to Communion with the Congregation for the first time.

This is all I have been able to write about us poor children. Our goal and purpose is to belong completely to the Saviour and to live for Him and His dear Congregation. We are grateful that right up to this day they have loved us poor children and carried us with patience. May the Lamb keep us in His bloody wounds, that no harm come to us until we can see Him and kiss the wounds in His hands and feet. Until the kiss of His side wound."

Note: According to her own reckoning, my Martha was born in October 1723.

Dear Brother Mattheus,

I want to take this opportunity to send you and your dear sick Anna Maria many hearty greetings and kisses in the dearest wounds of our Lamb. We have thought of you a great deal, especially of your dear wife. We are happy that she is feeling better now.

I'm sending you a short report of my and my dear wife's biography. I see that I have not been too successful at it. I hope that it contains what you wanted to know. We, especially my dear Martha, are sorry that she knows nothing about her birthdate. She has written about that to Augustus Hix, because he may well know it.

I have nothing else to write. We are blessed and content in our Lamb's wounds here in Gnadenhütten. We greet you and your dear Anna Maria and everyone many times. We remain your poor brethren, Abraham and Martha Büninger.

27. April, 1752

Margaretha Edmonds, née Anton
1721–1773

Like Martha Büninger, Margaretha Edmonds also became acquainted with the Moravian Church through the New York Society. In her memoir, Margaretha recounts how she met all the leading Moravians of the 1740s in New York City and also how she was awakened by George Whitefield's sermons while there. As a young woman, Margaretha lived with her aunt and uncle, Lucas and Judith Brasier, who became members of the Moravian Society in New York City in 1744. In New York, she heard the sermons of some of the most famous Moravian preachers of the time, Owen Rice, James Greening, and Hector Gambold. She moved to Bethlehem to marry William Edmonds, who was later to run the Bethlehem Store. In October 1755, her husband was elected to the Assembly of Pennsylvania as the second representative from Northampton County. He served in that capacity long past his wife's death, negotiating between the Assembly, the Moravian congregations, and the Indian nations.

Margaretha dictated the first part of her memoir to her husband on March 31, 1755, before the birth of their first child. In it, she clearly points out that she is awakened not by attempting to achieve salvation, grace, or faith through her own efforts but rather, as a true Moravian, through complete dependence on Christ for His freely given grace.

Particulars of the departed sister Margaretha Edmonds, née Anton, as the same dictated to her dear husband:

I, Margaretha Edmonds, a daughter of Henrich and Eva Anton was born in New York on March 7th, 1721, baptized in the Dutch Reformed Church, and raised in my dear parents' religion. Until my eleventh year, I enjoyed my mother's guidance in the things proper to the female sex; for then when she died I came to my father's half-sister (Judith Brasier) who was married to Lucas Brasier. When I was older, I was awakened by Mr. Whitefield's sermons, and on a pleasure trip to Albany on which my mother's sister had taken me to visit a few relatives, the dear Saviour led me to understand that the amusements that occurred there were nothing but vain things that brought the heart no true pleasure. The Saviour then also gave me the grace to begin to feel for myself the hardness of my heart and my own inability to believe in Him; for I then applied all my strength in

order to receive a believer's heart for my Saviour until I became convinced
in another way in the Brethren's sermons. In particular, Br. Greening's[8]
English preaching and his and his wife's cordial relationship with me were
a blessing for my heart. After some time, Br. and Sr. Gambold[9] came to
New York, and the words that he once said to me, that the Saviour was to
be found neither in heaven above nor here below in some place or other
but rather in the heart, pierced me to such an extent that I cried many
tears for grace. Now and then, the faithful Saviour allowed me to feel His
nearness and love as well as my lack of faith. At last, through the sermons
of Br. Rice, I began to understand better the Brethren's teachings about
the Saviour's free grace towards poor sinners, and I was able to give myself
up to the Saviour, just the way I was, and He allowed me to find grace in
His blood.

In the year 1753, I was received into the Congregation in New York, and
when, after some time, Sr. Anna Ramsberg[10] came to us as our Choir
Helper, I experienced many blessings for my heart in my open-hearted
relationship with her. She also gently advised me to be patient, when I
confessed to her my great desire for Holy Communion, and to wait for
the dear Saviour's own good time. In the year 1754, on Good Friday, I
experienced the great grace of enjoying the Holy Sacrament of his Body
and Blood for the first time with the Congregation in New York. Now, I
thought, everything was in order, for I did not yet know my great fall and
the ruin of my heart. But the Holy Spirit taught me to understand it ever
better and from day to day to look to the Saviour and His Grace, and so I
went my way, sinner-happy and blessed. After some time[11] I thought about
going to the Congregation in Bethlehem but, because my aunt,[12] Judith
Brasier, was a very dear sister and also weak, I decided to stay with her out
of love until she went home. However, in February 1755, I unexpectedly
received a call to come to Bethlehem, to marry my dear husband, and to
help him in the Store there.[13] On March 31, I entered into holy matrimony
with him in Bethlehem. Now I hope that my dear Saviour will keep me in
Him and in His wounds and in His dear Congregation, and always wash
me in His costly blood until I receive the grace to see Him face to face and
to kiss His pierced feet, Amen.

Thus far her own words.

In the year 1756, in October, a daughter was bestowed upon her who
received the name of Judith in Holy Baptism. From November 18, she also
had the joy of having her with her, to teach her in housekeeping matters.[14]

In the year 1763, she and her husband moved from the Bethlehem Store to the store house in Plainfield,[15] which had just been built, until they could move on October 27th last year into the house that had been built in the new little Place Congregation. We cannot, at this point, be silent but, rather, must say truthfully that she applied all her loyal diligence and care wherever she worked with her husband in the Store and took care of the household with the same untiring loyalty. According to her heart, we have found her to be tenderly attached to the Saviour and His people, and she was regarded in her life with respect and love. Nonetheless, she recognized and often admitted her mistakes and shortcomings and soon sought forgiveness and absolution from the Saviour when she found something false in herself. She was most concerned to enjoy the Opportunities [services] with the Congregation. When she was still living in Plainfield, she often longed tearfully, or regretted it from all her heart, when circumstances prevented her from coming to the meetings. When the new house was hardly finished, she hurried to move in and, when she lived here, she really proved that the Opportunities were her concern, just as she had so often declared.

Two weeks ago she participated in the meeting where her step-daughter Margaretha was bound together in holy matrimony with Br. Schlöser, and she cared for her as a true mother to her both before and after. On the Tuesday after the wedding she was about to go with her daughter Judith to the liturgical Opportunity in the Hall, but shortly beforehand she was overcome with such a severe chill that she could hardly get up the stairs to the upper floor and soon had to lie down. From then on she did not get up again for[16] a severe fever followed, which kept growing regardless of the fact that one did what one could and what was prescribed[17] by the doctor in Bethlehem. But nothing else could be done because a severe inflammation started, but she still remained mostly conscious (and knew everyone who visited her). Finally, she enjoyed Holy Communion on her sick bed exactly a week ago with great reverence, and was very grateful for this great grace and gave herself up childlikely to the Saviour's will and whatever He wanted to do with her. The hour of her parting came ever closer and her dear husband, the present widower, came and gave her up into the arms and lap of her eternal bridegroom, who took her on the 26th. The day before yesterday in the afternoon in the second hour, as she was read the verse "as your lips pallid grow . . .", at the words "so go to the Congregation, your body will live again" she grew pale. Her age was 52 years, less 8 days.

Johanette Maria Ettwein
1725–1773

Johanette Ettwein was the wife of Johannes Ettwein (1721–1802), one of the leading organizers of the North American Moravian communities in Pennsylvania and North Carolina. (illus. 12) He was born in Freudenstadt in Württemberg on June 29, 1721, and joined the Moravian congregation at Marienborn in 1739. Seven years later, Johanette and Johannes were married in Zeyst and sent to London to serve the Moravian community there in 1750. They were called to Pennsylvania in 1754, and then, from 1758–66, they served in Wachovia (North Carolina). Johannes and Johanette returned to Bethlehem after the break up of the General Economy to assist Bishop Nathaniel Seidel in the running of the reorganized Bethlehem congregation, at which point Johannes was ordained Bishop. He was best known for his leadership of the Bethlehem congregation through the Revolutionary War period.

Unfortunately, Johanette's "short essay" referred to in the first paragraph of the text is no longer extant. She died while her husband was on a trip to Europe, and in his absence the memoir was pieced together by a scribe from her own essay and notes. The fact that Johannes's comments would have been needed to compose the memoir reflects a significant change in the role of the spouse in the Moravian practice of memoir writing after the reorganization of the Bethlehem Economy. Prior to the breakup it would have been the Choir Helper who would have completed the memoir (as the person who knew the deceased best). After the breakup, with the institution of family households, it was the spouse who assumed that role.

The life story of our departed sister Johannette Maria Ettwein née Kimbel would best and most reliably be told and maybe still can be told by her dear husband, our dear Brother Johannes Ettwein, who is at the moment in Europe or on his way to us.[18] But as a short essay about the conditions of her life exists in the departed sister's own hand so we cannot do otherwise than to mention something of her life, albeit in an incomplete fashion.

She was born on September 26, 1725, in the county of Sayn in Westphalia.[19] God blessed the testimony of Brother Wredow, the preacher there, and the visits of Sisters from the Congregation passing through as the instruments of her awakening. She herself writes of this:

I was already awakened in my childhood, and from my twelfth year I knew that I must love the Saviour. My late father took great pains to raise us children for the Lord, and my late mother, who was ill for nine years, told me that there is a Saviour who can help. Her faith made her well. I often saw her lying face down and praying, a sight that always touched me and made me think, if only I were like her!

At my confirmation for my first Holy Communion my heart felt a particular blessing, although it was not the same as what I felt at my first communion in the Congregation. In 1739, in my fourteenth year, I had a special experience one night, when I felt that the Saviour had forgiven me everything. This caused me to live a blessed life, although I still often felt my faith to be weak. My best friend did not leave me, however.

In 1741, my dear father Peter Kimbel died happily in the Saviour. During his last hours he blessed each of his children as a farewell and said to me, "You are going to the Congregation," which pleased me greatly, and he also asked that Pastor Wredow help me in this. I stayed with my mother until March 1742, and then came to Marienborn into the Economy.[20] In 1744, I went to Br. and Sr. Schellinger,[21] who looked after me like their own child and took me with them to Holland. In 1745, I became an acolyte and on March 11th 1746, I was joined in holy matrimony with my dear husband.

After this I travelled with him to Holland, where I visited my dear mother again, who was very ill and longed for her dissolution, and was very pleased to see me once again. Shortly after this she died peacefully. In Zeyst[22] we were ordained as deacons and went to England, where we stayed with our beloved Johannes and Benigna.[23] In 1747, it was back to Herrnhaag, where my dear husband was very ill. After various journeys to Herrnhut and back again, the Saviour blessed me in Herrnhaag with my first daughter, with whom I lived in Lindheim[24] in 1749, and in 1750 I travelled to London with my dear husband where, in the following years, we had a happy time in the Disciple's House. In 1754, we went to Pennsylvania, and in 1759, I travelled to North Carolina with my dear husband, but left my two sons, Christian and Johannes, in Nazareth. Thus far her own words.[25]

Because, in the following years, her husband made many, sometimes distant, journeys in this country, on which she sometimes accompanied him, some information could be added to her own memoir if she had noted down what she experienced. She has put a few conversations down on paper, which she had with her invisible friend, and from these one can see how, even during the absence of her dear husband, her heart faithfully participated in everything which he did in the service of the Saviour, and how she frequently prayed for him and commended him and his service to the Saviour.

From these conversations, one can also see how the Holy Spirit brought her to accept the painful truth that the cause of all disturbances in her own blessed thoughts lay in the fact that she was not always a true poor sinner in her own eyes. It was her true heart's joy and her life to serve with joy and tirelessly her dear husband, all brothers and sisters, especially the pilgrims and visitors, in fact, everyone at every Opportunity, day and night.

She had no desire in her heart to accompany her husband at the beginning of this year to the Synod in Germany, to which she had been invited along with him, because she thought that because of her seasickness she would be more of a burden then a help, but she let her dear husband go with a childlike devoted heart.

In Spring, a great constriction of the chest manifested itself that stemmed from attacks of the dropsy. However, God blessed the use of medications, not only those of our doctors but also some from a visiting doctor from Philadelphia, who was consulted about it, so that she was liberated from this by summer, and her faithful belief that she would live to see her husband return was strengthened.

But, in August, this illness returned anew, and her strength declined to such a degree that all the faithful efforts of the doctors and all the possible care from her children and other sisters no longer had the desired effect.

She herself began to doubt that she would see her dear husband again, as her heart desired, and resigned herself to this. The Saviour Himself claimed her and she said, "I believe that He Himself will also comfort my dear husband when He calls me home to Him.[26]

On the festival day of the Married Choir, September 7th, she was so weak that she gave up all hope of participating in the Choir Communion. In the evening, the Saviour granted her relief from her chest pains, so that she could enjoy her part in this and after many sleepless nights also a gentle and peaceful night's sleep, even if in great weakness. In this night, one heard her speaking in her fantasy to her dear husband, as though she had him with her, and sympathize with him, that he had nearly been shipwrecked, and finally say to him, "I will now not be there any more when you come. This is the work of the Saviour and He will comfort you over this."

On the 8th, in the eleventh hour in the morning, a great change took place in her. Her completion neared and, with that, her heartfelt feeling of peace and proximity to Jesus and the blessing of the Lord in the name of the Congregation, which she had served with such a glad heart; all this could be told her absent dear husband. And so, this maid of Jesus gave up her spirit into Jesus' hands. Her age was 63 years, 11 months, and 13 days.

Sarah Grube, née van Fleck
1727–1793

Like Margaretha Edmonds and Martha Büninger, Sarah Grube was one of the early members of the New York Moravian Society. She was born into the van Vleck (here spelled van Fleck) family, which had close connections not only with the Moravian society but also with Count Zinzendorf himself. Her father, clerk to the New York merchant Thomas Noble, would have known all the leading Moravians of the time, and Sarah and her aunt, Catharina van Fleck, were listed as contributors to the costs of building the first Moravian Church in New York City in 1751.

In the memoir, Sarah's description of her vision of Christ in a dream is quite striking and, in fact, unusual in Moravian memoirs. Despite her earlier support of the Moravian Society, she claims that her actual awakening did not take place until she heard Peter Boehler preach in New York in 1755; and it is then that she realized that she must join the Moravian congregation in Bethlehem. Once a full member, Sarah worked throughout both her marriages in many of the smaller country congregations in Pennsylvania, New Jersey, and Maryland. She led something of an itinerant lifestyle, moving on to a new congregation every few years. Of particular interest is the text of her funeral service, a combination of Biblical texts and original poetry, which was attached to her memoir.

Personalia of the late sister Sarah Grube, née van Fleck, January 16, 1793.

I was born on December 11, 1727, in the city of New York and baptized into the Dutch Reformed Church, in which my father was an Elder. My father loved the Saviour and often laid his children to his heart with prayer and tears. His edifying life was a constant sermon to me and, from my youth on, I felt the traces of the Holy Spirit in my heart. From my 6th year onwards, I went to sewing school at my aunt Catharina van Fleck's, who also loved the Saviour and later became a member of the Brethren's Congregation. Because she was single, she often tried to persuade me to live with her; but such a lonely life did not appeal to me. In 1742, my dear father went blessedly to the Saviour, and I moved to live permanently with my aunt in answer to her constant pleas. She took me on as her child and often prayed for me in tears to the Saviour.

In 1744, as I was just at the point of being carried away by the vanities of the world, the faithful Saviour blocked my way and made me very uneasy about my condition. He took advantage of the situation one Sunday, as I was listening to a sermon (of *Domine Ritzema*) [27] in the Dutch Church on the text, "To as many as accepted Him He gave the power to become children of God, they who witness His name" [John 1:12]. I felt very clearly that I had not received the Saviour in faith in my heart and therefore was not yet a child of God, and this made me very unhappy. The following Sunday I went to a Brethren's meeting for the first time, but I was very scared that one of my relatives or friends would see me because at that time the Brethren were much despised, especially by the Reformed pastors. I sought peace for my soul, prayed and read a great deal, went diligently to church and in the evening went to the Brethren's Meetings. I fought against sin and tried all sorts of things but found no solace in anything. Once I decided to make myself holy, but at that hour I felt my depravity more than ever, for everything I did, yes even my prayer, became a sin for me, because I could not believe in the Saviour. In this my sorrow and misery I called to the Saviour with these words, "If you do not have mercy on me, I will be lost forever." Immediately, I felt the peace of God, and my heart was filled with love for the Saviour and for all people. However, in the next four years my state of bliss was not constant, for whenever I felt the misery of my sin, I became quite cast down and despondent, and when my Saviour once again looked mercifully upon me, I once again became full of life and contented. In 1748, when I became severely ill, the Saviour appeared before my heart, and it seemed to me as though He were stand-ing right in front of me in person and was showing me His hands with the marks of the nails, and said, "Look, into *these* hands I have inscribed you," and He assured me that everything He had done and suffered was also done for me. O, with what sweet feeling was I able to lay my head down on His head that was crowned with thorns for me: I heard in my heart the words, "It is finished!" [John 19:30] Yes, I often felt as though the Saviour were look-ing at me and saying, "You are truly beautiful and pure." The answer of my heart was, "Dear Saviour, it is with your righteousness that you have clothed me; [28] now I can believe that you are my God and Saviour." I desired to die soon in this blessed state of heart and to be at home with my Lord.

Now I was greatly concerned that my mother should also enjoy the blessed state of which I now partook. Therefore, I prayed to the Saviour for her, and He gave me the assurance that He would regard her with mercy and this He has kept to faithfully; for some years before her going home she came to love the Saviour dearly and found comfort in His suffering and death. In 1757, she departed this life very blessedly on September 29th—her 72nd birthday.

In 1755, when Br. Peter Böhler was preaching in New York, and especially when he announced the text, Psalm 45:11–12: "Hearken, O daughter, and consider, and incline thine ear; forget also thine own people, and thy father's house. So shall the king greatly desire thy beauty; for He *is* thy Lord; and worship thou Him", these words pierced my heart like an arrow, and I felt a call to give myself up completely to the Saviour and the Congregation. When I stayed away from the Communion in church for the first time, the preacher was most worried and sent his wife to me to ask why I had stayed away. I answered her that I had decided to join the Brethren. The preacher came himself and testified to his pain that I wanted to leave his church. However, when he saw that I was seriously determined to go to the Brethren, he said that he did not want to stop me but rather give me the Lord's blessing. My two eldest brothers also asked me how I could justify leaving the church into which I had been born and raised and enjoyed Holy Communion. I answered them, "If we were to appear once before the dear Saviour, He would not ask to which church we had belonged, but rather whether we were clothed in the righteousness of His blood." At that they let me go.

On October 6, 1755, I was received into the Congregation, at which point I felt the blessed peace of God in my heart. In 1757, the Saviour gave me a hard schooling and revealed my basic depravity to me more than ever before. It was, however, very hard for me to feel so sinful and to recognize that I had experienced so much grace for my heart already. But it did become clear to me that I should always come to the Saviour just as poor and miserable as on the first day, since He had forgiven my sins and taken them upon Himself. In 1758, on February 19, I became a candidate for Communion and on April 16 I was confirmed. I had such a strong desire to go to the Congregation in Bethlehem, however, that I had no peace day or night but did not know how I was to get away from my aunt because we were as one heart and soul together. Because I was used to visit Bethlehem often, I used that as my pretext and arrived in my dear Bethlehem on May 11. I soon revealed my desire to the brothers and sisters and requested them to ask the will of the Saviour as to my staying here, and to my great joy I received my permission to stay on May 22 and moved into my dear Choirhouse. On June 10, I went to Communion with the Congregation for the first time.

By staying, I incurred great displeasure from my aunt, for she loved me tenderly and had destined me to be her heiress. But that was all too venal for me, and the Saviour detached me from all my friends in the flesh.

After I had happily spent a year and a half in my dear Choirhouse, for which I cannot thank the Saviour enough, I was sent to the children and served them with pleasure but had a special schooling there for my heart. In 1761, I was given the grace of joining the Hourly Intercessions, which was a blessing to me. In 1762, I was accepted as an acolyte. In 1764 after I had served with the children for five years, I entered into matrimony with the single brother Nicolaus Heinrich Eberhardt. After our marriage we travelled to Lititz where my dear husband served in the Diacony and was Br. Mattheus' assistant in preaching, and I took over the running of the communal household. In 1765, we were called to Old Man's Creek in the Jerseys to serve the little flock there. I felt myself very inadequate for this task but trusted that the Saviour would give me the necessary grace and gifts to do so, which I have indeed received in full measure, and it has been a blessing for my heart. We had to endure some hardships as we were both often ill with the fever. In 1768, we were sent to serve the little congregation in Monakasy, now Graceham, in Maryland where the Saviour revealed Himself to us as full of mercy and let us experience much joy with our brothers and sisters.

In 1770, on April 18, it pleased our dear Lord to take my dearly beloved husband home to him, which caused me deep pain, but the comfort of my Best Friend became clear to me in a way that defies all description. After this, I moved to Bethlehem into the Widows' House where I enjoyed much that was a blessing for my heart, despite the fact that I had to earn my own bread. In 1778, on February 19, I was married by Br. Mattheus in Lititz to Br. Grube, and we took over the office of Married Choir Helper in which position the Saviour gave us His grace and support in all our shortcomings and frailties. In 1780, I was ordained Deaconess. In 1784, we were relieved by Br. and Sr. Denke and came to Gnadenthal for a few months and in December, after Br. Neusser's going home, we went to serve the little congregation in Philadelphia, where we stayed for a year and were relieved by Br. and Sr. Meder, whose position we took in Hope. After a year and a half, we finally returned after many years' absence to Bethlehem, where we stayed for four years and I enjoyed many blessings for my heart, until Br. and Sr. Martin Beck from Emmaus were called to Graceham and we had to fill their position *ad interim*. For the first year I was quite well, but in the beginning of 1792 I began to sicken and suffered much pain from cramps in the legs, especially at night. The pains then went up into my abdomen and every day I had a creeping fever, and although all kinds of medicines were used, the illness could not be alleviated.

Thus far her own essay. Her dear husband adds:

She was a loyal and dear helper to me, whom I received from the hands of the Saviour and returned her today with tears to His arms and lap. We had a happy and blessed marriage for almost fifteen years. She had a very cheerful disposition, could love with all her heart, and was loved by everyone in return, and she had a special love for the children. The brothers and sisters here, who visited her diligently, would have liked to see her recover, but there was no hope for that as the pains in her body and the sores on her legs multiplied, and then, in the final days, there came the unbearable stomach cramps. She called ardently to the Saviour and also asked the brothers and sisters to do likewise. Yes, she often called out, "Dear Saviour come, oh come, and fetch your poor little lamb who is sick and full of pain, I am yours and want to lay myself at your feet as your poor sinner." Throughout her whole long illness she was very patient and had a constant relationship with the Saviour and prayed diligently for the Congregation. She took a tender, sinnerlike farewell from her husband. And so she completed her life down here on January 16 after midnight in the 3rd hour, as the blessing of the Lord was given to her by her dear husband in the feeling of Christ's proximity and so she fell asleep gently and blessedly after she had completed her pilgrimage down here for 65 years, 1 month, and 8 days.

After such pain and anguish, sleep peacefully, thou dear heart,
In the Blood and Wounds of the Bridegroom, in which you found your
    salvation
At the pierced feet you will ever enjoy
Unspeakably sweet pasture, eternal bliss, peace, and joy.

At the burial of the happily departed Sister Sarah Grube in Emmaus,
    January 20th, 1793.

A. *After the Address and the Memoir*
Chorus: You are come unto Mount Zion and unto the city of the living God; the heavenly Jerusalem, and to an innumerable company of angels, to the general assembly and church of the first born, which are written in heaven, and to God, the Judge of all, and to the spirits of the just men made perfect and to Jesus the mediator of the new covenant, Jesus, and to the blood of sprinkling [Heb. 12:22–24 (AV)].

B. During the Love-Feast

Chorus: So rest now in Jesus' lap, O blessed one, your joy is truly great,
To stand among that number of the perfected, where constantly the
   words resound
We are redeemed by the Blood! The Lamb who died for us Has brought
   us Life. So rest now in Jesus' lap
O blessed one! Your joy is truly great.

Chorus: For the Lamb which is in the midst of the throne shall feed them,
   and shall lead them into the living fountains of water, and God will
   wipe away all tears from their eyes [Rev. 7:17 (AV)].

Response: Yea, beloved handmaid of the Lord, who has departed from us
We would dearly see you still among us here below but we do not
   begrudge you the gentle peace at Jesus' very wounds
In which your heart has hitherto found peace here below
Oh how gladly you laboured in love for your Friend
How willingly your efforts were dedicated to Him
How the salvation of every soul concerned your heart
How tenderly you took a part in their joys and pains
How edifying and how beautiful to regard your life
Even in your days of pain, you were never heard to complain
Your look remained happy and cheerful even in pain and suffering
And how you valued your joy of going soon to the Lord
Oh the Friend you can now see, to whom you cleaved
Who was beautiful to you above all, Now shall your desire
Be quite fulfilled; May nothing disturb your enjoyment of the pleasures
Which in the Vale of Sorrows mingle with the sufferings
The memory of you remain blessed here
Until up there we with you can see what we here believe.

Jacob van Fleck

Anna Hasse, née Chase
1743–1786

Anna Hasse's memoir, of which there is an identical copy in the Bethlehem Diary
*(vol. 35, 57–64) provides extremely important insights into the working of the early
Moravian Church in Great Britain. Anna, born in Westminster, London, and
baptized into the Church of England, was introduced to the Moravians by her
mother, Sarah Chase. Sarah took her two daughters to the children's services held by*

the Moravians. Gradually, Anna lost interest in their teachings and was seduced by the ways of the world. It was not until she was in her mid-teens that, one evening when on her way to meet some friends, she walked past the Fetter Lane chapel and heard John Gambold preaching. This was a major turning point for her, and she returned to the Moravians. According to Church records, she was admitted to Holy Communion in 1764 (not 1763 as she remembered) after having had to wait for three years. She traveled to Holland with Zinzendorf's daughter, Benigna and her husband, Johannes de Watteville, where she married. With her husband she took over the running of the mission at Carmel, Jamaica. Anna appeared, however, not to have led a completely happy life with the Moravians; in fact, from the scribe's comments she and her husband appear to have been excluded finally from the Congregation.

Memoir of the Married Sister Anna Hasse who died blessedly on March 16th in Bethlehem. She herself had the following written down on her sickbed:

I was born on January 4, 1743, in London. My father, John Chase, was a milliner and sergeant in the cavalry of the royal Grenadier Guards, a Presbyterian, and my mother Sarah, née Copper, belonged to the English Church. The latter, who as far as we know is still alive and belongs to the Congregation in London [29] and has known them from the very beginning when the Brethren came to England, occasionally took me as a child and also my eldest sister, to the children's services in secret, against my father's will; in them I got my first impression of the Saviour. In the same year, 1747, my aunt, Sr. Church, took me in for a few weeks, and then I had the opportunity to attend the children's services without any impediment. In my 8th or 9th year my father made the acquaintance of Br. Ockertshausen [30] and thus my mother and we children gained more freedom to associate with brothers and sisters. From then on I visited the Brethren's schools. But my very lively spirit gradually lost the impression of the Saviour and was often frivolous and dissolute because of the company of other children. From my thirteenth year on, I went into service with other families, both to help my parents make ends meet and to seek my own fortune. Since it was too quiet and religious in one family, I went to another where things went more according to my inclination towards the fashions and diversions of the world. I then carefully avoided all fellowship with the brothers and sisters, and I wished to be able to lose completely all impressions of the Saviour and all my attachment to the Congregation; but, against my will, something remained, and the Saviour did not allow me to become completely entangled with the world. Also, my mother and relations did not rest until they had got me away from this family and had brought me into service with Br. and Sr. Mail[31] to look after their little daughter because they saw my ruin before their eyes. Once, when Br. and Sr. Mail were away, I desired to go to a public amusement in the company of other like-minded people, and our way went through Fetter Lane,[32] it occurred to me out of curiosity to attend the evening preaching in the Brethren's Chapel, which was being held by Brother Gambold on the text:[33] "Come unto me all that labour and are heavy laden, etc" [Matt. 11:28 (AV)], and this made such a deep impression on my heart that I forgot my companions, went home, and spent the whole night in tears. It is from this point on that I date my complete awakening and gained the assurance that the Saviour would not leave me.

Now I visited the Single Sisters more often than before, was received into the Society in January 1761 and in June of that year into the Congregation.[34] I wanted in earnest to flourish for the Saviour and my gracious election remained with me steadfastly even through all subsequent vicissitudes. In 1763, I became a partaker of Holy Communion and soon thereafter moved in with the Single Sisters, where I enjoyed many good things, especially through the faithful care of the Sr. Elisabeth von Seidlitz.

In that year my father, who was regularly visited in his illness by brothers, whom he had come to love, went blessedly into eternity. Because the Single Sisters Choir had to give up their house and a part of them went into the world, I also came into temptation to do likewise, particularly because I had an ample income from my sewing work. The Saviour preserved me, however, and, out of worry that I would not remain faithful, I asked for permission to go to a German congregation. This I received in 1767, when our dear Br. Johannes and Sr. Benigna were in London, who took me with their company to Zeist where, although only for a short time, I was very content and happy in the Choir House. Then, in October of the same year, marriage with my husband and, at the same time, the call to go to Jamaica with him were proposed to me, both of which were difficult to accept, but the Saviour made it so happen that I resolved myself to do this. We were married on November 27th of the same year and had a blessed time in the loving care of Johannes and Benigna.

Thus far her own words.

At the beginning of February 1768, they travelled via England to Jamaica, where they arrived in Carmel in June and assumed the running of the Economy, in which she served diligently and profitably with her sewing and piece-work, in which she was very able. The hard and unpleasant external and internal circumstances of this post caused them to request the Unity Elders' Conference to replace them.[35] Their request was granted, with the instruction to go to Bethlehem, in 1771. They arrived on May 30th of that year while Brothers George and Loretz were here [36] and were cared for and accommodated as well as was at all possible. They could never quite find peace, however, with this their destiny, and there was always something that prevented them from thinking about any other. Here, God gave them four children, who are still alive and in the care of the Congregation. Their subsequent progress in this congregation often caused us much pain and sorrow, and it even went as far as them losing recognition as members of the Congregation. One must say in the late sister's favour that, with all the vicissitudes and her otherwise free way of thinking and acting that was not easily restrained, there was always a soft spot in her heart where she could be touched. Thus she felt the last painful step that one had to take with her so deeply that she thereby came to a thorough return to her election by grace. She was already seriously and painfully ill, as she had been as if crippled from rheumatic fever attacks every year since her last confinement, and because this was especially serious this year and she guessed that she was nearing her end. Nothing was more painful for her than to know and to see herself separated from the Congregation to which the Saviour had brought her and through which He had shown her so much mercy. The Saviour had led her heart to appreciate her guilt, and she found comfort and peace in finding the cause of everything in herself and to think of herself humbly and like a sinner. This drew the heart of the whole congregation towards feeling sympathy for her. We all forgave her from the bottom of our hearts, and in answer to her ardent pleas, she was assured that we would regard her as a sister if the Saviour should bring her life to an end in this illness and remove her from all dangers. This was a great comfort for her heart and from then on she did not desire to become well again. The condition of her heart was a true joy to those brothers and sisters who visited her assiduously. Childlike, natural, light and sinnerlike were the expressions of her comforted heart. She considered the hymn "I will never do anything but rejoice blushingly over my blessed state, etc. etc." to be the most beautiful hymn in the hymnbook because it concurred with the feeling in her heart so perfectly. Her illness turned into dropsy and became more painful. She showed great patience, but one could also grant her occasional touchiness amid great pain. She expressed herself as grateful to the Saviour, who was so gracious to her, and to all the brothers and sisters. She was afraid that when her parting approached she would become anxious. But the closer it came, the more she longed for it. She took a tender and motherly farewell from her two oldest children and was happy that her children were well looked after for the most part and recommended to the one daughter who still lived at home with her that she should ask the Saviour to take care of her also. In the last night, between the 15th and the 16th, when verses were being sung to her, she chose one herself and with broken voice began the singing of the verse, "Beneath Jesus' cross would I lie, there should His pierced foot receive a thousand little tears of thanks and love, with the warmest sinner's kiss, etc. etc." at which point she showed her strongest desire to be blessed for going home and when the same had been done in the tangible presence of the dear Saviour, she kissed her husband, children, and every sister present with a very contented and bright look and from that moment on called out as long as her lips could move "Come, come, oh come." She fell asleep very gently to the verse, "Your soul now goes over into the pierced hand, and He loves it so much more, as He has done much for you," with the beautiful and remarkable watchword that she had turned to in her most desperate hour as a comfort: "He will be very gracious unto thee at the voice of thy cry; when He shall hear it, He will answer thee." [Isaiah 30:19 (AV)] Her age was forty three years, two months, and twelve days.

Margarethe Jungmann, née Bechtel
1721–1793

Margarethe Jungmann's memoir is one of the longest in this collection. Written in her own hand, it tells the story of her early awakening, her acquaintance with the Moravians, especially Count Zinzendorf himself. However, the scenes of her life that are perhaps most vividly described are those of her work in the Moravian mission to the North American Indians.

Margarethe Jungmann's whole life was shaped by the Protestant evangelical awakening in Germany and America. Like so many other Protestant children in the 1720s, she was brought up by an extremely strict pietistic father whose daily prayers relied on Johannes Arndt's True Christianity *and hymnbooks for guidance, and whose decision to move to America was prompted by a desire to practice faith in a truly "philadelphian" manner. Johannes Bechtel, Margarethe's father, made the acquaintance of Count Nikolaus von Zinzendorf when he arrived from Europe in 1741 (in fact, it appears to have been at Margarethe's prompting that this meeting happened). After this initial meeting the Bechtels were regular supporters of the*

Moravians (their house in Germantown acted as one of the resting places for the mail riders from Bethlehem to Philadelphia). Margarethe joined the Congregation in Bethlehem, married, and began a life of service in the mission to the Indians (see illus. 13). It was one for which she readily admitted she was not prepared but she learned quickly. She became fluent in both Delaware and Mohican languages and served at Schekomeko (New York), Gnadenhütten (Pennsylvania), Pachgatgoch (New York), Wihilusing (Pennsylvania), Languntouteneunk (Pennsylvania), and Lichtenau (Ohio). She died at the age of seventy-two after many hardships, perils, losses, and adventures, and after ten pregnancies and eight children. Attached to her memoir are the verses sung at her funeral, which pay original homage to her work among the Indians.

Memoir of Margaret Bechtel, Mrs Jungmann.[37]

I was born in 1721, on September 13, at Frankenthal in the Palatinate, where my father, Johannes Bechtel, was a burgher and master craftsman (his profession was that of a turner). My mother, of the Marret family, was expelled from France on account of her religion. They were both Reformed and, therefore, had me baptized in the Reformed Church. Because my father had heard much about America, he resolved to move there with his family. He undertook this journey, then, with my mother and three children: my two eldest sisters and me. At that time I was in my fifth year. In the Spring of 1726 we embarked upon the journey and arrived the same year in Philadelphia. We purchased a piece of land and a house in Germantown where we then lived. My father, who was awakened and very uneasy in his heart, and who still did not know the true way to salvation, gave us children a very strict and moralizing[38] education. He kept us so that we were allowed no fellowship with other children but rather had almost continually, but especially on Sundays, to read spiritual books, like the Bible, Arndt's *True Christianity*, hymnbooks, etc. Every morning and evening we had our family worship when my father each time read us a chapter out of the Bible, and then fell on his knees and prayed aloud, often for a whole hour, which several times made him faint. This often brought me into great fear and perplexity, for, I thought, I should never become so pious. Whenever I did anything wrong, I dealt very strictly with myself, believing that I had committed a transgression and offended the good Lord. However, whenever I read the history of the dear Saviour's Passion in the New Testament, I felt so well in my heart that I was sometimes almost in an ecstasy. Yet it never lasted long before my uneasiness and anxiety returned because I plagued myself with it day and night.

It finally went so far that I became so ill that I almost died. At that, the anxiety in my heart increased to such a degree that I gave myself no peace, so that I would almost have lost my reason. In my distress, I turned to the good Lord because all the consolation and comfort from my father was of no help and I promised Him that I would lead a better life and become pious, I also besought Him with many tears to restore me to health and not to let me die until I was converted. I was richly comforted by Him and became well again. After that the fear in my heart left me a little for a while, but I could not attain any true peace.

In 1741, Count Zinzendorf arrived in Philadelphia from Europe. He wrote immediately to my father that he should come to him, as he wished to see him and speak to him. At first, my father had some reservations about it and appeared not to want to do so. Also, other people, such as Separatists and the Inspired[39] with whom he associated a great deal, sought to discourage him. But I was in a state of rapturous joy and, therefore, did not leave him any peace until he promised me that he would go. I myself fetched his horse for him from the field, saddled it, and thus it was for my sake that he sat himself upon it and rode to Philadelphia.

I had a quite particular feeling in my heart about the Count's arrival but did not know why. Now my father came back very soon, which gave me concern; but to my great joy the Count followed him the next day and came to our house. As soon as I saw him I was convinced that he was a true child of God and only wished to hear a great deal from him straight away. On the Sunday following he preached at the Reformed Church, with spirit and power. What I felt then, I cannot describe. The gospel of the dear Saviour's love for sinners penetrated deep into my heart, especially the verses: "Just as you are, you may come to the Lamb, and if only you come, you'll be accepted. Be you so sinful, so full of shame—There's so a thirsting heart ready for you." Very often did I repeat them to myself. I now presented myself before the dear Saviour as sinful and as depraved as I felt myself to be, and I received the forgiveness of my sins from Him.

Soon thereafter, the Count rented a house in Germantown, which became a School for children.[40] I thereby came into nearer acquaintance with the brothers and sisters who had come with him into this land, especially with the two sisters, Anna Nitschmann and his daughter, Benigna von Zinzendorf, with great blessing for my heart. It was also an especial grace to me that I could now and then watch a night with the children. When afterwards the Congregation was settled in Bethlehem, all the brothers and sisters moved there, which pained me greatly, because I felt as if I had been abandoned and I thought that now nothing more would come of my complete conversion, for I did not yet quite fully know how to keep myself close to the Saviour. Soon thereafter my father gave me permission to go

with my mother on a visit to Bethlehem. It so happened that the Congregation was just then celebrating Holy Communion and leave was given to me
and my mother to be present as observers. I was so overcome by the grace
that prevailed on that occasion that I could do nothing but weep. It was
remarkable to me that I had imagined it before in a dream at home just
the way I was seeing it here.

Now I wished for nothing more than to stay here immediately and to be
accepted as a member of the Congregation. At this point the late Count
called me to him and asked what I had in mind and what my desire was. I
now had the opportunity to lay before him my whole past conduct and my
present concern. He wrote immediately to my father that I belonged to
the Congregation and should now stay here. But my father thought otherwise. He wrote back immediately that I should come home without delay,
which then had to happen. A few weeks later, the Count travelled to Germantown again and spoke with my father personally, and gave himself
great pains on my behalf, but he had to use quite serious arguments to
persuade him. At last, the dear Saviour guided my father's heart so that he
himself brought me to the Congregation in Bethlehem, which was to my
great joy and shame.

I was immediately received into the Congregation and soon attained to
the Holy Communion. I had hardly been here a couple of months when a
proposal of marrying my first husband, the late Br. Büttner, who was then
the preacher in Tolpehoken, was made to me. Because I was completely
given up to the will of the Saviour, I was immediately willing to accept and
we were married by the late Disciple.[41] A few days later, it was decided that
we should go among the Indians at Schekomeko.[42] We set off and soon
arrived. You can imagine how I felt. I did not yet myself really know what I
wanted. I did not yet know the Saviour and the Congregation well enough
to value them fully and was now to be a blessing to other souls! Not only
that, but in my parents' house I had had everything I had wanted. Now I
found myself placed in a situation of the utmost poverty. Many a day we
hardly knew where we should find something to eat. And this and some
other circumstances made me feel very unsettled. But I learned the language of the Indians very quickly and soon gained a love for them and was
loved by them in return; and this cheered me up again and made my
course a great deal easier. When I then thought back on how the dear
Saviour had led me from youth on, how often He had shown mercy to me,
how He had brought me to the Congregation through so many difficulties,
etc., I could do no other than thank Him from my whole heart for my
election of grace thus far.

When I had been here for not quite three years, I had the great pain, which seemed to me almost impossible to overcome, that my dear husband, who had been ill for a long time with consumption, went home on February 23, 1745, when I was in the sixth month of pregnancy. In March I travelled in the company of Br. and Sr. Martin Mack, their child, and Sr. Post and her child, grieving that we had now to leave our beloved Indian Congregation, from Schekomeko to Bethlehem. On the journey we had much to endure from hostile people, of which some account is given in the History of the Indian Mission.[43] In June I was happily delivered of a little son, but after three weeks the dear Saviour took him home to Himself again. That was once again a testing time for me. At that time the Saviour's ways were still almost impenetrable to me, and I hardly knew what I should think about what had happened.

In that same year, on August 24 according to the old style, I was married for the second time, to my present husband, Johann Georg Jungmann. A few days later we set off for Frederickstown, to serve there in the Children's School. The following year the Saviour bestowed a little daughter on us. But when she was only three months old we received a call to the Indian Congregation at Gnadenhütten. We accepted this and moved there. We served there for six years. During that time I was once for a while on a visit at Bethlehem of which I must mention some particulars because it remains unforgotten by me. It was namely in the year when the first Elder's Festival was celebrated there, and that day was a very noteworthy day for me, for, while we lay on our knees before our dear Saviour in the first meeting and I felt my poverty and distress in a particular manner, it was as if I heard the dear Saviour say to me quite distinctly, "Thy shame is mine, all my merits thine, You shall be saved." What I felt in my heart at that is beyond all description. It was the most blessed moment of my life. This grace has attended me ever since, and the covenant that my dear Saviour and I made with each other at that time has been renewed many times since then. I will thank Him in eternity for this—it was my comfort again and again when I was uneasy or worried about myself.

After some time we moved back to Bethlehem. Here we were refreshed for a while by the grace prevailing in the congregation. Then we received a call to Pachgatgoch in New England.[44] We set off on our journey quite refreshed and strengthened and served the small Indian congregation there for three-and-a-half years. In the first two years we had a very blessed time until the war of that time caused great confusion among our Indian brothers and sisters.[45] We were then relieved by Br. and Sr. Schmik[46] and returned again to Bethlehem. Then we moved to Christiansbrunn where we served on the farm for one-and-a-half years. From there we came back to Bethlehem. Here we took over the soap manufactory and stayed there for nine years. Then we received a call to Wihilusing on the Susquehanna.[47] At our sending out service I was ordained a deaconess. We were there for a year and a half, then we came back to Bethlehem, where we made a brief visit to our children and the Congregation and celebrated our Choir Festival.[48] In 1769, strengthened anew, we then set out by way of Pittsburgh for Languntotenunk.[49] On this journey I experienced quite a particular preservation as I had two falls from my horse. The one time was so dangerous that my dear husband did not know whether I would come back to life again or not, for I lay a considerable time as if dead. It was no small fright to him, for we were quite alone and in the thickest bush. However, we arrived at Br. David Zeisberger's[50] and the Indian Congregation to great mutual joy (illus. 14).

When we had been there for a year and a half, we followed Br. Zeisberger to the Muskingum.[51] He had already made the beginnings of an Indian congregation there. We were there for almost five years and then moved on to Lichtenau[52] where Brother Zeisberger had also already made a beginning. We stayed there until the war between the Americans and the Indians broke out.[53] This war caused much unease among us. One day the Captain came into our house with five of his warriors. We did not know what he had in mind. He looked at us, was very friendly, gave us his hand and told each of his warriors to shake hands with everyone. They stayed with us for a few minutes and then left. We heard afterwards that they intended to proceed to Wheeling,[54] to fight in the war against the white people. On the following day, fifty more were supposed to follow them and then one group after another, all through our settlement. The brothers and sisters therefore thought it unsafe for us to remain here any longer because I was the only white sister there, and it was resolved that for the present we should go to Bethlehem.

Therefore, that same evening we had to embark on our journey through the bush. We were given six Indians to accompany us. One of them had always to ride a mile ahead of us to see whether it was safe. We then followed him and covered six miles by that evening. In the beginning we had a little moonlight but then it became so dark that we could get no further but rather had to tie up our horses and sit there the whole night under the trees. We did not dare to speak one loud word nor to make a fire. That was a long night. At last day came. We set off and travelled to the Muskingum Creek where we were supposed to cross. Our companions went in one after another but found to their astonishment that it could not be crossed without the horses having to swim. They could not understand why the creek was so swollen at that time of year (it was August) when it had not rained for a long time. They, therefore, resolved to travel the way by land through the bush, where we had to make twenty miles out of ten. The way went over mountains and through valleys, bushes, and herbage higher than the horses, so that we passed only in great danger.

On the following day, we arrived in Gnadenhütten. As we dismounted we saw the very same warriors who had previously been in our house, and about whom we had heard that they had marched to Wheeling. The second lieutenant immediately ordered his men to fire on us because he thought we had come from Pittsburgh. But the Captain, hearing it in the house, shouted immediately that they should hold their fire, as he first wanted to see what kind of people we were. We went into Br. and Sr. Schmik's house. He came out after us, recognized us immediately, and asked where we wanted to go. Brother Schmik gave him the answer that we were his friends and had come to visit him. He [the Captain] said, it was no time for that kind of thing, for if his warriors had met us in the bush they would have killed us on the spot. We spent that night with Br. and Sr. Schmik. Meanwhile a messenger sent by Br. David [Zeisberger] arrived in great haste to inquire whether we had arrived safely. This was because he was very frightened when he had heard that the warriors were returning the same way as we had wanted to go with several prisoners and scalps. It now became clear to us why we could not cross the creek. We thanked the dear Saviour for preserving us by His grace in this wonderful fashion and Brother Schmick sent a few Indian brothers after the warriors to observe at a distance whether they had set out in the direction of Wheeling. They stayed out until they were certain and then brought us the information. After this we continued our journey, although I was very weak, sick, and exhausted. Of all the journeys I have undertaken, it was quite the hardest. But I depended completely on the dear Saviour to help me through.

We continued on via Pittsburgh until we arrived at Lititz, glad and thankful for the kindness, faithfulness, and preservation of our dear Lord on this so dangerous and arduous a journey. We remained there for a few days to our mutual joy, experienced much love and friendship from the brothers and sisters and then travelled on to Bethlehem, where we arrived on August 29th, the Single Brethren's Festival, to our joy and that of the brothers and sisters. We stayed here for three years until Br. David Zeisberger visited from Indian country and requested that we return with him. We were also willing and ready to venture there again, trusting in the help of the dear Saviour and in the hope of concluding our lives with the dear Indian Congregation, to which I felt a particularly strong attachment.

Brother Reichel, who was here as a Visitor at that time, encouraged us to do this and we thus set off on the journey with the blessing of the Congregation. It was June 8th, 1781, and on July 12th we arrived at Schoenbrunn, to our joy and that of the dear Indian Congregation.

Thus far her own account. Her dear husband, Br. Jungmann, adds: I must give her the testimony that she was immediately at home there again and in her element. (Our dear sister was very practised in the Indian languages, so that she could speak with the Mahikan and the Delawares quite fluently.) Nothing could move her heart more than when she saw or heard a soul concerned for our Saviour. Then her mouth was directly open to testify what the blood of the wounds does for sinners. But we were hardly there for six weeks when the greatest crisis came—we were all taken prisoner and the three Indian congregations were destroyed. That was hard and painful for us. However, she immediately looked to the Saviour, believing that nothing happened without the permission and the government of Him to whom she had given herself up completely. And she was bright and cheerful and comforted the other sisters who were with her. Thus she continued, as long as she had Indians around her. When it came about, however, that we had to leave them and we were brought to Detroit, her pain about that became great, until we settled by the Huron River again and the Indian congregation gathered again; then she came back to life.

That continued for a few years until it was resolved to leave the place and to cross Lake Erie again. She found herself unfit to do this because she felt very weak in all her limbs, especially in her arms and hands. This made her think that she wanted to come back to the congregation. The brothers and sisters, although painfully sad to lose her, consented to our journey and, accompanied by Br. and Sr. Sensemann, we arrived on July 8th, 1785, at Bethlehem, the place congregation that had always been of great importance to her. She derived some benefit for herself from the congregation meetings and never missed one lightly, as long as she was able to go.

For the last two years she had a painful sickbed, on account of increasing paralytic pains: yet even when the pain was so strong that she trembled, she prayed with so much heart and feeling to the Saviour or started to sing the most beautiful verses so that tears fell from those present. Thus she spent her time day and night until her blessed end. On November 22th, 1793, in the evening in the company of all her family resident here in Bethlehem and several other brothers and sisters, she received the blessing of the Congregation and her Choir with the blessed feeling of the nearness of our dear Lord and then passed away gently and blessedly at midnight. Her age was 72 years and 2 months. She had lived with the present widower for 48 years in a contented marriage, in which she had brought eight living children into the world and one premature child, of whom the eldest daughter, whose married name was Bruckner, went home in the Saviour's service in St. Thomas. The others are all still living. Five are here in Bethlehem (including her daughter Susanna, who served and cared for her in her painful illness very lovingly and in a childlike fashion), two sons have left the Congregation, a fact that cost her, as a true mother who cared deeply about the welfare of her children, many tears because she often thought and said to the Saviour "you know, I would give up everything, except you and the Congregation." She lived to see eleven grandchildren, of whom three have gone to Saviour before her and eight, as far as is known, are still living. She heartily hoped that these would flourish.

> How well our Sister now will fare
> From all her pains to repair
> And Jesus Himself to see
> The one who chose her for His maid
> Stands among the blessed company
> Who now with tears do sow
> And willingly their heads do bow
> To him, in praise and service
> In his sermon of assurance.

> When the Saviour's Wounded place
> She kissed for her election of grace
> And sees in the companies on high
> The Mohicans, and Wampanos
> The Delawares and Shawanos
> Who have gone home blessedly
> Oh how she with one voice
> With the redeemed ones will rejoice
> Who accepted His teachings and comfort.

> In Schekameka and on the Kent
> At Pachgatcoch, whither she went
> On Beaver Creek, the Muskingum River,
> On the Mahony, she travelled thither
> Everyway in this vale of tears
> With her husband of many years

Oh yea, there, there, she will see
Standing majestically,
Whole hoards slaughtered for the Lamb.

Each and every Indian nation
Will sing to God with elation
Oh Lamb, for us you have died
And with your blood holy
Our redemption gained, most costly
Amen! Amen! To your name
Let us give praise and fame
That we from you heed your teaching.

There she will surely join in our song
And be enthralled with the throng
To sing such hymns:
She sees God in His son
And before His throne she sinks down
Full of shame and delight
Sunshine, joy, and sounds of rejoicing
She will e'er have, her Saviour embracing.

Marie Elizabeth Kunz, née Minier
1732–1769

Although Marie Kunz's memoir was written when she was still a Single Sister, the editor's comments that frame her words speak of her life as a married woman. Her own short account of her life provides an excellent example of the language of spirituality during the Sifting Period. For example, her description of Christ as her bridegroom, for whom she desires to keep her virgin state, and the Holy Spirit as the Mother reflects Zinzendorf's notion of the sexualization of the Holy Trinity, a fact also recognized by the scribe who calls her essay "her heart's intercourse with Him who loves her soul."

Personalia of the late Sister Marie Elisabeth Kunz according to her own, albeit somewhat brief, account.

She was born Minier and came into this mortal life in 1732, on January 5, in Cannestoga[55] in the Province of Pennsylvania. When her father moved to Heidelberg, she had the opportunity of hearing Br. Wagner[56] and was strongly awakened during a sermon. After closer acquaintance with Br. and Sr. Wagner and other brothers and sisters who came to visit, she had no peace until she received permission to come to the Congregation in Bethlehem. After she had received the same, she arrived there on June 2, 1745, and thus in her 14th year. In 1749, on January 6 (the day after her birthday), she was accepted into the Congregation, and on February 2 of the same year, she partook of the flesh and blood of the Bridegroom of her soul in the Holy Communion with the Congregation for the first time. When she had been in the Single Sisters' Choir for a while, she noted down the following in her own hand about her heart's intercourse with Him who loves her soul:

In 1754, on November 2, the good Saviour began a special work of grace with my heart. With body and soul I could give myself up just as I was and want nothing else in this world than to depend on Him: for this grace could be felt so strongly in my heart that I thought "there is nothing more for me here"; and it was just as though the tormented body of the Bloody Saviour were hanging there right before my eyes. Now, because it was Communion day, I could hardly wait until I got to enjoy His Body and Blood in the Sacrament, and as I was actually enjoying it I could hardly remember whether I was still here or already in the marriage hall. That was a great day of grace for me, which I shall never forget. And thus the Holy Spirit, the dear Mother, continued His work of Grace, and this was so powerful that sometimes I thought that I cannot remain here any longer. During the Passion Week,[57] in 1755, I could neither hear nor meditate enough about all that my dearest Friend of souls had suffered for me during these days. My heart swam in tears, and it was amazing to me that the good Saviour had shown so much grace to such a poor maid as I am. For my poverty and my many sins became clear to me in my heart, and it saddened me greatly that I was not yet completely as my true friend wanted in His heart, as befitted my virgin's state, which was very great and important to me. I begged the Saviour with tears to give me the grace to keep my soul and body chaste until I reached His arms and embrace.

In 1762, on November 21, she was joined in Holy Matrimony to Br. David Kunz, the present widower, with the watchword: "Be content again my soul, for the Lord does good to you. Do not forget it, o my heart!" This marriage she conducted contentedly and blessedly until her death.[58] The Saviour also blessed her with three children, namely two sons, David and Jacob, of whom the latter was not seen long in his earthly tabernacle, but the former is in our children's home. She was safely delivered of her last child, a daughter, on the 9th of this (year) and remained quite healthy until the 20th. On that day, however, she had a severe headache and thereafter such a high fever that she was conscious of little around her and took notice of nothing. Last Saturday it appeared to be improving somewhat, but in the middle of the night her condition changed so that one could see clearly that her last hour was at hand, as she had been prepared right at the beginning of her illness for her going home.[59] Last Friday she saw her little David one more time and last Saturday she took a heartfelt farewell from her husband. She has now reached the end of all her affliction and now rests in peace after she had lived this mortal life for 37 years, 5 months, 2 weeks, and 2 days.

Anna Marie Worbass, née Schemmel
(1722–1795)

Anna Worbass' memoir is a remarkably eloquent testimonial to her life of faith. Born into a tanner's family, Worbass came to the Moravians during the awakening in Württemberg in the 1740s. In a dream she heard a message that she should join the Congregation and, once her father had died, she packed up a few things and walked to Herrnhaag. She was refused permission to stay. On the road home a voice told her turn around and try again; however, she did not heed the voice. She returned to Württemberg to work for Georg Schlosser with whom she eventually traveled to America as his maid. Once in Bethlehem, she was released from service to the Schlossers and became a maid to the Single Sisters. In 1758, she married Peter Worbass, and they moved from Moravian settlement to Moravian settlement for the next twelve years. In 1770, they were instructed to build the first family house in Nazareth. Anna's memoir was written in her own hand. It has neither an editorial framework nor emendations. For example, no information is added, as is usually the case, about her two sons who, as she says, "have gone astray and have been corrupted."

I wish to tell something in praise of my true Saviour and good helper of what He has done for me, His poor and wretched one through the course of my life.

I was born on January 19, 1722, in Württemberg in a small district town Vaihingen on the Entz. My father was called Johann Georg Schemmel, a tanner, my mother was born Mätz. I was carefully raised by my dear parents and strictly made to attend school and church and to read the Bible. In my childhood years, I felt a love to my Creator and Saviour. In my thirteenth year, I was catechised,[60] and when questions came up about the Saviour and His death and passion, it so made an impression on me that I thought to give myself up to Him and to live as His property only; and this I promised Him at the confirmation before the first communion but also with trembling, and I looked forward to the enjoyment of Holy Communion, at which I had a blessed feeling and I felt good inside. I said to my mother that I wished I was allowed to go to Communion every four weeks. It was too long to do without it for a quarter of a year, and I was happy when I was allowed to enjoy it again. But it did not last long before my heart was carried away with the love of the world and the most sinful vanities. Then I lost the blessed feeling, and my soul became restless within me. I often resolved not to go on like this any more. But I was carried away again several times. But as the disquiet of my soul became stronger and stronger, so I kept myself from all those things where I thought they made my soul so unquiet. I searched alone in peace and thought if only I could get back again to the blessed feeling that I had before. And so I spent three years.

When I was in my twenty-second year, there arose an awakening in my town, and my eldest brother was one of those involved. One Sunday I went to visit him, and there was another awakened man with him. They were singing together the hymn, "Halleluia, praise, glory, and honour." I sang along confidently, but when the hymn was over the man asked me whether I too had already experienced something similar in my heart and if I could be comforted by the friendship and communion and blood of Jesus. Then I stood there ashamed and said I did not know, and my heart became weak and cried. I went home and told my mother. She wanted to comfort me and said that I was sprinkled with the blood of Christ as a child in Holy Baptism and we also enjoyed it in Holy Communion. The next day my brother came to our house. I was even more convinced by him that I had fallen completely away from God's grace, and I saw myself to be in a lack of grace. He showed me the way to the Saviour and that I as a sinner would seek grace and forgiveness of my sins from Him and would also find it, and also that already in this life my salvation in Him could be guaranteed. I was happy to hear that and turned to the dear Saviour as a sinner. He gave me trust in him and I went to the meetings of the awakened people. It was a blessing to me. I was concerned about getting a reconciled heart and becoming acquainted with the Saviour. He soon made Himself known to me in grace. Once, when I lay before Him in prayer and tears, it seemed to me as though I could not stand to be without His pledge to me any longer, and I asked for grace and mercy, a little drop of blood and faith that He had also died for my sins, and I came to Him in a struggle and said, "I will not leave you, you bless me." Then He allowed Himself to be felt in a heavenly and blessed way, and my heart was filled with comfort, peace, and joy and praise and thanks, and it was spoken to me as though into my heart, "I take onto my back the burdens that weigh you down much heavier than a stone. I would curse against them. I honor you with my blessing, my pain must be your refreshment." I felt good inside. This bond of grace and peace which He then has made with my soul remains unremoved forever, but how deeply ashamed I feel when I think how often He has been hurt on my account. In this shine of grace I continued on for a while and kept myself to grace. But because my father's depravity in sinfulness was still unknown to me, I also lacked the pleasure of the salvation that lies in the bloody sacrifice of Jesus and in His death and passion. I came to my own works, and selfishness was also at work. My mood often changed. When I felt grace I was blessed beyond measure. When my sinfulness confronted me I became troubled and downcast. Once, when I was praying to Him to become completely as He wished and to live only for Him, there came the answer, "If you want to give yourself to me completely then go to the Congregation." I was taken aback at this and thought, why then can I not attain this here as well, but I was repeatedly reminded of this. I asked my father about this. He did not want to allow it.

On February 13, 1746, my father left this life blessedly as a sinner full of grace—it was given to him on his sickbed. Then, that same spring at Easter I went to visit Herrnhaag. I liked it. I also felt the demand in my heart that I should stay here and give myself up to Him completely. But I was like a wilful child. I came into doubts and also felt a great attachment to my mother and returned home again. I became confused. The text also came into my mind, "He that loveth father or mother more than me is not worthy of me" [Matthew 10:37]. My mother also became worried and let me go. In 1747, I went again, took bedding and clothes and thought to stay in Herrnhaag. But when I got there I did not receive permission. That pained me. I also cried sometimes and thought that the fault must lie with me, but I could not find it. At the end of the same year I went there again. Again I was dismissed. When I left again and was hardly outside the town, I felt a strong movement inside me, as though someone wanted to turn me around and was saying, "Do you want to go away again? Turn round, turn round, and ask small and humbly and you will definitely be able to stay. Then I saw myself in a great pride and under a mountain of unbelief, so that I could not trust the Saviour in this. The three men with whom I was supposed to go home were already going on ahead. Then I thought, "If I turn around and nothing comes of it, I will lose my travelling companions." Then I found the fault in me. I went around the whole day heavy and downcast. In the evening, when I was alone, before falling asleep I asked the Saviour to have mercy on me and, because he could not now be finished with me and I was now going away again, to forgive me and give me a little drop of blood in my heart to protect me until, when I belonged to His people, He could get me there in another way. It became easy for me. I felt His forgiveness and fell asleep peacefully. He comforted me and I also felt His dear closeness. After that I was with my mother for a half-year. I was tired of travelling around on foot and I thought, "Now I want to wait until the Saviour acts." Thereafter I went to Georg Schlosser in Pfortzheim in the Durlach (he was one of the three men with whom I went home from Herrnhaag the last time) to help with the household (he had two children to care for). He had a mind to come to the Congregation. In the beginning I thought that perhaps this could be an opportunity for me. But it was delayed. In the meantime Herrnhaag was disbanded. Then I became troubled. I wrote to the Sister's Labouress. She wrote to me and said that because I was already with this man, I could go with him to Pennsylvania. If I had belonged to the Congregation the Saviour could also have brought me to do this. I resolved to do this, trusting in the Saviour, although I thought that I was hardly worthy of it. In 1751, we arrived in Holland just at the time when the Congregation was ready to sail and was waiting only for a number of brothers and sisters. They took us in to carry us over the sea. It was a comfort to me and humbling. Towards the end of September we arrived in New York. There I received permission from Br. Nathaniel (Seidel) to go with Br. and Sr. Graff and Br. and Sr. Busse[61] to Bethlehem. We arrived there safely on October 6, and I received permission from the dear Saviour to live there. On November 3, I moved into the choir house of the Single Sisters with a feeling of shame and was happy to have found a little place for, after so much fluttering around, my foot could now rest. On July 11, 1752, I was received into the Congregation. I felt touched anew by the dear Saviour in my heart and was especially content and happy for some time. But because things were delayed with Holy Communion I entered into another time of trial. My deepest basic depravity was revealed to me and also all the disloyalty and deviation since my first experience of grace. There was many a sad and distressed hour before I could lay myself down before Him at His feet as a poor sinner and ask for His blood in forgiveness to wash over my whole heart. He comforted me in his bloody deathly form. Soon thereafter He gave me the blessed enjoyment of His body and blood in Holy Communion, to be desired in His arms and at His breast. My eyes could not remain dry at this enjoyment, in shame, thanks, and humility at the love, patience, and forebearance with which He had carried me until this hour. And He said to me, "See, I would have liked to give you that long ago if you had not stood in my way." From that time on I walked the path of a blessed sinner through His grace and support. Although sometimes something of the remaining sinfulness came to the fore, I always found with Him comfort, help, and advice. My worldy business was whatever turned up in the Economy, and latterly I was a cook for the sisters for two years in the Sisters' House. In 1758, it was put to me that I should change my state, and I gave myself up to the will of the dear Saviour, and on July 29 I was joined in holy matrimony to the single brother Peter Worbass. The dear Saviour accompanied me into this state with His dear nearness and made of all the conditions connected with this state a blessing to me. In December we came to live in Gnadenthal, where the dear Saviour gave me a little son with the name of Joseph. In 1760, we returned to Bethlehem to the newly built inn to start the business. From there we came to the inn across the Lecha. We were there for only four months; then in 1762 we came to live in the Bethlehem mill. There the dear Saviour gave me my second son, named Werther. There I had an especially peaceful and blessed time. The dear Saviour gladly let Himself be known to me in grace. In 1769, we came to the Jerseys, now named Hope, to be in charge of the business. It was a little hard for me there in the business, which I was not used to, but the dear Saviour made everything bearable and easy for me through His frequent unexpected visitations of grace and His dear nearness. In 1771, we were called away from there and were told to move up to Nazareth and to live for ourselves up there. I became downcast, cried and held myself to the Saviour in shame. He let me know that it was His will and I was comforted by Him. He accompanied me here to Nazareth on July 27, 1771, with His dear nearness, and I took from His hand the place He had thought for me to live in and experienced His merciful help and support in everything that happened, and, according to the inner endurance of my heart from Him, I feel His work of grace making me more and more into a poor being, hungry and thirsty for Him, yes needy of blood, so that He can come every day and comfort, bless, and nurture me. He is my comfort and my advisor about my two sons who have gone astray and have been corrupted, who knows how to keep me even in this plight and to think of them with grace in His own time and hour according to His grace and mercy.

1. Itinerary map of Pennsylvania. Ink drawing. Courtesy of Moravian Archives, Bethlehem, Pennsylvania.

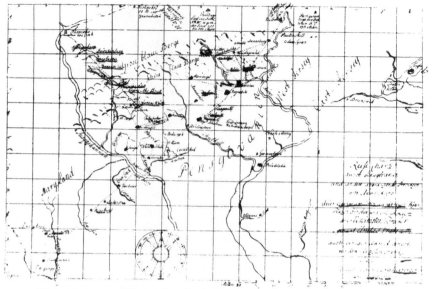

2. Unknown artist of the Kupetzky studio, ca. 1748, *Nikolaus Ludwig Graf von Zinzendorf (1700–1760)*. Oil painting. Courtesy of Archives of the Unity of the Brethren, Herrnhut, Germany. Zinzendorf was the founder of the Moravian Church.

3. Johann Valentin Haidt, *Moravian Lamentation of Christ,* 1751. Oil painting. Courtesy of Archives of the Unity of the Brethren, Herrnhut, Germany.

4. Unknown artist, *View of Bethlehem,* from the *Kurze zuverläßige Nachricht . . .* (1757). Copper etching. Courtesy of Moravian Archives, Bethlehem, Pennsylvania.

AUFNAME. in die Brüder-Gemeine.
A Der Pastor der die Liturgie verrichtet B.B Die Pastores und Diaconi die die neuen Brüder mit dem heiligen Kuß aufnehmen. C.C. Die Diaconißen die die neuen Schwestern auf eben die selbe aufnemen DD. Die Brüder und Schwestern von der Gemeine

RECEPTION dans la Communauté des Frères
A. Le Ministre qui celebre la Liturgie B.B Les Ministres, Pasteurs qui reçoivent les nouveaux Frères par le saint baiser C.C. Diaconisses, qui reçoivent les nouvelles Sœurs De la même Maniere DD. Les Freres et Sœurs de la Commune

5. Unknown artist, *Reception into the Moravian Church,* from the *Kurze zuver-läßige Nachricht . . .* (1757). Copper etching. Courtesy of Archives of the Unity of the Brethren, Herrnhut, Germany.

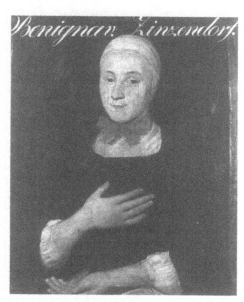

6. Johann Valentin Haidt, *Benigna von Zinzendorf (1725–1789).* Oil paint-ing. Courtesy of Archives of the Unity of the Brethren, Herrnhut, Germany.

7. Johann Valentin Haidt, *The 24 Single Sisters Choirs of the Moravian Church in 1751 Are Introduced to Christ by Anna Nitschmann*. Oil painting. Courtesy of Archives of the Unity of the Brethren, Herrnhut, Germany.

8. Johann Valentin Haidt, *Anna Rosina Anders (1727–1803)*. Oil painting. Courtesy of Moravian Archives, Bethlehem, Pennsylvania. Anna Rosel was the Single Sisters' Labouress from 1748 until 1764.

9. Unknown artist, *Maria Barbara Horn (1729–1797)*. Silhouette. Courtesy of Archives of the Unity of the Brethren, Herrnhut, Germany.

10. "Nun trinkt deine Seel . . ." Verses attached to memoir of Benigna Zahm. Manuscript. Courtesy of Moravian Archives, Bethlehem, Pennsylvania.

VERHEIRATUNG von zwölf Paaren Colonisten.
A. Der PASTOR, der Sie zusamen gibt B.B.B. Ut. Die Bräutigame C.C.C
Die Bräute D.D. Die Brüder und Schwestern von der Gemeine

MARIAGE de 12 Couples de Colonistes.
A. Le Ministre qui benit le Mariage B.B.B. &c. Les Epoux C.C.C. &c.
Les Epouse D.D. Les Freres, et les Soeurs de la Commune

11. Unknown artist, *Wedding of 12 Couples Destined for the Colonies* from the *Kurze zuverläßige Nachricht . . .* (1757). Copper etching. Courtesy of Moravian Archives, Bethlehem, Pennsylvania.

12. Johann Valentin Haidt, *Johanette Ettwein (1725–1773)*. Oil painting. Courtesy of the Moravian Historical Society, Nazareth, Pennsylvania.

13. Unknown artist, *Baptism of Indians in North America,* from the *Kurze zuverläßige Nachricht . . .* (1757). Copper etching. Courtesy of Moravian Archives, Bethlehem, Pennsylvania.

14. Johann Valentin Haidt, *David Zeisberger (1721–1808).* Oil painting. Courtesy of Moravian Archives, Bethlehem, Pennsylvania. Zeisberger was the leading Moravian missionary to the Delaware.

15. Johann Valentin Haidt, *The Widows Choirs of the Moravian Church Represented by Their Choir Labouresses Are Presented to Christ* (1745). Oil painting. Courtesy of Archives of the Unity of the Brethren, Herrnhut, Germany.

16. Johann Valentin Haidt, *Ferdinand Philip Jacob Detmers (?–1803)*. Oil painting. Courtesy of Moravian Archives, Bethlehem, Pennsylvania.

17. Unknown artist, *Maria Theresia Stonehouse (1723–1751)*. Oil painting. Courtesy of Archives of the Unity of the Brethren, Herrnhut, Germany. Maria Stonehouse was an influential benefactress in London.

18. Johann Valentin Haidt, *Anna Johanna Seidel, née Piesch (1726–1788)*. Oil painting. Courtesy of Archives of the Unity of the Brethren, Herrnhut, Germany. Anna (Piesch) Seidel was one of the leading women in the Moravian Church in the eighteenth century.

19. Johann Valentin Haidt or copy of Johann Valentin Haidt, *Benigna von Watteville, née Zinzendorf (1725–1789)*. Oil painting. Courtesy of Archives of the Unity of the Brethren, Herrnhut, Germany.

20. Johann Valentin Haidt or copy of Johann Valentin Haidt, *Anna Nitschmann (1715–1760)*. Oil painting. Courtesy of Archives of the Unity of the Brethren, Herrnhut, Germany. Anna Nitschmann was Zinzendorf's life-long companion and second wife.

Memoirs of the Widowed Sisters

THE WIDOWED SISTERS
An Introduction

Young men and women, either married or single, made up the bulk of Bethlehem's population in the early years of the settlement. The few widows that there were either remarried or else lived in a log house in Nazareth. However, by the beginning of the dissolution of the General Economy in 1762, the need for a larger choir house for the widows became pressing. In 1768, the Widows' House on the south side of Church Street was constructed. At the same time, the Elders of Bethlehem recognized the financial straits of the Choir and founded a society to sustain the poorer of them. In 1771, The Widows' Society of Bethlehem was constituted, one of the oldest beneficial societies in North America.

As can be seen from the following memoirs, widows frequently remarried (see Anna Boehler, Anna Fenstermacher), thereby easing the burden on the congregation of their upkeep. If they did not remarry they would provide services in the congregations where they could (for example, widows like Maria Rothe were asked to care for aging widowers in other congregations). Widows moved into the Choir House when they wanted to spend the rest of their days in peace (see Juliana Horsfield). The older, more sickly sisters were given a separate room to sleep in which could be also be heated in winter. The other widows slept in a dormitory. Widows, when physically capable, were expected to work in the kitchen or laundry or to clean the rooms and care for the infirm.

From the concluding remarks of each memoir written by the Helper of the Widows' Choir, we can obtain a picture of life within the Choir House. The actual physical existence of a Widows' House was considered to be a gift of grace from Christ, for without the ability to live in proximity with one another much of the spiritual and physical support the widows gave one another would be impossible. The widows aided one another in their state of bereavement, their own special liturgies sustained their faith (see

Anna Boehler), and devotional paintings depicted the widows' own particular relationship to Christ (see illus. 15).

The "Instructions to the Helpers of the Widows Choir" insist that the Choir Helper take into account the differing circumstances of the widows' married lives. Every effort should be made to understand the background from which the widowed sister had come (sometimes a good marriage, sometimes not, sometimes from mission work or other responsibilities within a congregation, and sometimes from quite humble labor) as these differences in circumstances could affect the sister's presence within the Choir. However, despite these varying external circumstances, the widows were considered to maintain their own special spiritual relationship with Christ. Their own experiences of the loss of their earthly husband helped them to understand the enormity of Christ's suffering for them as their Eternal Bridegroom.

Anna Boehler, née Rose
1740–1809

Anna Boehler was born in Germantown in 1740. Her family was one of those who left Moravia and settled in Herrnhut in the 1720s. Her father, Peter Rose, was one of the group of Moravians who travelled to Georgia in 1735 to attempt to set up the first Moravian settlement in North America. However, this endeavor failed for a variety of reasons; disease and internal dissent played their part, but the war between the British and Spanish and the refusal of the Moravians to bear arms meant that great pressure was put on them. The settlement was disbanded in 1740 when the remaining Moravians dispersed, some of them to Pennsylvania. Rose moved to Germantown, but died soon after his arrival on March 12, 1740. Anna's mother, Catharina Huber, then moved with her two children to Bethlehem, where she is listed as an "unattached" woman and is also described in the Bethlehem Diary *as the "first Moravian sister who engaged in missionary work." Anna Boehler's sister was, in fact, the first Moravian child to be born in Pennsylvania. Until now it has been assumed that the Rose family had no more ties with the Moravian Congregation after the father's death. However, as we can see from this memoir, this assumption is incorrect.*

In this memoir, Anna provides a detailed description of the institution of the Kinder-Anstalt *(Children's House or School — literally "Institution") which was effectively the children's choir house. Although the children were taught here, the* Anstalt's *primary purpose was not that of education but rather the freeing of both*

*parents of young children for full-time church service and, as with the other choir
houses, the development of the children's spirituality and fellowship. It is also worth
noting that at this time the Bethlehem married men and married women lived in
separate dormitories, not in couples — another reason for a* Kinder-Anstalt. *As is
clear from Anna's memoir, the work with the children appears to have taken second
place to the other concerns of the fledgling congregation in the early years. The
children were housed somewhere in the* Gemeinhaus *(Congregation House) until,
in 1743, the boys were taken to Nazareth by John Christopher Franke to start the
forerunner to Nazareth Hall while the girls remained in Bethlehem.*

*Having passed through the various schools Anna joined the Single Sisters' Choir
at the age of eighteen and herself became a teacher for the Greater Girls. She married
for the first time at the age of thirty-one and moved with her husband to Philadelphia,
then Lancaster and Heidelberg, Pennsylvania. In 1780, she was widowed and left
with two young children and another one on the way. She returned to Bethlehem
and five years later married Franz Boehler, the brother of the famous preacher Peter
Boehler, who ran the school at Old Man's Creek in New Jersey.*

*Anna's memoir provides a long and detailed account of how a woman's life in
the eighteenth century was shaped and affected by the political and denominational
issues of that time. Whether as a founding member of the Children's School in
Germantown or as a worker in the various Moravian congregations during the War
of Independence, Anna's life exemplified in so many ways what Zinzendorf meant
when he said that the real history of the Church was constituted in individual lives.*

Memoir of our widowed Sister Anna Boehler, née Rose, formerly Unger,
who fell asleep on May 10, 1809, in Bethlehem.

I was born on January 1, 1740, in Germantown in the county of Philadelphia in the state of Pennsylvania. My late father was Peter Rose, a native of
Bohemia, who left Moravia for his freedom of conscience and to ensure
his salvation, as did also my dear mother Catharina Huber, and both came
to Herrnhut.[1] When I was three months old, my father went home in
Germantown, where they recently had moved from Georgia because the
brothers and sisters could not stay there any longer, owing to the disturbances from the war.[2] He left behind my late mother with their two small
children; she was still a stranger in this country, until the late Count Zinzendorf came to this country in 1742. He soon sought her out, and when
she heard that a congregation was being started in Bethlehem she was
happy and moved with my sister and me, when I was a little over two years
old, to Bethlehem. We were the first two children here. Later on, when
more children arrived, they started a Children's House with us, which soon

increased in size so that the whole Home moved to Nazareth because there was not enough room here.[3]

I still remember with great pleasure the blessed times that I had in my childhood years. Although we had very hard and strict treatment, the blessed feeling that reigned among us predominated. I had not yet been baptized and, therefore, during the baptism of some children of my age I had a great desire for this, and I begged the Saviour like a child for this grace, which was granted me on September 18, 1748, in my eighth year, by our dear Br. Spangenberg. Although I did not understand it properly straight away, I really did feel in my heart the power of the Blood of Jesus that overstreamed me. I was deeply contented and I was childlikely grateful to the Saviour that He had heard my plea. Soon after, a Children's House was to be started in Emmaus[4] (this fact was announced to us during a meeting).[5] Since Br. Spangenberg wanted to have a few glowing coals (as he put it) for this task from our midst, I was sent there with two other children to start it up. That was a hard test, to move from our lovely Home in Nazareth to an empty house in the bush. I could not get accustomed to my new surroundings. We certainly received many visitors and encouragement from Bethlehem, but our desire always remained to come back to our Home. Soon, in response to our constant pleas,[6] we succeeded in moving back to Bethlehem. And when the Children's House had to move from Nazareth to Germantown, we moved with it, and there too I had a truly blessed time. The Home grew quickly because of the many children who moved here from Philadelphia, and it was especially agreeable to us that Br. Spangenberg, who was at that time living in Philadelphia, visited us very diligently. Once we also had the pleasure of going there on foot and having a children's Prayer Day[7] there. In April 1750, I again moved with the whole Children's House back to Bethlehem, where we had to live for a short while on the other side of the Lecha until the house that was being built for us was ready.[8] In 1751, we moved in. On March 25 of the same year I was accepted into the Great Girls' Choir. During this time I strayed a great deal. I really just lived from day to day and forgot what the Saviour had done for my heart during my childhood years. Yes, I thought that my having been born and raised in the Congregation was the clearest proof that I could not be lost. I was not wholly unaware of my bad condition, but I tried with all my might to suppress this reminder. But the faithful Saviour pursued me tirelessly, and in my 17th year He gripped my heart so strongly that I became very frightened. I felt myself to be lost and damned, but at the same time He gave me a childlike trust in Him so that I could confidently believe that He still had thoughts of peace about me and the door of grace still stood open for me; but it cost me much anxious pounding of the heart and hot tears to think about the time that I had spent in indifference, since in my childhood years I had already loved, tasted, and felt Him and now once again had to pray from the heart and sigh "O, where do I find Jesus?". Then doubts were mixed in as to whether He would take pity on me again and accept me out of grace. The good Saviour helped me, though, and gave me trust in Him that He had forgiven me everything about which I was worried and embarrassed. On my birthday, January 1st, 1756, I became a candidate for Holy Communion. That was my happiest birthday since I had left the Children's Choir. I felt such a peace of God at this that I almost lost consciousness. The sight of the congregation and what I saw in the Hall[9] filled my heart with a deep reverence and passionate longing to partake of it immediately with them.[10] This feeling stayed with me until I experienced the grace of going to Holy Communion for the first time, but only after three months, namely on April 7th of the same year, that is, on Maundy Thursday. O, I was so happy! I felt so ashamed and grateful to the Saviour, that I could have poured out my thanks eternally at His feet. After this I had unspeakably blessed times; the relationship with the Saviour was truly all that I desired. Yes, it often seemed to me as though I only had to do with Him alone. Soon I joined the Hourly Intercessions,[11] which brought me even closer to Him, and the hours, which I never missed unless I had to, did much for my heart. In particular, I became accustomed to talking fully with Him about both great and small matters.

In 1758 on May 4th, I was received into the Single Sisters' Choir and the following year went to work with the children, where there were things of all sorts to learn. The Saviour graciously helped me through all the difficulties that I had to experience. In 1761, I went to work with the Greater Girls. In that period I got to know myself very well for the first time. I became greatly troubled in spirit about myself. I no longer felt trust in the dear Saviour in the way in which I was accustomed. I even believed that there was no other person in the world as bad as I felt myself to be; but I kept all this to myself and tortured myself day and night, believed myself to be lost and thought, "I am not elected to be saved." I could not pray either and was in such a jam that I did not know what I should do or where I should turn because I had lost my trust in the Saviour almost completely. O God, what a state I was in!

Then I had a strange dream. It seemed to me as though two angels were walking around the Hall during Communion and were pressing a seal onto the brows of all the brothers and sisters, but they passed me by. I gathered up the courage to ask them what that was supposed to mean? Answer: Those that had the seal on their brow would soon see their Lord. Trembling, I asked, "Won't I see Him then?" Answer: Without faith no-one can see the Lord, for not to believe is the greatest sin. I answered quite timidly, "But I have wept for Him!" And I burst into such tears that it woke me up, and I got out of bed and went into my room,[12] and there I emptied out my fearful heart in a thousand tears before my faithful Saviour but could say nothing except to call out with David, "Create in me a clean heart, O God; and renew a right spirit within me."[13] But my heart came alive again. I could see how He had endured great suffering on the Mount of Olives even for me, and I could make it my own. And He gave me the grace to believe that He had also trembled and shaken for me and had atoned for my sins also. Then I could say with a feeling of consolation, "O Jesus, my friend in times of need, I thank you from my heart for all the pains of your soul and martyrdom until death."[14] From that time forth, by His grace, I knew how to apply His merits and passion properly to myself, and all the doubts and disbelief that had plagued me for so long disappeared. I also gained trust in my Choir Labouress,[15] and I could talk to her in depth about everything, and it was a blessing to be able to tell her how I felt, and the Saviour definitely laid a particular blessing upon this because I felt like a completely different person. Deeply ashamed, of course, by His great compassion toward poor me, but at the same time completely comforted, I was able to continue my course through life and cleave to Him like a child through all misery and affliction, through all the bright and dark days He was my comfort, in whom I placed my trust. In general, I must admit that during the nine years in which I lived with the Great Girls, whom I loved tenderly, I experienced many blessings for my heart. Their growth and development lay close to my heart, and the Saviour allowed me to have much joy in them. (Many of them have since become useful sisters in the Congregation, about which I rejoice with all my heart.)

In 1771, on October 15th, I received the call to enter into marriage with the now departed Br. Friedrich Unger and, at the same time, the call to serve the congregation in Philadelphia with him. I accepted this, trusting in the Saviour, although it cost me dearly. On the 25th of that same month we were married and then moved to Philadelphia and served the little congregation there for several years. The Saviour blessed us here with the birth of a daughter Anna Friedericka, who is now married to Br. Nathaniel Brown (from whom we have two granddaughters).

In 1775, we received a call to Lancaster, where the Saviour blessed us with our second little daughter Maria Rosina, who later served in the Boarding School here. A few years later we went to Heidelberg.[16] This time was very hard generally because of the disturbances of the war.[17] Great anguish and misery were everywhere and all correspondence was held up because noone was allowed to travel without having sworn the oath,[18] and so we had to live without hearing anything from a Congregation.[19] Everything was in a state of confusion, and we did not know where to turn. In this situation my late husband became ill, but nobody believed that his illness was dangerous. He did not think so himself, but I was continually concerned and, when I told him this, he comforted me with the words, "I am not so ill that I think I will go home. But if that should happen, then only have faith that the Saviour has never neglected anything in His kingly rule, and whatever He does and allows to happen, has a blessed end. The Saviour will take care of you and our children. He is the best father."

On Good Friday April 2nd, 1780, I experienced the indescribable pain of him going to his eternal rest. That was a hard trial for me, as our marriage had lasted only seven-and-a-half years, which we had spent very happily. So I was put in the state of widowhood with two small children and one on the way. I can write no more about this time. I opened the hymn book at the verse that always makes a deep impression on me: "God has given you your lot with His own hand because your capacity is known to Him; and He will also not forget always to embrace and support you with faithfulness, mercy, and love." That was truly a comfort to me, but dark thoughts, dark days, and sleepless nights could not be avoided.

A few weeks later, I moved to Bethlehem and, on July 27 of that same year, my third little daughter was born, Johanna Elisabeth, who died in her seventh year here in the Children's House of the scarlet fever that was rampant at that time. In the first year of my widowed state it was indescribably hard for me to see myself and my three small children so abandoned and crying for their dear father, and I often felt as though my heart would break. But in the second year the Saviour granted me the grace to keep myself closer to Him, and He often comforted me in an indescribable manner. I derived much pleasure from my dear children and slowly became accustomed to my sad state, and I must admit that in my eight years of widowhood I experienced much good for my heart, because of which this time will remain a blessed memory.

In 1785, on May 21, I was married for a second time to the widower Brother Franz Boehler who had his Plan[20] in Jersey near Old Man's Creek.[21] A few days later we set off for there by way of Philadelphia. We were received with much love, but after only two months I came down with the fever that made me quite despondent. We served this little congregation for almost ten years during many severe illnesses, but I must sing praises to the Saviour that with His comfort He raised my all too often low

spirits and my sighs that always were aroused by the liturgy of the Widows'
Choir: "Strengthen me with the spirit of your joy because you know of my
frailty, He has graciously heard us and helped us through all difficulties
and through all the frailties." But, because my dear husband had almost
completely lost his hearing through a severe illness and we considered
ourselves to be unable to do the Plan justice, we asked permission to be
relieved of our position, which we received after some time, and on December 6, 1794, arrived here in Bethlehem, our little place of rest. I was very
depressed and weak from my last severe illness, but gradually I recovered
so that I could go out once again. And the pleasure of seeing my dear
daughter after such a long absence revived me.

My dearest wish was now to use the rest of my days or years in the
Congregation in peace and for the benefit of my heart. I still had to go
through an experience of my own for it pleased the Saviour to have me
experience a dark time and true days of trial.

> Oh God, what was it, that I there felt
> What difficult hours were they
> Nothing on my side there dwelt
> But grief and vanity.
>
> Before Jesus' gaze, so I thought,
> There is no deception,
> And that to me such sadness brought,
> And to my heart confusion.
>
> No good there was in me to be found,
> But my sins they were forgiven,
> For this I bowed low to the ground,
> From God, this knowledge given.
>
> Amid a thousand tears, I must say,
> My Saviour, fail me not,
> On the right path help me stay,
> To love you is my lot.
>
> Strengthen my faith that now is weak,
> Let no foe me of it deprive,
> Bent and weary, thee I seek,
> With your succour, so gladly alive.

This He did; He strengthened me,
Oh time of celebration,
In Him I could rejoice, happy
That prepared was my salvation.

As unexpectedly as this came
So gladly did I take it,
So deeply did His grace me shame,
Oft asked for, my thirst slaked.

How dear His goodness was to me,
To heart and soul a solace,
When I could again myself clearly see
Living life to its fullest.

Now dear Saviour, give me the grace,
That on my future way,
I your hand may take and go quite safe,
Till I see you on that day.

Until that day, when I can thank you dear
For all that you have wrought
For me, your sick one, in this vale of tears,
For my grace you have bought.

I continued on with my life happy again in the hope that my faithful Saviour would keep me by His hand and thereby let me go my way safely as long as it pleased Him, until we resolved to make a visit to Lititz[22] to visit our youngest daughter there. We travelled there towards the end of May 1806 and were looking forward to seeing our dear children soon. But, on the way, my dear husband became ill and then actually went home in Lititz on June 4. That was once again a hard trial for me; my expected joy was transformed into true sorrow. And so I returned to Bethlehem, once again in the widow's state. This visit cost me many thousands of tears, and the only comfort that came to my aid and set me on my feet again was that, without the Saviour's will, nothing can happen to His children; and also the words my dear husband used to say to me often: "All my days are written in His book. I will not die an hour before my time here is up."

Thus far the departed sister's own words.

She lived here in the settlement for quite a few more years and then experienced the pain of the death of her dear daughter Maria (who was married to Brother Constantin Miller) in the year 1807, on February 27. This gave her some hours of grief and often aroused in her the desire to be reunited soon with her in the presence of the Saviour, and she needed many words of comfort for her loss that went very near to her.[23] At all times, it was a comfort and joy to her that the dear Saviour saw fit to have her children serve Him, and she often declared this in quite an edifying fashion and supported them diligently with prayer. She herself was a useful sister in her service in the town and country congregations and was generally loved by brothers and sisters and friends, for she carried out every task laid upon her with an earnest devotion, and she only complained about anything that was unpleasant and difficult to her best Friend, whom she had come to know as her Redeemer and Helper through the many experiences she had gone through, in the same way as she had come to know herself to be a poor sinner and sought help and salvation only from Him (her memoir is clear proof of this) and He never let her hope in Him come to naught.

On September 5th, 1808, she moved into the Widows' House in order, as she said herself, to spend her final days in this life in undisturbed peace. She soon became accustomed to her surroundings and, apart from her sickliness, she was of a cheerful and lively disposition, which provided many pleasant hours to both herself and those who came into contact with her.

At our last Choir Festival Day she was extraordinarily happy and cheerful, and the following day she declared to a sister among other things, "That was a truly blessed day, and the blessing that I received from the Saviour should stay with me into eternity, for I know that I shall soon go home." On the Monday she put her outward affairs in order and made arrangements for her sick bed. On Tuesday, she visited various friends in the town, and in the same night a violent headache overcame her, accompanied by stabbing pains in the side, but she seemed to improve with the help of useful medications from the doctor, until after a few days a high chest fever started up. She had to suffer much, but the comforting hope of soon being released from all pain and transported to the realm of health gave her the courage and strength to endure it with patience. If one said to her that it seemed as though she would go home at any time, so she would say amiably, "I wish it were so! But I submit myself to the will of the Saviour and whatever He does I accept."

On the 8th she asked to receive the blessing of the Congregation and her choir for her going home. This was bestowed upon her with a blessed feeling of the nearness of the dear Saviour. But her consummation was delayed and she had another two hard days and nights of constrictions in the chest which did, however, became weaker and weaker until on May 10th in the morning in the 11th hour the moment arrived which she so dearly longed for, as her faithful Saviour came and took her redeemed soul into His eternal joy and put a gentle and blessed end to her suffering at the age of 69 years, 4 months, and 10 days.

Magdalene Beulah Brockden
1731–1820

Magdalene was born in Little Popo on the Guinea Coast and was captured by slavers when still a small child. She was bought by Charles Brockden, Recorder of Deeds for the City of Philadelphia and Deputy Master of the Rolls of the Province of Pennsylvania, as a maid for his wife. A close friend of Zinzendorf, although himself not a Moravian, Brockden was also associated with Benjamin Franklin and Anthony Benezet, the famous antislavery campaigner. In 1743, Brockden sent Magdalene to Bethlehem to save her soul (in itself an ideological act in a century in which the very existence of a soul in the African was the subject of debate). He manumitted her nine years later, although in that document he reserved the right to rescind the manumission if he considered that Magdalene (or any children she might have) were in danger of being enslaved by someone else. He finally revoked the right to rescind the manumission in 1758. Magdalene lived a long life in the Moravian Congregation in Bethlehem. She married Andrew, an Igbo, in 1762, and they had three children (although only two sons are mentioned in the narrative), none of whom survived infancy.[24] From the various records in the Moravian archives it appears that Magdalene worked mainly as a laundress, taking in work from the Single Brethren. Her memoir is probably written in the mid-1750s, making it the earliest extant writing by an African woman in North America.

Our Negro sister Magdalena, who happily departed on January 3rd of this year, left behind the following report.

I was, as is known, a slave or the property of the late Mr. Brockden who bought me from another master, when I was ten years old and from then on I served his family until I was grown. Because my master was much concerned about the salvation of my soul and he saw that it was high time that I was protected from the temptations of the world and brought to a religious society, so he suggested to me that I should go to Bethlehem.

Because I had no desire to do so, I asked him rather to sell me to someone else, for at that time I still loved the world and desired to enjoy it fully. However, my master said to me lovingly that I should go to Bethlehem and at least try it. He knew that I would be well treated there. And if it did not suit me there so he would take me back at any time. When I arrived here I was received with such love and friendship by the official workers and all the Brethren that I was much ashamed. (She arrived on November 23, 1743 in Bethlehem.) I soon received permission to remain here. My behaviour in the beginning was so bad; I really tried to be sent away again, which did not happen. The love of the Brethren, however, and in particular the great mercy of the Saviour that I came to feel at this time moved me to stay here. Some time after, my master came here and gave me his permission and blessing, and I became content and happy.

The Saviour showed great mercy to my poor soul, which was so deeply sunk in the slavery of sin that I never thought that I would be freed from these chains and could receive grace. How happy I was for the words, "Also for you did Jesus die on the stem of the cross so that you may be redeemed and eternally blessed." I understood this in faith and received forgiveness for my sins.

In 1748 on the 19th May she was baptized in the death of Jesus and on the 26th January 1749 she attained the pleasure of Holy Communion with the congregation. On 21st January 1762 she entered into matrimony with the Negro Brother Andrew, and this marriage was blessed with two sons who have both gone home. In 1779 on March 30th she became a widow. She enjoyed lasting health until her old age. About fourteen days ago she became seriously ill, and it soon became clear that this illness was to be her end, and this became clear to her also. She fell asleep the above day in the 89th year of her life.

Catharine Brownfield, née Kerney
1716–1798

Catharine's memoir gives a detailed account of the Moravian congregation in New York City in the early eighteenth century. Here she met several of the leading Moravians of the time, such as the preacher Russmeyer and his wife, and also Owen Rice, an evangelist, who came originally from Haverfordwest, Wales. Rice, ordained a deacon in 1748, served as an itinerant preacher in the English-speaking parts of Pennsylvania, New Jersey, New York, and the New England colonies. He also worked as the English language preacher for the Congregation in Philadelphia and Bethlehem before he returned to Europe in 1754. He died in Gomersal, Yorkshire, in 1788. It was Owen Rice who inspired Catharine to visit Bethlehem and join the Congregation. After initial resistance from her family (she is kidnapped away from Bethlehem by her brothers) she settled in the congregation and married John Brownfield, an Englishman. At this point her memoir breaks off.

Catharine's husband, John Brownfield had entered General James Oglethorpe's household and was eventually appointed as his secretary. It was, of course, Oglethorpe who planned to open up Georgia as a British colony by sending debtors and people escaping religious persecution there. Zinzendorf secured an agreement with him in 1733 that settlers from his lands in Saxony might also settle in Georgia. In February 1737, John Brownfield accompanied Oglethorpe to Georgia. Here he became acquainted with the Moravian Brethren about whom he had already heard while he was in London. When the Moravian settlement in Georgia failed, Brownfield followed the settlers to Pennsylvania and came to Bethlehem in April 1745 where he was employed as a bookkeeper. He was ordained deacon in 1749 and died in Bethlehem in April 1752, leaving Catharina as his widow at the age of thirty-six. She remained with the Widows Choir for the next forty-six years until her own death in 1798.

The original English version of Catharine's memoir mentioned in the opening sentence is unfortunately no longer in existence. The following text is a translation of the German memoir, of which two identical versions exist: this copy and the entry in the Bethlehem Diary, *vol. 39, 52.*

Our dear widowed sister, Catharine Brownfield, née Kerney, has written the following about her life in the English language.

I was born on February 4 (new style), 1716, in New York and baptized and raised in the Church of England, to which I remained faithful. And I can truly say that I was concerned about my salvation right from my childhood. I believed that, if I were to go to Holy Communion, then I would find complete peace. For that reason, in my fifteenth year, I went to classes or catechism but, when the day came when I was to enjoy it, I became so troubled in my heart that I did not dare to and said to my teacher that I wanted to wait until the following Easter, in the hope that our Saviour would then give me His blessing. The following year, it pleased the Saviour to open my eyes, so that I saw my natural, lost state through the preaching of a Dissenter, the first whom I had heard and whose sermons at this time were a blessing to many and especially to my heart. It then pleased the Lord to open my ears as he had done with Lydia,[25] so that I became more and more concerned about my unconverted state, although I sometimes gained some comfort from the sufferings of my Saviour, but that did not last. Again and again, fear and doubt overcame me. I remained in this uncertain state for almost four years, until it pleased my gracious Saviour to reveal Himself clearly and in a particular way to my poor heart. In faith I saw how He had become man for me and had died for my sins on the cross. I am unable to describe the sweet enjoyment and assurance that I received through the Holy Spirit. I lived in this blessed state and enjoyed what my dear Lord Jesus had done for me, that He had removed me from the vanities of the world and transported me into His heavenly light.

The only thing that hurt and pained me was that I had saddened my dear parents greatly by leaving the church in which I had been raised, but the daily comfort that I received from my dear Saviour made everything bearable for me. I often thought, "Oh, if only they knew the sweetness that I enjoy, then they would gladly deny everything that the world calls happiness until they enjoyed the peace of God which passes all understanding."

Without the knowledge of my parents, I now kept the company of awakened people. Here I heard much against the Brethren, which affected me greatly, and I warned them not to speak about them like that; although I did not know them at all and had not yet seen nor heard any of them, still I felt a secret love for them. The fear of offending those whom I considered to be eminent Christians kept me away from the Brethren for two years. At last I opened my heart to Sister Russmeyer, who was a true friend of the Brethren, and I decided not to believe the opinions of other people but to hear the Brethren myself!

The first brother I heard was Brother Owen Rice. He explained the sixty-third chapter of Isaiah[26] and the Holy Spirit applied it to my heart, so that I could say from experience that they and they alone are the people for hungry souls. In 1744, I came on a visit to Bethlehem, and although I did not understand the German language, in all the meetings that I attended I nevertheless felt the sweet peace of God in Christ Jesus my Lord. In 1745, I came here to live, was soon received into the Congregation and admitted to Holy Communion. During the praying of the Litany of the Wounds, the wounds of Jesus became so clear and so strong in my heart that I am unable to find a better expression than in the verse, "Oh, love filled with Jesus, Oh, my heart day and night, Oh, how with waking desire I think on him at dawn and dusk." Thereafter, I lived in Nazareth.

In September 1745, my two brothers came to visit me with the news that my mother was ill and wanted to see me before her death and that she had been given up by the doctors, all of which affected me greatly. If only I had immediately given heed to the spirit of truth, then I would saved myself much anguish and distress. My brothers often went walking with me, and in my heart I was warned not to trust them. As they were about to depart and I was about to take my leave of them, one climbed up onto his horse and the other took me and sat me behind him and thus they galloped away with me and took me to Brunswick,[27] where my mother was waiting in her carriage for me, her lost child, as she called me.

I was also warmly received by my dear father. However, it was as though there were no life in me. I felt no peace in my heart, as though my dear Saviour had abandoned me. I kept to myself as much as possible. After I had been there for two days, I knelt and begged my parents, who were very disturbed at my melancholy, just to send me to Mr Keiler. At this, my father asked me if I were bound by some oath to spend my days with the Brethren. I answered: "No, but I have often earnestly asked the Lord with a broken heart not to allow me to lose my blessed state." On the fourth day I got two servants, who brought me in a canoe to Mr. Keiler, who treated me like the merciful Samaritan and got two horses and that same night we rode twenty-eight miles on the way to Nazareth, where I arrived safely the following day. Here she writes herself in German: "You, my Jesus have carried me through the desert, where various temptations pressed upon me, your sweet comfort has, in times of hesitation, so refreshed my poor heart with a new strength. If I know aught of the burden of sorrow then I also know how you stood by me." In 1747, I was married to Brother John Brownfield, one of the best of men.

So far her own words.

Her marriage was blessed with one daughter who passed on before her. On April 23, 1752, she became a widow and moved to Nazareth to live with the widows, until the Choir House was finished in Bethlehem, into which she then moved with them. Her heart clung to the Saviour and the Congregation. In all the frailties which she had in herself, she always maintained a steady trust in Him. She always had a real taste for the meetings. It pained her greatly when she could no longer attend them because of her weakness. As the years went by, she was very wretched and weak, so that she was unable to leave her bed for any length of time. During the last six months her illness became a burden to her and other sisters. She would often pray to the dear Saviour that He should end her misery soon. A few days before she went home, because she was still conscious, she requested that she be given the blessing and this took place. And so, on the 5th, she went gently and happily. She reached an age of 82 years, 2 months.

Christiana Dorothea Detmers, née Morhardt
1730–1814

Christiana Detmers was born during the Protestant revival in Swabia where her father introduced her to the Moravian Brethren. However, during her teenage years, Christiana's mother suffered from a severe depression, which obliged Christiana to take over the running of the household and which caused Christiana to resent heavily the influence of the Moravian brethren on her mother. It was not until she fell down the cellar steps that she realized the strength of her mother's feelings towards her and the power of Christ. Christiana now turned to the Brethren herself, spoke with Brother Dörrbaum (1713–1756), who was one of the leading young men in Herrnhaag at the time, and joined the congregation in Herrnhaag in 1747 (not 1744 — the copyist has clearly mistaken a 4 for a 7). Five years later she traveled to America with Anna Johanna Piesch (Seidel) where she worked as a teacher in Bethlehem. She married the warden of the congregation, Ferdinand Detmers, in 1763 and had her first and only child at the age of 34. Her daughter died at age five.

Christiana's memoir provides the reader with an example of the different kinds of life available to a Moravian woman in the eighteenth century. For example, she spent her first thirty-three years as a single sister working as a teacher. She then married one of the leaders of the congregation in America and fulfilled the duties associated with this position. Of further interest is Christiana's attribution of God's will to her fall down the cellar steps as a teenager. She understood it as God's way of bringing her to understanding.

Our late Sister Christiana Dorothea Detmers, née Morhardt, has left us the following memoir of her life.

I was born in Stuttgart on June 22, 1730, and baptized and raised in the Lutheran Church. My father was Friedrich Morhardt, a burgher[28] and baker in Stuttgart, and my mother Christiana Dorothea was born Meyer. As the first child of eleven, I was an important gift of grace from God to my parents because He had heard the prayers which, before my birth, they often said to Him on bended knee. I spent my childhood years partly with my parents and partly with my grandparents on my mother's side. I showed an aptitude for learning at school. It was important to my parents to raise their children for the honor and joy of God. I, however, was a bad child and was open to all temptations, despite the fact that my upbringing by my parents was very strict.

From my 14th year on, however, my heart was not without good emotions. It often occurred to me that in my present state I could have no such blessed end if I were to die now. In the year 1745, my father became acquainted with the Brethren's Congregation.[29] With his frequent encouragement, he convinced me also to visit the Brethren's meetings, which were held in Stuttgart, although I considered it to be unnecessary, especially because of my youth. A year later, my mother became almost inconsolable about the condition of her heart. But, through the Saviour's grace and with the encouragement of the brothers and sisters, she was able to pull herself together somewhat. However, because she remained somewhat melancholy for a time, I had to run the household, of which she felt herself to be incapable. This turned me so against the Congregation that I wished my parents had never heard anything about them. I denied my mother the dutiful obedience of a child. Yes, I saddened her so, that even I became anxious and frightened about it myself. But the Saviour was merciful to me and employed a serious means to change my attitude to her. On Easter Sunday morning, I fell down the cellar steps and lay at my mother's feet, to her great horror, for I lay there a while unconscious. When I came around again I begged my mother for forgiveness for my bad behavior towards her hitherto, which I then gladly received. The revelation of her feelings, as she saw me lying there, moved my hard heart and humbled me.

Just then, Brother Timaeus was visiting us, and I wished to hear from him whether I could still be saved. His encouragement was most comforting to me. My memory and especially my hearing had suffered from the fall. This worried me, because I was afraid that I would not pass the examination before confirmation leading to my first enjoyment of Holy Communion. The preacher, who was not well disposed towards my parents because of their acquaintance with the Brethren, was very hard on me, but I could answer all his questions with a calm confidence. I enjoyed Holy Communion trembling. But I still enjoyed participating in every opportunity for foolishness and dissipation, as long as it remained hidden from my parents, and I was not allowed to say anything about this in the meetings, which were held in our house. I knew that things did not stand well with me, and I often resolved that things should get better, but this did not last. And so it went on, until the Saviour brought me into great distress about my lost state, so that I did not know what to do. I made it very difficult for the Holy Spirit, though, to make me into a truly poor sinner who wanted to accept Jesus' merits through grace. But He did not relent in His care and effort, until I cried for mercy and pleaded with the Saviour to take care of me, for I seemed to me to be the greatest sinner. To the amazement of my parents, I asked to speak to Brother Dörbaum who was on a visit from the Congregation. I could tell him honestly about the condition of my heart. He comforted me and directed me lovingly to the Saviour, who turns no sinner away. Oh, if He, the true friend of sinners, had not clung to me first, I would never have sought Him out.[30] Brother Dörbaum received from me a promise to visit him soon Herrnhaag. My mother really wanted to help me in this, but my father believed that I could not leave because of the running of the household. After much pleading he finally gave me his permission. However, it should remain hidden from my grandmother. But because she was troubled about my convictions, she found an opportunity to talk to me by myself when my parents were not home about my feelings toward the Congregation. I answered her questions in a friendly manner, but she wanted to distract me from my intentions with a marriage; I assured her, however, that she was too late, I could not retract my promise. On the very same day she arranged for my mother to be questioned by her confessor. After this my mother said to me, I cannot allow you to go to the Congregation. I cried loudly and, after I had pulled myself together again, I said to my parents that grandmother had been with me and told them what we had talked about. They approved of my conduct, and I explained to them that I now wanted to go to the Congregation. The Saviour also helped me, so that I was able to fulfill my aim.

I arrived in Herrnhaag in August 1744[7]. The Saviour made Himself known to me as such a friend, that I often had to cry in shame and submission. I also felt a great love towards the sisters; I asked each one who visited me to pray that the Saviour would soon secure me my little place in the Congregation. In the meantime, it saddened me greatly that many of those who also waited with me for permission received it before I did. But I was even more saddened when I was told that I could go home again for the time being. I thought that this could not be possible, but I became calm and felt the comfort of the Saviour in my heart and also reassurance that I had honestly revealed my base nature to the sisters. When it came to my actual departure, I felt dissatisfied. And I had hardly left the settlement for fifteen minutes when I was called back with the news that the *Jüngerin* wanted to speak to me. Among other things, she demanded that I should write to her when I wanted to come for a visit again; I asked that she should rather just keep me there straight away. She asked me, "Is it really the desire of your heart to become nothing but the Saviour's?" I answered this with tears, "Yes!" "Well," she answered, "in that case let us keep you here for a trial period." On September 16, to my great joy, I moved into the Sisters' House and savored the love of the sisters in spite of the fact that there was nothing lovable about me. In the days leading up to November 13, when everyone was required to examine carefully his or her heart before Jesus' gaze, I thought seriously about myself and found so much in me that was unlike my Saviour that I became frightened, and I believed that I would not be able to stay there and even packed my things. I bewailed my troubled state to my Labouresses amid many tears; lovingly, they guided me as a sinner to the Saviour, and He comforted me. But I had still, through faith, to make His merits my own. On March 10, 1748, I was received into the Congregation, and I was thoroughly convinced by this that He loves sinners.

In April, I travelled to Herrnhut with several sisters and, soon after our arrival there, moved to Hennersdorf, where I served in the household. Here I enjoyed much in my relationship with the Saviour that was a blessing for my heart. On August 13, I enjoyed Holy Communion for the first time with the Congregation, which was a true blessing.

In the same year I travelled through Ebersdorf back to Herrnhaag with a company of sisters who were bound for Bethlehem in North America, and once again I moved into the Sisters' House. In 1749, I came to work with the small children in the Children's House and then became one of the hourly intercessors; I was also employed as a Labouress with the Greater Girls and accepted as an acolyte. In April 1750, I travelled with Sister Eleonora von Schweinitz [31] to England and to the Disciple's House in London.[32] After we had left, on the same day my dear mother arrived in Herrnhaag to visit me. It pained her greatly to have missed me, as it also hurt me, when I discovered this, not to have seen her again. But the fact that she had allowed herself to be comforted also reassured me. It cost me many tears to become accustomed to my new surroundings in London but quietly I cleaved to my Saviour. When the late Disciple returned with his household to Germany, I came to work with the children at Mile End, where I also had to go through a fair amount of sorrow. Upon his return in 1751 a newly blessed time began for me. Twice I had declined to go to Pennsylvania; this made me timorous in the face of my sisters, so when the request came a third time, in a moving letter from the *Jüngerin* herself, I could not resist. This gave rise to a few conversations with the Saviour. I will never forget His witness to poor me in these circumstances.

On September 28, 1752, I departed from London with a convoy of sisters under the leadership of Anna Johanna Piesch[33] and on November 25 we arrived here in Bethlehem. The loving reception in the Single Sisters' House did me much good and the ways things were then also made me content. I soon came to work with the older girls, where I had trouble settling in and learned new lessons, which, however, did much for my heart and caused me to depend even more on the Saviour and be even more in love with His martyr figure. I paid great heed when the Holy Spirit showed me still more of my bad habits.

In time, I came to work with the children; also here I often made mistakes and had many opportunities to be ashamed of myself and to ask for forgiveness. On July 19, 1763, I was married to Brother Ferdinand Philip Jacob Detmers[34] who was employed here under the Warden (illus. 16). In December 1764 we were blessed with the birth of a little daughter Christiane Sophia, whom the Saviour took to Himself again in her 6th year. In March 1772, we moved to Nazareth where my husband had been called to be the Warden of the Congregation. In October 1784, we moved to Lititz to fill the same office. In the year 1796, on grounds of his age and frailty, my dear husband asked permission to be relieved of his duties, which was granted, and in October of the same year we moved back here to Bethlehem. On August 28, 1801, I entered the state of widowhood. Now and in my former married state the Saviour has done much for me and bound me even closer to Him through many experiences, for which I worship Him in humility and in the dust.

Thus far the late sister.

On September 29 of that same year she moved into the Choir House of the Widows here and spent her time happily and cheerfully. A few years ago she survived a severe illness, which everyone thought would cause her to go home. She appeared to have recovered fully until about four years ago when she was beset with rheumatic pains, which disturbed her especially during the night. But her cheerful and lighthearted nature did not leave her, as she kept out of bed as long as was at all possible and attended the Meetings as long as her strength lasted. A few years ago, Sister Elisabeth Standz moved in with her to care for her in her frailty and was her loyal sickwaitress until the very end, a fact for which the dear departed often thanked her. Through all her faults, shortcomings, and afflictions, which she knew very well herself, she held to her belief in the Saviour, who had ensured her of the forgiveness of her sins through His Spirit, and she was certain that He would preserve this beautiful gift for her until that day [of judgement]. Three weeks ago she had to lie down completely, her weakness increased from day to day, and one could clearly see that the Saviour would soon release her from her pain and bring her home to Himself. On Tuesday, the 26th of this month, toward evening, she asked to be blessed for her journey home, which then happened immediately in the presence of Jesus, during which she was quite conscious. Thereafter, she lay quite still until about half past eleven, when she fell asleep quite gently at an age of 84 years, one month and four days.

Anna Barbara Fenstermacher, née Rente
1709–1790

Anna Fenstermacher was born in the Palatinate and claims to have been awakened during her first experience of childbirth. At the age of eighteen, she and her husband decided to move to America with their family, but not before her mother gave her some sound advice about snakes and told her to look out for the Brethren. Fifteen years later she and her husband and their nine children moved from the countryside into Philadelphia where soon thereafter she was widowed. She was received into the Congregation in 1744 and sent four of her children to Moravian schools. Her memoir includes touching details such as her mother's advice and also the help given her by a concerned neighbor when she and her children had nothing to eat.

Our departed sister Anna Barbara Fenstermacher had the following written down about her way through this life.

I was born on March 28, 1709, in Erstett in the Palatinate, where my father, Martin Rente was a burgher and a blacksmith. My parents raised me as a good Lutheran, and it was also my great pleasure to go to church. In my twelfth year, I went to Holy Communion for the first time and, soon thereafter, I went into service.[35] In my eighteenth year, I took my first husband, Michael Leibert, and bore him ten children, six sons and four daughters.[36] I had my first son while still living in my father's house and, during this birth, I was awakened. As I cried to the Saviour in my soul's troubled state, he forgave my sins, and then I really felt my salvation. When I had recovered, I was crying a great deal, and my mother asked me, "Why are you crying so much? You have a son!" I answered her, "Because I did not die, and I am so blessed, and now I have to go back into the world." And from that time forth I was always concerned as to how I would maintain grace.

In 1727, we moved to this country and, when we had already said our farewells and I was leaving, my mother followed me and said she had something else to say to me, and we sat down, and she began: "When you arrive in the land, don't think about gaining great wealth, but rather first take care of your children, and see that they come to no harm and don't get bitten by snakes or the like. Second, I have heard for a long time that a congregation of God is to be founded over the ocean, just as it was in the Apostles' time, and when you hear about it, don't think about the fact that you were brought up in such and such a religion (her husband was Catholic) but rather join with them. They think much of the sufferings of Christ; they move from place to place, but when only three are gathered together, remain with them, for it must be again as it was in the beginning." And so on. That made an such an impression on me that I always thought about it.

Once, when I was very ill, I felt my salvation again, and it was always in my heart as though those people would come, about whom my mother had spoken, and when the Brethren came into the land, I believed that they were those people even before I saw them. I heard Count von Zinzendorf himself preaching first of all; but I was also persecuted enough.

Thereupon in March 1742, we moved in to the city[37] where my husband lived for only another six months. There I was, a widow with nine children, until I had four of them with the Congregation. Thereafter, I was married to my late husband, Christian Fenstermacher. In September 1764, we moved to Lititz, which was hard for me to do because I had children in Philadelphia, and was still attached to the world.

Thus far her own account.

In 1744, she was received into the Congregation in Philadelphia and admitted to Holy Communion in 1746. In 1768, in Lititz she became a widow for the second time and, in answer to her dearest wish, she received permission to move to Bethlehem and was one of the first inhabitants of the Widows' Choirhouse, where she was quite contented and happy. She often gave witness to the fact that she was now living the most peaceful and contented part of her life and was content with everything. The beautiful services in the congregation were of immeasurable value to her and, for as long as she could, she did not miss a single Opportunity. With thanks she often testified how the dear Saviour had granted her a childlike care and steadfast trust in Him through all her troubles. One of these times had remained with her quite clearly, when she once had had nothing to give her children to eat and had been most worried about this in the night. Early in the morning, a neighbour came as she was in great despair and said "Barbara, during the night I was wondering whether you had anything to eat for yourself and the children." Whereupon she wept and said to him that she had nothing, and if he could lend her a couple of bushels of fruit so she would be very grateful to him. Whereupon he said to her, "I want to give you flour and fruit without expecting payment."

As long as six years ago she had a stroke and, although she recovered straightaway, from that time on we noticed a paralysis on her right side and a weakening of her senses. She often prayed to the Saviour with many tears to help her. Four years ago, she had a heavier stroke and from then on was robbed of most of her senses, could not talk coherently anymore, and from then on had to be cared for like a small child. Her nurse, Christina Segner,[38] did this with great love and loyalty day and night. For the last year she was in an especially wretched state, that one could hardly look upon or hear her whimpering without heartfelt sympathy. One could understand nothing other than, "Oh, Lord Jesus, oh my Saviour have pity and help me."[39]

Recently, she often got open sores on her body, for which the doctors remained loyal in the attempt to dull her pain, for her bodily suffering was very great. On December 15th, the daily watchword for the congregation was "though I walk in the midst of hostility, thou dost stretch forth thy hand [Psalm 138:7]. I can be comforted with you when my distress is greatest of all. Your care for me your child is more than fatherly." One could see that she was nearing her release from all sorrow, and the blessing of the Congregation and her Choir was given to her with the feeling of the nearness of Jesus, with which she passed away on the morning of the 16th quite gently and blessedly in the 82nd year of her life.[40] Now, in harmony, she will sing above, as we do here, "One thing has brought my through, little lamb, that slaughtered were you!"

Mariana Höht
1737–1772

From warnings about the dangers of snakes in America we move to Mariana's story — one of murder, kidnap, life with the Lenni Lenape, subsequent escape and return to the Moravian congregation in Bethlehem. After the attack on Gnadenhütten in November 1755, the Indians moved north east and descended on the Höht farm, killing Mariana's mother and father and capturing her and her sister. During her captivity in Tioga (Diuoiga), an area in Northern Pennsylvania near the New York

*border that from 1755–60 had no European settlers and therefore served as the
destination for captives, Mariana witnessed the murder of Susanne Nitschmann,
the wife of Martin Nitschmann, one of the missionaries at Gnadenhütten who had
been seriously injured by a bullet during the raid and taken prisoner. Mariana
married one of the Lenni Lenape, had a child, and eventually escaped back to the
Moravian congregation.*

*Although Mariana's memoir is listed among those of the widows, she was techni-
cally still a married woman when she died, even if estranged from her Delaware
husband. Her son, whom she brought back with her to Bethlehem against the wishes
of her husband, died at the age of five and a half. She herself seems to have spent
the last years of her short life in quite a state of melancholy. This memoir, composed
probably sometime in the 1760s, is full of personal detail and reflective comment in
addition to the exciting captivity narrative. Mariana, when held captive by the
Indians, prayed to her Heiland to deliver her. Her decision to marry the Indian
could be interpreted not as capitulation but as an acceptance of God's will (the term
she uses is* resolvirte*).*

The personalia of the dear departed sister Mariana Höht.

Our late sister Mariana Höht had the following account of her life
written down.

I was born in 1737 on May 24 in the town of Lichtenberg in the duchy
of Zweibrücken,[41] where my father was a burgher and master baker. In
1748, I accompanied my dear parents to America, more exactly to Philadelphia, where we soon became acquainted with the brothers and sisters from
the Congregation. It was not long before my dear father, who was very
concerned for the salvation of his children, sent us to the Brethren's
school. I soon became very fond of the brothers and sisters and liked to
hear them tell me something about the Saviour, which was also not without
blessing for my heart. I often tearfully begged the dear Saviour to have
mercy upon me and give me salvation. Worldy desires, however, also grew
within me; I often sought pleasure in them, but always with the disquiet of
my heart, because my dear father, who was very strict, became concerned
that we might fall too deeply into worldy ways. He, therefore, resolved to
move out of Philadelphia over the Blue Mountains. There we were often
visited by the Brethren. Their conversations with us were also a blessing to
me. I became familiar with my sinner's heart and felt that I needed the
Saviour and that I must turn to Christ and receive grace, or else I should
be lost. I also thought that nothing would come of me until I went to the
Congregation. I often told my parents this and asked them to let me visit

Bethlehem. They granted me this wish and in November 1755 I went on a visit to Bethlehem with my dear mother. I liked it very much, and my only wish was that I could stay there. I asked my mother for her permission and received it. I was to come as soon as my mother, who was about to give birth, could do without me. This made me very happy.

As soon as we arrived back home, we heard that the Indian wars were about to break out. I was very alarmed and often begged my father to flee to the Brethren; but, he refused. He was not going to flee, for he had done the Indians no harm but rather good. He, therefore, did not believe that they would do anything to us. He put his faith in our dear Lord, that He would help him and his children. I thus had to yield to him, but I was in constant fear because they were not far from our house, and when I fetched in the animals at night I could see them close by the house. Three weeks later, we heard that the Mahony[42] had been burned down by the Indians and that many of the brothers and sisters had perished in the flames, and that they had even murdered some of them. Then I said to my father, "if it happened to the brothers and sisters, and if our dear Lord allowed that to happen to them, then we would not fare better." I begged him once again to flee, but he did not want to. As I realized that I could do nothing to change my father's mind, I decided to be content but not without trepidation. I was not concerned about being captured but I was afraid of being murdered, especially because I was not sure of my salvation. Two weeks after the Mahony was burned down, they came in the evening, as we were sitting at supper, and fired shots. My father did not think that the shooting was nearby but rather wanted to go outside and see what and where it might be. As he went through the front door he fell into their hands. They killed him straight away. Mother and we children leaped out of the back door. My mother jumped into the water and was shot and my youngest sister was also killed immediately. They captured me and my two sisters and took us away with them. I cannot describe what I felt at losing my dear parents in such a fashion and at seeing myself among the wild, unruly Indians. I did not know what was happening to me. I had to go with them. It didn't matter what the weather was like, they showed no mercy, for they tried to torment us however they could. After we had travelled for a few days, I met Susanna Nitschmann, who had been very badly treated and was in great difficulty and despair. That was a painful sight for me. I looked after her as well I could and was often of great comfort to her. After a rough journey, they brought us to Diuoigo, where Susanna was killed and my two sisters and I separated. That also was very painful for me. I was given to the Indian who had captured and murdered Susanna. He was a very wild and evil Indian. I had a rough time with him; I received nothing. Others gave me something to eat, and if he saw it he took it away from me again. I also had to sew new clothes out of Susanna's things, which was also very painful for me. Because many of the Indians felt sorry for me, they took me away from him, particularly because he was very dissolute. They gave me to an old mother as her child. That occurred very solemnly in the presence of many Indians. Her son also accepted me as his sister.

By Indians standards, things went well for me here. The old mother was very good to me, as if I were her real daughter. Oh, it did me so much good to have a little peace and quiet. Also, I was sometimes allowed to visit my sister who had married a Frenchman in the Fort.[43] Because he was well known to the Indians and they liked him, I was allowed to stay with them for three months. In fact, I thought they would leave me there with them, which probably would not have been good for me, for there was such a bad and godless way of life there. My brother, the Indian, came to visit me often and wanted to take me away with him because the old lady asked for me a lot. However, I always begged him to leave me there. One time, however, he came and took me away with him by force. When I got back they told me that I would have to take an Indian as a husband. I said, "no, I did not want to." They said that if I did not want to then I would have to, otherwise they would kill me. For eight days and nights I lay in the snow and all kinds of weather in the bush and prayed and sighed to the dear Saviour that He might help me and tell me what to do. It seemed quite impossible to me to decide to do as they wished. I thought I would rather die. My old mother cried a great deal and told me I should do as they said; otherwise they would burn me, and then she would not have a child anymore. But I stuck by my refusal. Finally, they dragged me out of the bush into the house and said I was going to be burned now because I did not want to take the Indian. I let them carry on. They tied me to a young tree with a rope. My brother lit the fire, and then, as it started to burn and the smoke caught in my throat, I made up my mind and said I would do as they wished. They unbound me straight away, and with great joy brought me back to the house of the old mother, who was very happy to have me back. Now I had to marry an Indian. This too happened very solemnly in the Indian fashion. There was a big meal with many Indians. He was a good man. He loved me very much, and I had a son with him. He often wished that I were back with the white people. He even wanted to help me return, but he also wanted to keep the child. I could not bring myself to do that. However, I kept on hoping that the dear Saviour would clear the way for me to escape. I had been true to Him under the worst circumstances. He had often given me comfort and courage. The certain assurance was in my heart that He would yet bring me to the Congregation.

As the Indian was building himself a house in Koskoshin,[44] he wanted to take me with him. I, however, did not want to go but preferred instead to stay with my old mother, who was moving closer to Pittsburgh, so he left me. That made me very happy. I often received permission from my old mother to go to the Fort, as they thought that because I had a child I would not run away. But I always looked around for an opportunity to escape and eventually found one. Wagons that were taking flour to Pittsburgh under military escort took me along to Lancaster. Oh, how happy and thankful I was to see the brothers and sisters again. I lay there very ill for three weeks, but as soon as I was better the brothers and sisters helped me to get to Bethlehem. Oh, how I am overcome when I think of the love and warmth with which my child and I were taken in by the brothers and sisters and the tender care and attention paid me in the difficult convalesence I had to go through. As soon as I was better, I put my child in the Nursery and moved to the widows in Nazareth. I thank the dear Saviour for all that He has done for me, poor sinner, throughout my whole life. I will kiss His pierced feet for all His forbearance, patience, and forgiveness.

Thus far her own words.

In 1760 she moved to Nazareth. She was received that same year into the Congregation and enjoyed the Body and Blood of our Lord. She was very contented and grateful for all the grace that the dear Saviour showered upon her. She was happy until the dear Saviour revealed her complete corruption and showed her her wretchedness as a poor sinner. At that point she lost her feeling of well being and slipped into melancholy. She thought she had committed the sin against the Holy Spirit[45] but even then the Sinners' Friend gave her solace and courage. She was able to hold to Him in faith. From that time on she lived a blessed life again. In 1763, she was admitted to the Hourly Intercessions. She often said that these conversations alone with her friend were a true comfort. In 1765, she once again became distressed and was troubled about herself like the time before. But she was comforted and, again, the dear Saviour stood by her. He gave her a fresh assurance that she was His and that He was her Saviour now and forever. Several years ago she became sickly and this increased from year to year to such a degree that last summer she travelled to Philadelphia to receive treatment from a doctor. Her condition did improve but that did not last long, so that on February 12 of this year she moved into the sick room. She had completely given herself up to the will of the Saviour, whatever He wished to do with her, but she said, "if He wishes to take me to Him, that is what I would like best." There remained nothing for her to do but to thank the dear Saviour for her election to grace and that He had brought her to the Congregation. She had witnessed and experienced His comfort and words of peace many times. Her illness with large swellings on her legs worsened from day to day until it ended in violent bilious vomiting. She lost all appetite so that for four weeks she ate almost nothing but bread and water. Then came a consumptive fever in addition. She longed for her release and greatly desired to celebrate Easter with the dear Saviour. Her wish was granted her on April 13, in the morning in the eighth hour she passed away with the blessing of her choir and the Congregation. She had reached the age of 34 years, 11 months.

Juliana Horsfield, née Parsons
1737–1809

Juliana Horsfield was the daughter of William and Johanna Parsons (whose memoir appears on page 107). Her father was the Surveyor General of Pennsylvania and was strongly prejudiced against the Moravians. The cause of this great antipathy apparently lay in his wife's strong link to the group. Juliana described how once her father was certain that his wife with her children wanted to join the Moravians he took them away from her and moved into the depths of the Pennsylvanian countryside. During this difficult estrangement from her mother and the Moravians, Juliana survived by remembering the sermons she had heard while at the Children's services in Philadelphia and by reading the Bible her father used for his job as Justice of the Peace. Juliana did return to Philadelphia when she was twelve and eventually joined the Moravians at the age of twenty. Eight years later she married Timothy Horsfield, Jr., son of Justice Horsfield of Bethlehem.

Our dear departed Sister Juliana Horsfield, née Parsons, has written the following about her life:

I was born on November 19th, 1737, in Philadelphia. My dear parents belonged to the Lutheran Church. My dear mother, who was born in Saxony in Germany, had a good Christian upbringing. My dear parents lived together very happily until my mother became very disconcerted and anxious about her salvation and bemoaned this to my father. He, however, told her that it was just a melancholy, which she should not nourish inside her and then it would pass; he often felt like that. But that was little comfort to her. At that same time the Brethren started to preach in Philadelphia, and my mother sent us children to the Meetings, which they always held for the children, and I will never forget the blessing that I received there for my heart. At this time my eldest sister and my only brother died, both very peacefully.

My father was a great enemy of the Brethren, and for that reason he often warned my mother not to have anything to do with them—otherwise, he could no longer share a household with her. And, when he was certain that my mother, with her children, wanted to become members of the Brethren's Congregation, he left her and moved with me and my sister far away into the countryside to the Swatara,[46] where he had bought himself a country seat, and handed us over to a person of bad character to be looked after. That was a hard trial for me because I was only eight years old and here in a strange place, snatched away completely from the care of a tender mother; yes, I would like to say that I was also completely without a father because my father was the Surveyor General and often had to go into the most remote parts of Pennsylvania, and I was, therefore, often separated from him because of this business for long periods of time. And we were left with strangers, amongst whom I never heard God's name mentioned except to be misused, which was very unpleasant for me. My father always had the Bible to hand in his house because he was a justice of the peace, and in this I read diligently, which was a comfort and blessing for my poor heart. That was the sole grazing place that I had for my heart in the four years of my stay in this aforementioned place, for I never found the opportunity to hear an English sermon, and I understood only little of the German language.

At this opportunity, my dear Saviour often brought back to my heart and soul that which I had heard in the Children's Hours in Philadelphia, and these words, which were said to me about His love for children, left a lasting impression on my whole life, for His good Holy Spirit has never left me completely, and it is thanks to His repeated warnings that whenever my bad and corrupted heart wanted to lead me into evil things, which I knew would sadden my Saviour, it never came to pass. Both His and my mother's Christian exhortations were always before my heart and soul and kept me from sinning completely. Although I was still a child who much needed a mother's teaching and faithful care, I was still able to cry about the Saviour and bewail my whole plight in a childlike fashion; and I was always sure that He would hear me, for I have often experienced the fact that children are His special concern. And if I think back to my childhood years, I send the Saviour many, many warm thanks for the innumerable times He has protected me in many clear moments of danger and various scenes of my life which I shall never forget.

In my thirteenth year, my father brought me back to my friends in Philadelphia, where I lived for two years with my sister, who went home during this time and whose edifying end left a lasting impression on me, and the final words she said were, "I was one of the greatest sinners, but I am certain that even I have been dearly bought with the blood of Jesus Christ and that He has washed all my sins away with that blood and will now take me up in his eternal joy. I am now following His call." These words caused me to consider carefully whether I too did not have the same calling to give my heart completely to my Saviour and live in this world only for Him? But I spent several years more in constant indecision as to which way I should choose. Could I give myself up completely to the Saviour or to the pleasures of the world? But at this last thought a certain trepidation always overtook me, which I could never quite name. In this sorrowful state I often pleaded earnestly with the Lord that He would bring me back to my dear mother, and promised Him with a childlike simplicity that I would be a very good girl if He would bring me to good people. He did not scorn this prayer, and after several hard times of trial He brought me at the right time to the Congregation in Bethlehem, which at that time was outwardly poor and despised but inwardly blessed with love and unity. That was in 1758.

My dear mother and I now had the unspeakable joy of hearing that my dear father had left this world as a repentant sinner. He was still able to send word to my mother that he was sorry that he would not be able to see her again, but that her Saviour was now also his. He had forgiven him all his sins, and he hoped that she would forgive him everything also. Her son-in-law, Br. Jacob Rogers, who was here in Bethlehem, gave his funeral oration.

Thus far the late Sister herself.

In 1757, our late Sister was baptized in Philadelphia and, in 1759, she enjoyed Holy Communion for the first time with the congregation in Bethlehem. She lived here for quite a time with the children.

In October 1766, she entered into the married state with the Single Brother Timothy Horsfield, which was blessed with three sons, of whom one son (and one granddaughter of three she had during her lifetime through her son Wilhelm) went before her into eternity. She was particularly concerned to raise her children for the Saviour, an activity that her late husband gladly left to her because she possessed excellent gifts in that way. This was the case because the well-being of her children was the main object of her prayers and her maternal care. In 1789, she became a widow. That was very painful for her, for she lost a tender and widely loved husband. For several years she lived on in her own house in the settlement until 1797, when she moved into the Widows' House; here she wanted to enjoy her time of peace in quiet solitude and was quite resolved to end her days in *that* house. Although she found some things here not as she wished, she nevertheless gradually learned to accommodate herself more to everything and would often say, "I know my failings and weaknesses; we just have to have patience with one another, just as the dear Saviour has with me and us all." She was soon brought back onto the right path through the grace which she had experienced from the Saviour as her most faithful friend from her childhood on, and could, if she thought that she had hurt someone through persuasion, ask for forgiveness in a true sinnerlike fashion. She often spoke of her calling and election to the Congregation in a most edifying fashion, and in the last days of her life she could not acknowledge gratefully enough the wonderful way the Saviour had guided her. One can say of her that her body was a weak vessel but for that she had a stronger soul. For about a year now her strength had been noticeably diminishing. About a week ago a heavy chest fever befell her, but she complained about nothing except weakness. It was not clear to her that she would go home on that occasion, but she was very happy that her dear son Wilhelm and her dear daughter-in-law visited from Emmaus and the latter stayed with her until her blessed end, with which she was especially pleased. With her son, she put her worldly affairs in order and said: "Now I am finished with the world and free of everything." [47]

To one of the sisters who was visiting her she said, "Here I lie, like a child in a cradle, and wait to see what the dear Saviour does with me, for I am completely given up to His will." On the 17th, in the morning at around 11 o'clock, her last moment neared almost imperceptibly, and she fell asleep gently and peacefully with the blessing of the Congregation and her Choir at the age of 72 years and 2 months, less 2 days.

Martha Hussey, née Wilkes
1719–1790

Martha Hussey was the child of French Protestants who had fled to England in the early eighteenth century to avoid religious persecution. In her early twenties in London, Martha heard George Whitefield preach and quickly she became aware of her state of sin. She then became friendly with the influential Stonehouses, Maria

Theresa and her husband, George, who were wealthy members of the Fetter Lane Society. Maria Theresa Stonehouse (illus. 17) was later a leading member of the London Moravian Congregation and George Stonehouse was the Vicar of Islington. Both were supporters of the British Moravian enterprises and, as such, founder members of the Society for the Furtherance of the Gospel in London in 1741. Through the Stonehouses she met Bishop Spangenberg and then, at the age of twenty-three, was received into the London congregation. That same year she married Robert Hussey, an English farmer who had accompanied the evangelist Leonard Schnell to Georgia in 1743. Martha and Robert traveled to America with the First Sea Congregation, that is, the group of fifty-seven Moravians who sailed from Gravesend, England, on March 16, 1742, on the Catherine, *a sloop owned by the Stonehouses, and arrived in Philadelphia on June 7, 1742. The Husseys were some of the first Moravians to settle Bethlehem.*

Our late sister Martha Hussey, née Wilkes, told her Choir Helper the following about her life:

I was born on February 5th, 1719, in Paris, France. When I was four years old my parents fled to England with me for the sake of their religion and lived in London. In my childhood I already often felt the dear Saviour's signs of grace in my heart, but as I grew older, the corruption of Nature stirred itself, and I fell more and more into frivolity and dissipation. My parents, however, sought to protect me from bad company and always kept me at home. In 1739, I was awakened from the sleep of sin during a sermon by Mr. Whitefield, and I felt that I was a lost soul and an enemy of God. I fell into great disquiet and distress in my heart about this and could bewail my plight to noone. I went to every church but found no solace, and my fear and disquiet grew and grew. At the same time I had much to endure from my parents and friends because they thought it was just melancholy and that I would completely lose my reason over this. When my distress was at its greatest the dear Saviour allowed it so to happen that I became acquainted with the late Sister Mary Stonehouse, and, out of pity, she took me into her house and looked after me like her own child and showed me great love and loyalty. I attended Mr. Stonehouse's sermons; he prepared me for Holy Communion, which I enjoyed the first time in his church and felt at that time a powerful grace of God but still no assurance of the forgiveness of my sins. In this dear house, I became acquainted with the Brethren and many brothers and sisters, and especially dear Brother Joseph, who was like a father to me. He painted a picture before my eyes of the dear Saviour in His whole martyrdom and said, He has suffered that for your sins; He died so that you might live eternally! That went straight to my heart, I burst into tears, left, and threw myself with all my distress at the feet of my Redeemer, and then the merciful Saviour Himself appeared before my heart and gave me the merciful assurance that He had forgiven all my sins, that I was *His* and all His merits were *mine*. Then my soul found peace before His eyes.

Thus far her own words.

Soon after this blessed experience, she was received into the Congregation and, in 1742, married the Brother Robert Hussey. That same year, they travelled with the First Sea Congregation to Pennsylvania and were present at the settling of the congregation in Bethlehem. Even in her last hours, she still remembered the powerful grace that then reigned and the feeling of Jesus' nearness, especially during the Communion, which she enjoyed as a member of His body. She was put to use here in the Children's Home and for many years was the first Hall Servant[48] and considered it a blessing to serve the Congregation until her bodily frailty no longer permitted it. In 1762, she was ordained as a deaconess by Brother Joseph before he travelled to Europe. In 1775, on July 7th, she became a widow and then moved into the Choir House. Of her five children, four have gone before her to the Saviour. Her daughter Anna, who is still living, was a great comfort to her, and she was tenderly cared for and looked after by her in her long and difficult illness with untiring faithfulness and a willing child-like heart, day and night. For this the Saviour will repay her, in response to her mother's and our prayers.

The Choir Labouresses speak of the late sister as a happy and contented widow who spent her days in quiet conversation with her best Friend; she loved and was loved. She was sickly for many years, and three-and-a-half years ago it seemed as though tuberculosis had set in. A year ago she moved into the sick room and developed dropsy in addition to all her other afflictions. She was patient through all the pain in her long illness and often asked the Saviour in tears to stand by her so that she might bear it with patience until the end. But she also greatly desired to go to Him, to kiss His wounds for all the grace and mercy that He had shown to her in her distress. On December 19th, in the evening, her longing was filled after the blessing of the Congregation and the Choir had been given her with the feeling of the nearness of Jesus. And she went happily into Jesus' arms and lap in the 72nd year of her life.

Barbara Jag, née Holder
1747–1816

Barbara Jag's memoir is one of the shortest in this collection. It is included primarily for the sake of contrast with longer memoirs, such as those by Mariana Höht and Anna Johanna Seidel.

Our late sister, Barbara Jag, née Holder, left the following brief account of herself.

I was born on August 26, 1747, in Lynn Township (Northampton County), Pennsylvania. In 1757, on February 22nd, I received permission to go to the congregation in Bethlehem where I soon settled down and was quite happy and content among the children. In 1758, on May 8th, I entered into the Greater Girls' Choir, at which opportunity I gave myself with body and soul to the dear Saviour as His eternal property. In 1759, on December 9th, I was received into the Congregation, and the following year I had the grace to become a partaker of the Body and Blood of Jesus in Holy Communion. This first enjoyment and what my poor heart thereby experienced will remain with me as an unforgettable memory my whole life long. In 1766, on May 4th, I entered the Single Sisters' Choir. In doing so, my dearest wish was that I might become a complete joy to the Saviour. In 1779, on September 28th, I was joined to the Single Brother Johannes Jag, from Nazareth, in holy matrimony; thereafter, we moved to Gnadenthal [49] and several years later to Nazareth to live. We lived with each other quite contentedly until 1811 when, on November 24th, I was transferred into the widowed state by his blessed homegoing.

Whatever else could be said about my path through this time stands in the following verse:

> God be praised that He has brought me,
> A poor woman, out of pure love and mercy
> To His flock.
> God be praised, that it is He
> Who has made my heart His eternal property
> Down here on earth through His dear peace.
> Yea, God be praised, who will for e'er

Keep me by Him, until so e'er
That I joyfully will see Him, aye.

Thus far her own words.

On April 12, 1812, our late sister moved here into the Choir House and, despite her physical weakness, spent her time cheerful and contented in conversation with the Saviour whose redeeming grace she had experienced in her heart, and she sought to preserve the same carefully as a priceless jewel. This kept her in a mood of comfort even during the almost constant pain that she had to endure, especially in her back. She often imagined her homegoing to be near but was nevertheless quite resigned to the will of the Saviour.

On the 18th of this month she was overcome by a stong constriction of the chest which did, however, appear to ease off towards evening. On the 19th in the morning it started up again very strongly, and one soon saw that the Saviour was hurrying with her end. But she stayed quite conscious, and when asked whether she thought that she would go home at this opportunity, she answered that it was not in fact decided but that she desired it greatly and would go with joy to the Saviour, and she experienced this happiness at midday in the second hour when she fell asleep gently and blessedly. She had achieved an age of 68 years, 5 months, and 24 days.

Catharina Krause, née Ruchs
1724–1807

Catharina Krause, in sharp contrast to Barbara Jag, writes a vivid account of her spiritual life. From her awakening as a young girl, which was strong enough to withstand the threats both psychological and physical from her family, to her reception into the Moravian congregation at Herrnhaag at the age of twenty-six, and finally to her move to Bethlehem, she tells her story in old age in an engaging, conversational manner.

Our late sister Catharina Krause, née Ruchs, has written down the following about her life.

I was born on November 16th, 1724 in Alt-Eckendorf in Alsace. My dear parents were George and[50] Elisabeth Ruchs. I was their first child with whom they had much to endure; my dear mother often told me that I had caused her more trouble than her other ten children. From childhood on, I felt the dear Saviour touching my heart, and all the while I was diligently sent to school and kept to all good things by my parents. In my thirteenth year, I went to Holy Communion for the first time; for this I was blessed with the laying on of hands, during which I felt the power of God in my heart. The pastor gave us the text, "Have God before your eyes and in your heart your whole life long, and beware of willingly committing any sin or disobeying God's commandment." The dear Saviour also let me feel how much I needed Him, for I had opportunity enough to enter into all kinds of sin if He had not held His hand over me. I often fell ill, and during each illness I promised the good Lord that I would improve my life, and so it remained merely a matter of good intentions until my twentieth year. At that time the good Saviour took advantage of the fact that I opened the Bible at the text: "For I say unto you, That except your righteousness shall exceed the righteousness of the scribes and Pharisees, ye shall in no case enter into the kingdom of heaven."[51] This text was like a double-edged sword in my heart. I wept and sought to help myself by reading books, but that only made my anguish greater. I tried to go quietly to the pastor's house and bewailed my anguish to him in tears, and he told me: "That is what I believed of you." He comforted me with the words: "If you want to change, you will have much to endure from your grandparents," which is what happened. They became enraged and threatened me with blows if I did not desist from my visits to the pastor (this my grandmother did once and, as she hit me, such a horror overcame her that she was taken aback and said, "I have struck you this time but I will never do it again." My father and mother were watching this and my mother wept silently.) They were especially interested to see how I would conduct myself. I remained silent and found myself a little place where I could pour out my troubles to the Saviour. I did not desist from visiting the pastor because it was there that I heard the beautiful hymns from the Brethren's Congregation.[52] And thus a whole year passed, until the time I had a remarkable dream that cast me into such a state of distress that I went straight to my parents' bed and asked them to plead with the dear Saviour with me that He should have mercy on me. My dear parents did not know what they should think of me and became very distressed on my behalf. They thought I would lose my mind. My father, therefore, went to the aforementioned pastor to ask for his advice about my situation. He comforted him with the words, that he should not be distressed about me, I would not become a fool because of this, but rather I was on the right path. They should only try not to hinder me in this. The good Saviour had also heard my and my dear parents' prayers in this matter and moved my grandparents' hearts so that I was allowed to go unhindered to the pastor's house meetings as often as I wished; on one of these occasions the Holy Spirit placed my situation as a sinner quite clearly before my eyes. But I also got a glimpse of my Saviour, who comforted me and assured my heart that He had also shed His blood for me and had suffered on the cross for my sins too. At this I received joy in my heart and a great longing to live in a Congregation of the Brethren (about which I had already heard a great deal). But the opportunity to do so did not present itself straight away.

To my mother's comfort, I remained with her until her blessed end, took care of her until then, and had the joy of seeing her leave this world as a poor redeemed sinner with trust in Jesus' merits. In her last hours she also comforted me by saying that once she had gone home I could go to the Brethren's Congregation unhindered. But for another two years after my mother's going home I had to take care of household affairs for my dear father. During this time I often asked the Saviour to clear the way for me to go the Congregation. He was also so faithful to me and helped my brother to be of the same mind and, in 1750, with our father's permission and blessing, we set off and arrived happily in Herrnhaag on March 18th with the beautiful watchword, "Whosoever lays down his life for me shall find it again" [Matthew 10:39; 16:25]. That is why I gave up all life early. I was grateful to the Saviour with all my heart that He had now fulfilled my wish and had brought poor me to His Congregation and had helped me so mercifully through all difficulties, and this my lot remains great and important to me; for I thought, even if I only had bread and water I would keep going, in order to enjoy that for which my heart had yearned for so long.

At Herrnhaag I was employed in all sorts of ways—in the laundry, and at the well. I did everything with a willingness and faithfulness that made everything easy that was hard. In the year 1750 I was received into the Congregation. In 1751, toward the end of October, I was admitted to Holy Communion. In 1752, in June, I received a call to America, and I travelled with a large party to Holland. On August 12th we arrived in Zeist, where we celebrated August 13th with that Congregation. That day will always stay with me as a special day of grace for my heart. On August 29th we travelled from Zeist to England where I had a blessed time with the sisters there and where I also had the opportunity to speak to the late Count Zinzendorf. And after a tender farewell from him and the brothers and sisters there, we boarded the ship and arrived safe and sound in Bethlehem via New York on November 25th. In April 1753, I came to Nazareth to serve in the kitchen of the Nursery or Children's Home and from there I went back to Bethlehem where, on February 16th 1755, I entered into marriage with my late husband, Johann Krause.

In this state the Saviour showed us much grace and mercy and blessed our marriage with three children, whom I recommended to Him in the warmest fashion right away at their birth with the request that they grow up only for Him and that they flourish only to His honor and joy. To my joy, He has granted this request. One of the children went before me into eternity, and of the other two my son lives here in Bethlehem (from whom I have two grandchildren) and my daughter (who was married to Brother Schmück, who has already gone home) lives in Nazareth, from whom I have had six grandchildren, of whom two have gone before me into eternity.

In 1792, on April 28, I was translated into the state of widowhood when my dear husband was called home. On that occasion I thanked my faithful Saviour from my heart for all the mercy and faithfulness He had shown me and my late husband in our married state, and I gave myself over to Him anew as the best Husband of my soul for further guidance and leadership in my state of widowhood; that He might daily stand by me with His grace and help and remain my comforter in all distress.

Thus far the late sister herself.

As far as her life among us is concerned, we can give witness to the fact that her heart was very attached to the Saviour and the Congregation and she knew of nothing better in this world than to hear the word of God and to refresh and revive herself daily with it. That is why she never missed a meeting unless it was absolutely essential, and she would often say, "If I can no longer have this pasture, then how will it be with me?" She was often inconsolable when she became so weak that she was unable to go to the meetings in all winds and weathers, and her children had to repeat to her everything that was said or sung in the meetings, which pleased her like a child. Since the beginning of October of last year she was no longer able to leave her house, and her frailty increased more and more, so that since Whitsun she has had to be looked after like a child, which her dear daughter-in-law did willingly with an untiring care and faithfulness, something about which she often declared her gratitude to the dear Saviour and also to those who visited her, and wished her a thousand blessings for that. In all her frailty she never forgot to share in the warmest fashion in all festival days and other things that happened in the Congregation and to recommend the Congregation and all missionary posts to the Saviour assiduously in her prayers and also to lay her grandchildren on His heart for gracious preservation. It always gave her a special joy when someone read her something from Moravian publications, and each time she seemed as if newly enlivened and cheered by this. On June 25th an especial change in her condition made itself evident, so that it was thought that she was near her going home. To this end, she was given the blessing of the Congregation and her Choir on the same day. But she recovered again and we thought that she could stay with us for longer but last Sunday, September 15th she was overcome by a strong paroxysm. She lay there as though in a slumber, quite unconscious. In the afternoon, Holy Communion was brought to her, which she enjoyed with an especially blessed feeling—she was quite conscious, sang along with all the verses quite audibly, and from then on lay there quite still until the 16th and 17th when she suffered strongly from constrictions and asked her children and grandchildren to watch with her and pray. These [constrictions] slowly eased off and she lay as though in a gentle sleep until, in the afternoon, her breath became weaker and weaker, her children sang her going home verses and, at the last line of the verse "Come and take her spirit to yourself" (that is the end of the hymn), her soul flew gently into the arms of her Redeemer, to see Him in whom she had always believed and whom she had loved with her whole heart and soul. She had achieved an age of 82 years, 10 months, and 1 day.

Susanna Nixdorf, née Korn
1708–1800

Susanna Nixdorf's life spans almost the whole eighteenth century and the whole East-West breadth of the Moravian Church. Born in Silesia at the beginning of the century, she moved to Herrnhut with her husband, children, and mother after having come into contact with the Brethren (Brothers Andrew Lawatsch and David Nitschmann, Senior) in Breslau. Less than a year later, the family moved to America, where Susanna and her husband served primarily the congregation in Lancaster.

The memoir of our late widowed sister Susanna Nixdorf (née Korn), who died peacefully here in Bethlehem on November 28, 1800.

She was born on February 22, 1708, in Stolz, a village near Frankenstein in Silesia where her father, whom she lost early in life, was a miller and baker. My dear mother, she writes herself, was very concerned about my education; however, I had to go into service when I was only eight years old and went to my friends until I was twelve. Then my masters took me into service, and I stayed with them for eight years. In 1728, on November 28, I married my late husband, and in 1730 moved with him to Breslau. We both wanted to lead a pious and godly life and soon became acquainted with the awakened people in Breslau. After we had tortured ourselves by struggling in vain against sin for many years, it pleased the faithful Saviour in His great mercy to help us out of this misery. He sent us two brothers from Herrnhut, Lawatsch and Nitschmann, Senior, whom we took in with much joy. They showed us the availing merits of the Saviour and the free grace in His blood. It was made clear to us in our hearts by the Holy Spirit that we could believe it simply. Oh, how happy and thankful we were for this grace!

In 1742, having received permission, we moved with my dear mother and our two children to Herrnhut, where we arrived on June 5th. On July 8th, we were received into the Congregation and partook of Holy Communion with the Congregation for the first time on the following August 9th. In 1743, we received a call to travel to America and arrived safely in Bethlehem on December 8th of that same year.

We were employed in various places in the service of the Saviour, especially on two separate occasions with the dear Congregation in Lancaster where we were for twenty-two years in all (until we moved to Bethlehem). In 1778, we celebrated our golden wedding, with grateful and humble hearts for all the dear Saviour's grace and faithfulness which we had experienced and enjoyed from Him.

Thus far her own account.

In the year 1785 on September 29th her late husband went to his eternal rest in his 81st year. To the best of our knowledge, of the nine children, that is, five sons and four daughters, three are still alive; that is, two sons here in this country and one daughter, the widowed Sister Lauterbach, who is in a congregation in Germany. As a widow she lived a quiet and blessed life and was peaceable, loving and cordial in her ways. After she was no longer able to work she spent most of her time reading, until her eyesight finally became too weak. For several years now she had been unable to visit the meetings in the Hall, and Communion had to be brought to her. It was edifying to see the heartfelt devotion with which she enjoyed the same. The gradual decrease in her physical and mental powers was clear to see, although she was not ill as such. Yet she was especially alert and content on her last birthday with a group of sisters whom she had invited to celebrate it with her. Finally, though, the weakness of her old age increased to such a degree that she was put into a state almost of unconsciousness and had to be looked after and cared for like a child in every way, which was done with much loyalty and not without great difficulty, especially by her roommate and nurse, Rosina Müller, especially when she could no longer get out of bed. In this condition she was an object of sympathy and prayer and pleading with the Saviour that He should soon release her from all her troubles.

A few days ago we noticed a change in her condition, and[53] when her end seemed to be nearing, she was given the blessing of the Lord and her Choir. On November 28 her gentle and blessed departure occurred, in the 93rd year of her pilgrimage in the valley of sorrow here below.

Johanna Christiana Parsons, née Ziehich
1699–1773

Johanna Parsons, mother of Juliana Horsfield and wife of William Parsons, was the niece of the brothers John Henry and Ludwig Christian Sprogel, and it was through them that she first came to Pennsylvania in 1716. Initially a Baptist, she married William Parsons, Pennsylvania's Surveyor General in 1722. The marriage was troubled, not least by her husband's complete lack of sympathy with her spiritual needs. While living in Philadephia, she sought solace from the various religious groups then present in the city, groups such as the French Prophets.[54] Here, Johanna also heard George Whitefield preach and his words revealed to her her lack of faith. Finally, she heard the words of John Christopher Pyrlaeus (1713–1785), one of the original founders of Bethlehem and a missionary to the Indians of Pennsylvania and Ohio, and she decided that her place was with the Moravians. From her daughter's memoir (see above, Juliana Horsfield) we learn of the consequences of her allegiance to the Moravians. She herself makes no mention of it.

Our late Sister Johanna Christiana Parsons has left the following written account of herself:

I was born in 1699 in Quedlinburg where my mother had gone to visit her parents in the last months of her pregnancy. My parents lived in Eisleben [Saxony]. My father's name was Johann Julius Ziehich, and my mother's was Salome Margaretha, née Sprogel. My father was an awakened man and the religious upbringing of his children lay close to his heart. But my mother loved gay company, and although I also inclined very much to this, I still considered my father's way of thinking to be better. He often sent me to my mother's relatives, who were god-fearing people, and for as long as we were at home gave us children pious tutors. But when my parents finally came into such outward circumstances that it was very difficult for them to feed and clothe their children any more, first my uncle Gottfried Arnold took me with him to Berleburg, and I stayed with him from my 10th to my 13th year. Then I came to my other uncle who was a preacher in Westphalia. Through these circumstances I was in fact kept from the usual sins of the world. But I did not think a great deal about being saved, although I often thought about what my late father used to say to me; namely, that we were quite depraved by our very nature and if I did not ask dear God to give me a new heart, he did not know what would become of me.

In my 17th year my uncle Sprogel from America came to visit his relatives in Germany. He saw that I was in financial difficulties, and he asked me whether I wanted to go with him to Pennsylvania. I accepted this offer with joy, took my leave of my uncle, who earnestly warned me to keep really close to my dear God, as I was now coming into the wide world, where I would be in constant danger if I were to look away from him in the least, and I embarked upon my journey to Amsterdam, where my uncle Sprogel had left orders to send me on to join him in England. The preservation that surrounded me on this journey under such dangerous conditions became clear to me afterwards.

Here in Pennsylvania I first became acquainted with the Baptists, whose way of living with the Holy Scripture seemed to be the closest to mine. But, I thought, the true religion is not a particular sect but rather a work of the Holy Spirit in the heart.

In 1722, I married William Parsons, whom I bore six children, of whom only two daughters are still living, that is, Johanna Garrison and Juliana Horsfield. I had great love and esteem for my dear husband, and because I considered him to exceed me by far in virtue and other qualities, I hoped to be brought by him to the right way of blessedness. When I found nothing that gave my heart the peace it sought after, I gave up everything. However, the faithful Saviour did not abandon me. I entered into a great anxiety about my soul (I was then in my 26th year). My hell became so hot that I thought I would lose my mind, and I could find noone with whom I could talk about my situation. Once I revealed my great fear to my husband, and he told me kindly that I should just have patience for this would pass. But this was of no lasting comfort to me. Once, however, when I was quite alone and thought to find some relief if only I could cry my eyes out somewhere in peace (for my anxiety was so great that I thought that if my body were to be burning in flames it would be easier to bear than what I felt in my heart), I ran into the uppermost part of the house but could say nothing except "My God what should I do?" Immediately, the agony stopped and such a heavenly comfort and light filled my heart that I was assured that noone but God Himself, who had made me, could do such a thing. I was so full of wonder and amazement that I wished to remain so blessed all my life and to love my Creator above all. Just as I had felt myself to be in hell before, so now I felt as if I were in heaven, and the Holy Spirit presented the crucified Lord to me in such a manner that I felt as though I could speak with Him personally. But after some time I felt my depravity again and became very concerned that I would gradually lose such blessedness again, which then unfortunately happened. From that time forth I was never left entirely to myself and always felt the signs of His love, but I lost the connexion that I had had with Him.

I now looked around for religious people and became acquainted with some who were called the French Prophets (I read their books and found a great blessing for my heart in them). They held my lost condition up before me and showed me how I must grasp the atonement of my sins by Jesus Christ in faith and be like a child before Him and give over my whole heart to Him, so that He might work therein through His spirit and take hold of my powers of reason. But because I still lacked true faith in the meritorious humanity of Jesus I could attain no certainty or true comfort, but also did not know the hostility of the human heart towards this main point of our salvation, although I would have taken it very hard if people would have thought me a nonbeliever. The struggles and anxieties into which I placed myself through contemplating the different doctrines of humanity cannot be described, and I therefore gave everything up and thought, "If I am saved, then I am saved; I cannot help myself any further." I then fought with my corruption and comforted myself with the grace as well as I could, which I felt now and again, and diligently read virtuous books in which I found pleasure.

After a while I heard Mr. Whitefield preach and became convinced that I did not yet have the living faith in the merits of Jesus which he recommended. This made me once again very agitated and the absence of this simple faith caused me to fall into a great confusion of mind and soul, but I still had some hope that I would recognize the truth in Jesus. Finally, to my great good fortune, the Brethren came into the land. The society with which I had hitherto associated attempted to persuade me to visit their sermons. I, however, said that because I had gained nothing until now but confusion from the many religious opinions I had heard, from now on I had no intention of seeking out yet more people. Nonetheless, I was pleased that my children went to the Brethren's preaching. But my friends gave me no peace and only regretted the fact that they themselves could not understand German. So I went and heard Brother Pyrlaeus speak about the blood of Christ so impressively that it at once took my heart away. This, I thought, is what I have lacked until now. At the same time, however, such an enmity rose up in my heart against the Saviour as I had never felt before, but His grace was stronger. He did not leave me but rather put His peace in my heart as a footstool under His feet, and I appeared before Him as I was and said, "If you will not help me then there is no help anywhere." So then I enjoyed all the blessedness that He bestowed upon me and also had the happiness to enter into the fellowship of His children. "If something from what had been before tried to disturb me," I thought, "I have been given the unspeakable grace to come to know my Redeemer and to experience the power of His Blood." Now I can say, "Praise God that I am a sinner, if I am something else then let it depart." Since then, Jesus' blood is the only thing in which my heart finds peace. I have now experienced His love for thirty years, and whatever trials have come upon me, both outer and inner ones, He has always proved Himself a faithful Saviour. I now regard with praise the splendid work and grace that He carries on in the world and want to walk towards Jesus with joy when it will please Him to call my spirit to Him.

Thus far the departed.

When the Congregation in Philadelphia was settled anew by Brother Johannes [de Watteville] in 1749, she had the grace to enjoy Holy Communion for the first time with it. To her great comfort, her husband, who was not otherwise of her mind, went peacefully out of this life as a sinner relying on Jesus' merits in 1757. She led a quiet life and proved herself with the brothers and sisters as a widow who put her hope in God. In 1769, after receiving permission, she moved here to Bethlehem in order to spend what little remained of her mortal life in the Congregation, and she often expressed her gratitude to the Saviour for bringing her and her children to the Congregation. She lived a quiet, and blessed life, was of few words, and missed no Opportunity as long as she could still go out. At the last organization of the Hourly Intercession she was added to the company of Intercessors. This became an especial blessing to her and she often said, I always speak with my dear Saviour, but feel a special blessing when I talk to Him during my Hour of Intercession and lay my worries and those of all the brothers and sisters to His heart. On January 27 of this year she was present in the Hall for the last time. During her illness, she gave herself over to the will of the Saviour but, she said, If He were to take me to Him that is what I would like best. For I am of one mind with Him; there is nothing between Him and me. He has accepted me as a sinner and given me grace. The longing for her release increased day by day. When on the 9th she heard that Brother Horsfield had gone home she wished such good fortune soon for herself too, and often said, "Oh, how lucky he is." And the day after, on the 10th, at 4:30 in the morning she followed him gently and blessedly. Her age was 73 years and 10 months.

Susanne Luise Partsch, née Eller
1722–1795

Susanne Partsch was born in the Wetterau, the area around Herrnhaag. As a child the authorities removed her from her stepfather, presumably because of abuse, and placed her in the care of another family. After she began employment as a cook, she visited her mother near Herrnhaag and applied for permission to join the Congregation, which she also received. She married Georg Partsch in 1743, and they moved to Pennsylvania where she and her husband led a very different life from that in Germany. For example, in 1755 they witnessed the Indian attack on Gnadenhütten, which Susanna describes in vivid detail. Like Marianne Höht, Susanne also looked to the Savior for help and advice during this attack. The fact that the Indians did not see Susanne standing on the windowsill is attributed to the Saviour having averted their gaze. As she asked for guidance, Susanne wrote, "I felt as though I should go to the Lecha." In feeling the guidance of her Saviour Susanne has provided us with a perfect instance of Zinzendorf's ita sentio. After this ordeal, Susanne returned safely to Bethlehem, recovered from a fever, and left for the mission on St. Thomas with her husband.

Personalia of the late Sister Susanne Luise Partsch.
She dictated the following about herself:

I was born on December 4th, 1722, in Büdingen in Wetteravia. My father was Johann Just Eller, a slater to the Court, who left this mortal life before I was born. My mother raised me until my seventh year; but because during this time I had received a hard stepfather, I was handed over by the Büdingen rulers to Bailiff Schubert and his wife in Meerholz, with whom I stayed until 1740. During that time the Schuberts moved to the Ronneburg[55] and I went with them.

When the blessed Ordinary came there with his company it was said to me that these people loved God dearly. I soon became familiar with them through their friendly manner, and I felt as though I belonged to these people. I would dearly have liked to have gone with them immediately to Herrnhut, but my master did not want to let me go. Soon after that I came to Wächtersbach to the government counsellor Schmidt, where I served as a cook. In 1743, I returned to the Ronneburg to visit my mother, and there I became acquainted with Brother and Sister Vogt who lived there. I was taken hold of anew and became convinced of my lost state and the faithful Saviour, who had protected me from my youth, concerned Himself lovingly with me and did not allow that I should err into the world, whose diversions much pleased me. My visit lasted six weeks during which time I diligently visited both the meetings at Herrnhaag and in the Single Sisters' House to the true blessing of my heart; I was also received into the Congregation and attained the pleasure of enjoying Holy Communion with it.

In the same year I was married to my late husband Georg Partsch and, on August 26, set off from Marienborn with the other brothers and sisters destined for Pennsylvania. We arrived safely on December 6 in Bethlehem and, on January 2, 1744, in Nazareth where we lived for twelve years and were put to use in various tasks.

On November 18, 1755, we received a call to Gnadenhütten on the Mahoney to the Brethrens' Economy; I was to serve there as a cook. On November 24, Indians attacked our house. With the other brothers and sisters I retreated upstairs. When we got there it occurred to me that we could save ourselves if we dared to jump out of the window. I gave voice to my thoughts, upon which Brother Sturtius[56] dared to do this. Fortunately he succeeded, and I was then more strengthened to dare to do it and to climb out. I had to put my feet on the top of the window of the room in which the Indians were destroying everything; but their eyes were averted, so that they did not notice me. From there I jumped onto the ground and hurried into the bush and, because I did not know what to do (for I saw the Indians running from one house to another with firebrands to set them all alight), I asked the Saviour that He should let me know where I should go, and then it seemed to me as though I should go to the

Lecha, where I found a hollow tree under which I crawled until the next morning.

In the morning, in the ninth hour, I saw soldiers crossing the Lecha, one of whom, a German, saw me and came to me immediately and asked how I had got there. I answered that I had fled here from the settlement, which had been destroyed. Because he could see that I was frozen stiff, he put me on his horse and brought me back to the burned out settlement, where I fainted at the sight of the charred bodies, and they had trouble bringing me back to my senses. I asked the soldiers to bring me back to Bethlehem, which they promised to do. But to my unspeakable joy, as we came out of the bush, we met my dear husband and Sturgis both of whom had saved themselves by fleeing. My husband asked me to return again to the destroyed settlement with him, which I did. After a painful inspection of the same we started our journey back to Bethlehem, where on the 26th in the afternoon we arrived safely and unexpectedly, to the joy of all the brothers and sisters—they thought we had all been burned to death. I was very wretched and had to bear a serious illness, but recovered again. In 1761, we received a call to St. Thomas, which we accepted.

Thus far her own account.

They stayed in the West Indies only for a year and then came back to Bethlehem, where her dear husband died peacefully in 1765. Her marriage was blessed with six children, of whom three daughters are still alive; from two of her daughters she has had five grandchildren, of whom two are still alive. Her youngest daughter is presently in the service of the Saviour in the West Indies. In her widow's state she served for a few more years in the Congregation kitchen. In 1772, she moved into the Choir House.

She was sickly with consumption for many years, which often made her impatient; as she was of a lively disposition and also lost her hearing some time ago, she sometimes became bad tempered. But she allowed herself to be shown the right way again and held faithfully to the dear Saviour, in the steady hope that He would keep her in His arms and lap. And her fervent prayer was: "Nothing but the grace of Jesus Christ / nothing but His merits alone / allows me, a poor sinful maid / to be good, just, and blessed."

On February 1, 1795, the day for which she had been wishing so fervently came, when the Saviour put an end to all her troubles and, after the blessing of the Congregation and her Choir had been bestowed upon her, she fell asleep quite peacefully. Her age was 73 years and 2 months.

Maria Elisabeth Reitzenbach, née Spohn
1738–1809

Raised during the Württemberg awakening in the 1740s, Maria Reitzenbach became acquainted with the Moravians through soldiers who came through her town carrying Moravian texts. Maria's whole family wanted to join the Moravian congregation and, although Herrnhaag was already being disbanded, they did receive permission to move to Bethlehem. So the family sold off its property in Württemberg and traveled to America. Once there, Maria moved through the various choirs and remained a Single Sister until the age of forty-one, when she was asked to marry. This she did with great reluctance. With her husband she worked in the congregations of Heidelberg, Bethel, Hebron (today Lebanon), and Schoeneck, to return finally to Nazareth.

Memoir of the widowed Sister Maria Elisabeth Reitzenbach, née Spohn. She herself wrote the following about herself:

I was born on November 19, 1738, in Lauffen in Württemberg and was baptized in the Lutheran church and raised in the same religion by my dear parents Johannes Matthaeus and Lucia Spohn. During the great awakening in Württemberg, my parents were also strongly affected. At that time, several of the Brethren who were soldiers came to our town and brought with them tracts from the Congregation, which were read quietly in the evening in various houses to the edification of many. Subsequently, small groups gathered and discussed the condition of their hearts with one another, and a great blessing rested upon them. My mother kept me in seclusion and did not allow me to mingle with other children, which made me very discontented. And when I heard her praying on her knees day after day, "Oh, dear Saviour! Give me another heart! And have mercy on me and change my disposition," and so on, I sighed, "Oh, if only dear God were not to hear this her prayer! For if she were to become *better* than she is now, what then would become of *me*?" Finally I became so agitated myself that I did not know what to do. And when I was seven years old, and now went to school where I had to hear much scorn from the other pupils because of my parents' piety, I was driven by this to the Saviour, to whom I complained like a child about this trouble.

Once, when the preacher took this text for his sermon, "If I may but

touch his garment, I shall be whole" [Matthew 9:21], this same wish became so strong in my heart that, after I had returned home, I hurried into
the orchard and threw my self face down on the grass and begged the dear
Saviour with many tears for this blessing and, assured of my part in Him, I
stood up from the grass again, humble and full of joy.

At this time, the late Brother Michael Graf (who died in that town)
came on a visit to us from the Congregation and lodged in my parents'
house. During his stay, my grandfather (who was the village mayor) left
this mortal life peacefully (blessed by Brother Graf). The latter told me
much about the Children's Homes in the Congregation and how happy
and contented the children were in them, so that a great desire now arose
in me also to enter the Congregation and such a Children's Home. My
good mother, seeing the way of my heart, took my part in the most loyal
fashion, and when *she* and my father had visited the Congregation at Herrnhaag (where my mother had a sister), they were willing to bring me to
the Children's Home there, for which they received permission from the
Congregation. But, nothing became of this because the Brethren had to
leave Herrnhaag at the time when they wanted to bring this to pass, and
they themselves wanted to move to the Congregation. So my parents along
with several others received a letter of recommendation from Brother
Johannes de Watteville for the Congregation in Bethlehem, to which we
now received permission to move.

My parents sold their very nice property at a great loss and set off for
America contented and happy. They, that is, my brother Johannes Martin
(who went home quite contented and blessed in his 12th year in the
Children's Home in Bethlehem), my younger sister Anna Maria, the Christ
family and their children, and Christian and Ludwig Stolze arrived in
September 1751 in Philadelphia, where my mother lay sick for a while,
and they were thus delayed until we arrived in Bethlehem thankful and
happy in January 1752. Here I moved in with the children in the Home
but had a hard lesson to learn, for I had been raised very piously and,
therefore, took offense at this and that, so that in the beginning I did not
find the pleasure here that I had expected. This drove me to the dear
Saviour. But little by little I left off my strict ways and gained pleasure in
frivolity and similar things so that I learned to see that I was no better than
others.

In the following year, I was received into the Greater Girls' Choir with
the heartfelt plea to the dear Saviour that I might find His joy in *that* Choir!
But only now did I really learn a new, really thorough lesson through which
the faithful Saviour let me see and recognize my thoroughly depraved

heart for what it was. I greatly desired to be received into the Congregation, but I always thought, "all this will be of no avail, dear Saviour, if *you* do not come near to me." But, to my unexpected joy, I was received into the Congregation in 1755.

I was not so desirous of Holy Communion because I thought I was too bad to enjoy the same, and when I thought about it I became terribly frightened, and I was very worried about the same. But on August 13, 1756, I had the great joy of partaking of Holy Communion for the first time, during which my fear and anxiety and everything similar fell away. And so I lived as a quite blessed and contented maid, and, in the same year, was appointed to assist those in charge of the girls of my age. Oh, how small, how deeply humbled this made me before the dear Saviour!

On May 4 of the following year I was received into the Single Sisters' Choir. I thought, "now I want to be truly blessed and contented!" And hardly did I seem to be completely in my element when it was proposed to me that I move to Nazareth as the school mistress of the younger girls. There I spent two years and visited our Choir in Bethlehem from time to time with two other single sisters. I remained in this same position of service to children and older girls for 15 years, until the Home became smaller and several of the children moved back to their parents. At this opportunity I requested permission to move into my dear Choir House, where I spent my days quite happy and content until June 1779 when, during the visit of Brother Johann Friedrich Reichel, the marriage with my now late husband, Brother Philip Jacob Reitzenbach was proposed to me. I must admit that I found it indescribably hard to take this step and to leave my dear Single Sisters' Choir. Only the thought that it was my duty to do everything for the love of my dear Saviour who had forgiven me my sins and had taken me into a state of grace made me give myself up to this. We were married on January 21 by Br. Reichel, and soon after we moved to Heidelberg to serve the small congregation there. Here the faithful Saviour stood by us and helped us through wartime and great poverty for six-and-a-half years. In the beginning, we had nothing to show but poverty and weakness inside and out. But He proved that He is the Helper and Comforter of the poor and weak. In extraordinarily deep snow my husband had the misfortune to break his arm, and because no doctor was nearby it could not be set properly and only after three months was he healed through the care of Br. Adolph Meyers in Lititz. Our brothers and sisters in Heidelberg, whom we so dearly loved (as they loved us), did everything in the meantime to show us their sympathy. During the visitation of the (late) Br. Johannes we left Heidelberg for Bethel on the Swatara where the small congregation had been without Labourers since Brother Till's going home. In the beginning we found some things difficult here but we stood childlike and faithfully by our faithful Saviour, who soon granted us the joy of seeing that our brothers and sisters fared as we wished them to.

We stayed here for over six years and had a large school, which was quite according to my husband's wishes, because mixing with young people and educating them in the things that are good was a pleasant occupation for him. From Bethel we came to Hebron,[57] where we stayed for a year and a half (I was sick for almost all the time), until we were relieved by Br. and Sr. Gottfried Peters. (We returned to Heidelberg to remain there for a short time and then came to Bethlehem for a short while to recuperate. It was there that, after a year, we received the call to serve the small congregation in Schöneck.) [58] Here my husband found exactly what he wished for, namely a large school. We stayed for three-and-a-half years in Schöneck until we were relieved by Br. and Sr. Schaaf and we moved in December again to Bethlehem where we spent the winter quietly until in March the following year we were given the position of Helper in the Married Choir, in which we served for over two years until we moved to Nazareth in 1798 and remained there until, in 1802 (on September 22), I was made a widow by the calling home of my dear husband, after we had lived in marriage for twenty-two years happy and content and had shared joy and pain and had been a comfort and a cheer to each other. For this reason I felt his loss very painfully and noone could comfort me but *the* Friend to whom I had often told all my troubles and with whom I alone took refuge.

In the same year I moved again to Bethlehem and have now lived here with my dear brother-in-law and sister, Br. and Sr. Hornigs, to whom especially I wish the rich blessing of the Saviour for all the good deeds they have done to me, and for their love and friendship, which I have enjoyed from them. At the end of this essay I must add this, that whenever I consider my service before the Saviour, I remember with a grateful heart His merciful support and His faithful help in all the difficult circumstances and think back humbly and prostrate to the undeserved love and trust that I have enjoyed from the brothers and sisters in the various rural congregations. For I reckon that time to be the most contented of my life. The Saviour also gave me the grace that I could love the brothers and sisters from the depths of my heart, so that it hurt me each time I had to leave a congregation that I had served in.

Thus far the late Sister herself.

She lived through her widowhood here quite content and cleaved to the comforting words of the Saviour, "I will be the widows' provider and father." This she had experienced as true, to her comfort in her sickliness and other sorrowful events of her life. Last winter her strength diminished noticeably, and she suffered greatly from chest troubles, but she bore everything with patience because it gave her the sweet hope that she would soon be with her best Friend. Because she could not visit the meetings any more, she was pleased with every visit of her Choirmates and other friends, and it cheered her when they recounted what went on there. For she took a faithful interest in everything that the Saviour did in the Congregation, and all that the Congregation in turn did among Christians and heathens. Amid such occupations of her mind her days of sickness passed unnoticeably swiftly. On the 16th in the night she was struck by a nervous apoplexy and in the morning one could see clearly that she was nearing her consummation. She took great pleasure in the goodness of her Saviour, that He was making such an unexpectedly quick end to her suffering. As a morning greeting she said to one good friend, "Jesus accepts sinners, tell everyone this word of comfort!" etc. And that was the last thing that she could say intelligibly. She became progressively weaker. At twelve o'clock she received the blessing of the Congregation and her Choir, during which the peace of God could be clearly felt. She still understood everything and, when asked whether she was now going to the Saviour, she answered, "Yes!" She became weaker and weaker and lay now as though in a sleep until at three o'clock in the afternoon her redeemed soul passed into the arms of her Redeemer. She had brought her pilgrimage here to 71 years and 6 months, less two days.

Maria Agnes Rothe, née Pfingsttag
1735–1805

Like Maria Reitzenbach, Maria Rothe also accompanied her parents from Württemberg to Philadelphia. However, only when they were in Philadelphia did the Pfingsttag family become acquainted with the Moravians and, like Johanna Parsons, Maria was attracted to them by the preaching of John Christopher Pyrlaeus. She requested permission to join the congregation in Bethlehem and finally received it at the age of thirteen. At the age of thirty-five, she was asked to marry Johannes Rothe, and then her life as a missionary to the Delaware began. Her husband, Johannes Rothe (1726–1791) had arrived in America in 1756 and went to work with the Indians in the missions as one of David Zeisberger's colleagues along with Brother John Heckewelder, Brother Johannes and Sister Margarethe Jungmann, and Brother and Sister Grube. Their first mission together was at Schechschequanink (Shes-

*hequin), a Moravian mission that was a former Indian village on the west shore of
the Susquehanna, situated at what today is Ulster in Bradford County. From there
they moved through Ohio. After the death of her husband, Maria spent some time in
the Widows House in Bethlehem but was then called at the age of sixty-three to look
after the aging widower Brother Molther in York. It seemed as though in the later
years of the eighteenth century there was a shortage of single women in the Moravian
congregations and thus widows were asked to care for aging widowers in the congregations.*

The following may be quoted from a written account of the life of our late
widowed Sister Maria Agnes Rothe, née Pfingsttag who fell asleep here in
Nazareth on February 25, 1805.

I was born on April 4, 1735, in Wirsche in Württemberg. In 1737, my
parents came to America and lived near Philadelphia for about nine years.
During this time they became acquainted with the Brethren and later
moved near to Bethlehem on the Lecha Mountain[59] to be closer to the
Congregation. Because I had visited the school in Philadelphia held
by Brother Pyrlaeus,[60] I had already been gripped in my heart; and
now I visited Bethlehem diligently, and so the desire to move there completely was aroused in me and became stronger and stronger and this I
told my mother. However, she denied me this with the reply, "They will
not take you." But it remained certain in my heart that I belonged to the
Congregation.

When, after some time, Br. Pyrlaeus visited my parents' house, I asked
him whether he would put in a good word for me so that I would receive
permission to move to Bethlehem. He did make it clear to me that I would
have it better in material things with my parents than in Bethlehem with
their then poverty and humble way of life, but he finally promised to be
mindful of me. I could hardly wait until my desire was fulfilled. My mother,
whose permission I had to receive, wanted to test me first, to see whether I
was in earnest, and therefore said to me that they did not want to accept
me in Bethlehem. I started to cry bitterly over this. But the greater was my
joy when she finally said that I had received permission. So I moved in my
13th year to Bethlehem and was happy and content in a childlike fashion
and everything was of consequence to me.

In 1748, on November 17, I was received into the Congregation. Now
the Holy Spirit started a special work of grace with me and I received a
foundation in my heart. In March 1749, I partook of Holy Communion
for the first time. I lived my life contented and blessed, and if something

were to upset me, I would then talk about it with an open heart to my Labouress and was put back on the right path. My lot of grace to belong to the Brethren's Congregation remained unspeakably great and important to me, and the dear Saviour will keep this grace for me until I see Him face to face.

Because I had enjoyed much good in the Single Sisters' Choir and had lived in the same very contently, it was very hard for me when, in 1770, the call came to enter into marriage with my late husband Johannes Rothe. With many tears, I asked the Saviour to show me His merciful will; and I received in my heart a comforting confirmation and so could now decide for this with joyfulness. The wedding took place on August 16 of the aforementioned year 1770. Our dear Lord acknowledged this our joining with grace; we came to love each other tenderly; each sought to make things easy for the other, and we were of one mind to dedicate ourselves willingly to the service of the Lord.

On September 22nd of that same year, in accordance with our call, we set off from Bethlehem to serve the Indian Congregation in Scheschequanink on the Susquehanna. On the journey, when I saw the first Indian face to face I was alarmed at his wild appearance. And precisely this one was soon thoroughly awakened and is one of our dear brothers. I liked it very much at my post, and I came to love the Indians dearly.

Thus far from this account.

From a written account by her late husband the following can be added.

In the year 1772, they moved with the Indian congregation which lived in Scheschequanink and in Friedenhütten in the company of the late Brother Ettwein to Languntoutenank on the great Beaver Creek.[61] On the eight-week journey through the wild bush our late sister fell from her horse four times with her ten-month-old child, but both were kept from harm. They stayed here until April 1773, when they once again set off with the Indian Congregation and moved to the Muskingum River where Schönbrunn was built.[62] However, they soon came to Gnadenhütten,[63] where a portion of the Indian Congregation had settled. There they served until August 18 of the same year when they set off on the journey for Schönbrunn, having received a call, where they stayed until the end of May when they started their return journey to Bethlehem. After some difficulties and experiences of the Lord's protection and help they arrived safely in Bethlehem on June 24 with their two children. In the ensuing years they were employed in the service of the congregations in Mountjoy, Emmaus, and Hebron. Her husband finished his service and his pilgrimage in this life on July 19, 1790, in Yorktown, where they had moved for the second time that same year. This loss hit her very deeply, because she had led a very contented marriage with him. This (marriage) was blessed with four sons, who are still alive, from whom she has had nine grandchildren.

Thereafter she came to Bethlehem to the Widows' Choir (where she spent her time contentedly), until she received the call in 1798 to assist Brother Molther in the household and otherwise in his widowerhood in Yorktown. The Sisters who had previously enjoyed her care there were very pleased to see her again and to enjoy her pleasant and edifying company.

> How edifying was your pilgrimage
> Maid of Christ
> How sweet to regard
> That which filled your heart
> And your actions
> You loved the Saviour
> You were quite dedicated to Him
> Thus you were quite prepared
> For such an end.
> So cheerful, so childlike happy
> Can only a heart depart
> From this world that so
> Found its inner well-being
> In Christ's Suffering and His Blessedness!
> Oh, happiest state,
> Oh, eternal bliss and joy.

Anna Johanna Seidel, née Piesch
1726–1788

Anna Johanna Seidel was one of the most influential women in the eighteenth-century Moravian Church (illus. 18). At the age of nineteen she was made General Eldress of all Single Sisters Choirs, in which capacity she travelled extensively across Europe and America with Zinzendorf and her aunt, Anna Nitschmann. Her memoir contains some wonderful pictures of Zinzendorf in action, like, for example, her description of hearing Zinzendorf deliver his "Berlin Discourses on the Redemption of Man by the Death of Christ" (delivered in 1738, published in 1740).[64] Anna Johanna was also very close to Christian Renatus, Zinzendorf's son, and she re-

counts her desolation at his early death. Of equal interest to the reader would be her reaction to the deaths of her aunt Anna Nitschmann and Zinzendorf, which occurred within ten days of each other, however that passage is heavily deleted in the original manuscript. At the age of thirty-five the marriage to Nathaniel Seidel was proposed to her, which she accepted with great difficulty but recognized the administrative necessity of such a move with the departure of Zinzendorf and Anna Nitschmann. She and Bishop Seidel were, after all, two of the best known members of the Moravian Church in Europe and America and seemed perfectly qualified to help in the transition of the Bethlehem economy from a communal to household structure. Of particular interest is Anna Johanna's reaction to the effect of the break up of the communal economy on the lives of the Single Sisters.

I was born on January 12, 1726, in Berthelsdorf, where my dear parents were staying for the interim until their newly built house in Herrnhut was ready, for they had only arrived from Moravia the previous autumn. When I was six years old I lost my dear mother, who died very peacefully and quickly of an acute malady. I had two brothers who were younger than I, and we were all three placed in what was then the orphanage in Herrnhut. Our dear father was seldom at home because he was constantly travelling with the late Papa. Treatment in the dear orphanage at that time was hard and difficult. My poor little brothers grieved so much that they both got consumption and quickly followed their dear mother. Thus only I was left and spent my time there now and again until I was twelve years old. The dear Saviour was my only comfort; I cleaved to Him and He helped me through with His grace. In 1737, when I was eleven years old, I entered into the Hourly Intercession along with some of my playmates and was so faithful in this assignment that was given to me that I still think of this with pleasure. On September 13 of that year, I was received into the Children's Congregation. In January 1738, I travelled to Berlin along with various other children where the late Papa had already been staying with his household for several weeks. We were lodged in his house and, when he held his speeches to the women, we sat around the platform on which he stood and sang together the hymns that he had us sing at the beginning.

In May of this same year, we children travelled with Br. and Sr. Leonhardt [Dober] to Marienborn and formed a home there to which children kept coming until finally we were quite strong in number. When I was not yet quite fourteen years old, I was entrusted with quite a large room of children, whose superior I was. This was a hard school for me in itself and drove me closer to the Saviour in all matters.

In October 1739, I went to Holy Communion for the first time, which made an unforgettable impression and was a blessing to my poor heart. Fourteen days later I, along with several of my playmates, was confirmed or accepted as an acolyte.

In 1740, we moved to Herrnhaag to the house built for the Children's Home. In January 1741, I became the Children's Eldress and Joint Eldress of the Great Girls, in which offices I served in true poverty of spirit for several years. November 13, 1741, when the first Elder's festival was celebrated in Herrnhaag, was an extraordinary day of grace and blessing, which I shall not forget as long as I live, for the Saviour gave special grace and mercy to me, His poor child.

In 1742, when Papa was in America, the Labourers held a Pilgrims' Communion in Marienborn every month, which I had the grace to attend, and which was astonishingly important to me and which always gave me much blessing for my heart.

In 1743, Papa, my dear aunt [Anna Nitschmann] and dear Benigna [von Zinzendorf] returned from America. Then a whole new time of grace began that yielded much for every heart in the Congregation. In June it was off to Hirschberg [Vogtland] for a General Synod. I went there too, and on July 5 was named co-Eldress of the Congregation at the same. Filling this high office in the Congregation cost me innumerable tears, and I went about it small and sinnerlike. The love and true affection of all my brothers and sisters to me poor thing shamed and humbled me yet more.

After the Synod was over we travelled via Ebersdorf to Herrnhut and Silesia, and in the autumn of that same year we had a Pilgrim House in Burau. In winter I was in the Herrnhut Sisters' House. When Papa returned from Livonia[65] in 1744, there were blessed days of the Son of Man in Herrnhut, but the stay was short. We travelled from Herrnhut back to Marienborn and remained there until February 1745. We then travelled to Holland and had a Pilgrim Congregation in Amsterdam in the Schellingers' house for a few months. Then we travelled back to Marienborn, and soon after I moved completely to Herrnhaag to take over the office of Single Sisters' Labouress, which I filled until the end of September of that year, and then I travelled to England along with my dear father and Brother Leonhardt. The latter and I had the assignment of administering the whole work of the Saviour there and keeping the labourers together. In addition, I had the special task of gathering a Single Sisters' Choir in London and to be their special Labouress. In the beginning it looked difficult, but the Saviour allowed me to succeed, so that within a short time I had a quite beautiful Single Sisters' Choir. I also learned the language very quickly and, in a short time, felt completely at home. In July 1746, Papa, Mama, and many brothers and sisters came to London, and we formed a lovely Pilgrim House in Red Lion Square. Before the end of the year, Papa etc. went back to Germany. In April 1747, I travelled back to Herrnhaag, and on May 4[66] was consecrated by dear Papa and Mama as the General Eldress of all the Single Sisters' Choirs. I shall never forget these very months in Herrnhaag all my days for it was a quite specially blessed time. From there we travelled to Herrnhut and the Disciple's House stayed in the manor house at Berthelsdorf. In November I travelled with Johannes and dear Benigna to Herrnhaag. (See illus. 19) In autumn 1748, I travelled to Holland, and after a two month stay in Zeist I travelled with the late Mama via Barby back to Herrnhaag, where I spent the whole winter and had a very heavy time during the Sifting Period. Towards the end of May 1749, I travelled to England to the Disciple's House, which was at that time to be found in Bloomsbury Square. Soon after my arrival Christel[67] and I travelled with Papa and dear Mama to Yorkshire and stayed for two months in the new Congregation Place in Pudsey, which received the name Grace Hall during our stay. We laid the foundations of the Single Brethren's and Sisters' Houses and had a very happy and contented time with the congregation there. In August we returned to Bloomsbury Square and stayed there until 1750, when we travelled via Zeist, Marienborn, and Herrnhaag back to Barby and Herrnhut. In autumn of this year the children, namely the Girls' Home, emigrated from Herrnhaag. They were lodged in Hennersdorf Castle. I received my longest stay with them because the supervision of the whole insitution had been transferred to me, and it was a blessed time that we had with the children in this dear little place. In March 1751, I moved with the Children's Home to Herrnhut, in April I visited in Silesia and returned to Herrnhut on May 4, where I stayed until the middle of June. Then I visited Ebersdorf, and from there went to Herrnhaag and Marienborn, completely divided up my dear Single Sisters and dispatched some to Ebersdorf, some to Neuwied and quite a number to Zeist. From there I travelled via Holland to England where I arrived in Bloomsbury on August 23, and the following day Papa and the other brothers and sisters of the Disciple's House arrived also. Towards winter we moved to Westminster and had quite a difficult time. Christel became ill; in February 1752, he started to spit blood and thereafter he showed a rapid consumption, and on May 28, to our pain and grief, he went home to the Saviour. I, for myself, felt most deeply what I had lost in him. And if the Saviour had not been my comfort, I would have remained inconsolable at this loss.

Towards the beginning of October of this year I travelled with a group of single sisters to America. We sailed with the *Irene* and arrived safely and well preserved in Bethlehem on November 24, where we were received with much joy and experienced the grace of enjoying Holy Communion with the congregation on that same evening. In January 1753, I visited the town and country congregations. The Indian congregation in Gnaden-hütten charmed me greatly and actually everything pleased me greatly in America. In the middle of February I left Bethlehem again and travelled via Philadelphia to New York and enjoyed Holy Communion with the local congregation on the 25th. On the 26th I boarded the *Irene* again, and on March 25th I had the grace of enjoying Holy Communion in the Disciple's House in Westminster. A few days later we moved into Lindsey House. In the autumn of that same year, I visited Yorkshire to see and speak to my dear father, who went home peacefully to the Saviour on November 3. His going home cost me many tears, but I cannot begrudge him his happiness at being at home with his Lord.

In January 1754, I travelled via Holland to Herrnhut and Silesia to visit the Single Sisters' choirs, and in August I accompanied the late Mama through the Netherlands back to England. In autumn I was very sickly, so much so that the doctors had already rather given me up. And oh, how much I would have liked to have gone home, but it pleased the Saviour to allow me get well again.

In February 1755, a part of the Disciple's House went to Holland and another part stayed in Lindsey House. I travelled to Holland and we broke our journey in Zeist. In May we travelled via Neuwied, Marienborn, and Barby to Herrnhut. And the Disciple's House was in the manor house in Berthelsdorf.

In September, 1757 I travelled with Papa, dear Mama etc. via Barby and Marienborn to Switzerland. We arrived in Montmirail on October 3, in November we visited Geneva and Lausanne and had a blessed time with all the brothers and sisters. On the return journey we visited Bern, Aronne, Basel, Zürich, and Schaffhausen and travelled through Württemberg to Ebersdorf, where we arrived shortly before Christmas. Immediately after the holidays I travelled to Herrnhut and arrived there safely on the last day of December. In Spring 1758, I was once again very sickly and spent most of my time in my dear Single Sisters' House in Herrnhut. In August we travelled to Holland and the Disciple's House moved to Heerendijk, where we spent the whole winter and on into 1759 until May. We spent much time in Zeist and eventually moved there completely. In the middle of this month I travelled with Johannes and his dear wife to England for a visitation of the congregations and choirs, and at the end of that year returned with them to Herrnhut. When I arrived there I found my dear Mama very weak from total consumption and thus gave myself over completely to her care and attention and took little notice of much else. And that I did and held to faithfully. It was a pressingly hard time for me, but the Saviour, who was deeply close to me, through the pain and worry, helped me through with His grace. On May 9 our dearest Papa, who will never be forgotten by all who knew him and had the grace to be near him, went home. That was a pain that cut deep and demanded that the good Mama followed him on the 21st (see illus. 20). Now I was completely orphaned, and the sorrow and trouble of my poor soul was great not only about these two dear people but also mainly about the loss of the leading sheep of the congregations and choirs, and how things would fare in the future. [Matter deleted]

After the going home of these two dear people I now thought to dedicate my life completely to my dear Single Sisters' Choirs and to apply double faithfulness and hard work to them. But the Saviour had arranged things quite differently and gave me a quite different field to plough. I was offered my Plan in America and with it the dear Brother Nathaniel. We were to go there to take over the Economy and the property of the Unity. This plan had been destined for us during Papa's life and was as good as approved, and I myself had been informed of this. I was happy to go to America, but to enter into marriage! That cost me dear, and there was much bitter pain until I was able to give up my will to the intention of the Saviour. But He helped me through that also and stood strong by my side. We were promised to each other on June 15 amid a small company. This occurrence was not made known to the Single Sisters and Brethren's Choirs however until the end of August. We were engaged for five months. In the meantime Nathaniel travelled with Johannes to Barby, and I travelled with Br. and Sr. Marschall to Ebersdorf to visit the Single Sisters' Choir. On October 16 I returned to Herrnhut, and on the 30th we were bound in holy matrimony by our dear brother Johannes amid a special feeling of the presence and grace of our best Friend. As I have already mentioned, it was very hard for me to enter into this important state. But because it was the will of the Saviour, as I entered into it I asked Him in His mercy, that He would so shape me as to be a joy and an honour to Him and my dear husband and give me grace to be a faithful, submissive wife. I gave myself up to Him just as I was and I felt His peace and His merciful support for us whatever circumstances befell us.

That winter we visited Niesky and on March 2, 1761, we left Herrnhut via Barby for Holland. We were in Zeist for six weeks and our whole group gathered slowly. We hired a ship and travelled with the same to England, arriving safely on May 12 in Lindsey House. At the end of May our whole group of brothers and sisters, which now consisted of fifty persons, went on board the *Hope,* and Captain Jakobsen sailed to Portsmouth. My dear husband and I, along with Br. and Sr. Marschall, stayed for a few weeks more in Lindsey House because we had much to confer with Brother Johannes about. In June we too set off and went by land to Portsmouth and from there directly onto our ship. But then we lay at anchor for another seven weeks and had to wait for the fleet.

We made up a complete little congregation on our ship and had our meetings daily and Holy Communion at the prescribed time and spent our days and weeks blessedly. Br. Johannes visited us once more as did various other brothers from London. On August 4 we finally sailed with ninety-six ships in the fleet and had a passably good trip, but needed ten weeks until we laid anchor in the Hook on October 18 in the evening.

On October 23, we arrived in our dear Bethlehem along with our dear brothers and sisters, the Münsters and the Marschalls. The other brothers and sisters arrived safely during the following days. In the first weeks there was nothing but joy and sweetness but after this we turned to our work. In 1762, the first task was the turn around of the communal economy, which was a difficult job that caused my dear husband and me many a sleepless night. But the Saviour stood by us with His grace even under these difficult circumstances.

For the first few years I stood in true heartfelt trust with my dear Single Sisters' Choir here. My being married did not disturb either them or me, and through all of this I would gladly have stayed with them with all my heart. But the change in their Labouresses also caused a change in this, which pained me greatly, but with time I learned to fit in with this also through the support of the dear Saviour. My dear husband and I visited the town and country congregations diligently and experienced much preservation from the dear Saviour during our many travels. In 1764, we were in New York and on August 17 had taken a boat to cross to Staten Island. As we got to the water my dear husband immediately got into the boat but was in it for hardly a minute when he got into another. I called to him and said to him that the boat we were already in was the boat we had wanted to travel in. He, however, said, "No. You come here to this one. I want to travel in this one." I followed him silently. We sailed off immediately and crossed safely. There was a heavy storm in the sky that broke out when we were hardly a half-mile from land but we reached the shore without a problem. However, the other boat, in which we had been at first, capsized and seven people drowned when it did so. We thus saw for our-selves right in front of our eyes how the dear Saviour had protected us, in that He had told my husband in his heart to get out of that boat. I could give many similar examples but let this one suffice.

In 1769, I travelled to Europe with my dear husband to the General Synod. We left our dear Bethlehem on the last day of March and sailed from Philadelphia on April 17, arriving safely in London on May 29. After a few days' stay, we travelled on via Zeist and Neuwied to Marienborn, where we arrived safely on June 28. I experienced the great joy of seeing and embracing many of my dear old friends. And that was all, because for the rest I had no joy, nothing but great sadness and shed many, many tears there.[68] As soon as the Synod was over we hurried back and arrived safely in London on October 6 and would have returned gladly to America that same year. Indeed, we found a ship, which we actually boarded on October 11. I was on board this same vessel for about an hour with my good husband when we had to hurry from it in fear of our lives because it keeled over onto its side and was stuck fast on a sand bank. We went back on land and stayed with some brothers and sisters but asked that we should be called when the ship got free again. But the ship sank completely in the Thames, and we had to decide to spend this winter in England. So we made a trip to Yorkshire, Ockbrook, and Bedford and arrived in London again at the end of January 1770. We had a happy and contented time with the congregation there, and on March 20 we travelled to Gravesend and from there boarded a ship that was sailing to New York. We had quite a good journey and took ten or eleven single brethren with us to Bethle-hem and Christiansbrunn. My good husband was sickly on the journey and got the gout, the first time quite badly. But I was healthy and could care for him. On May 12 we arrived safely in New York, stayed there for a couple of days, and then travelled to Bethlehem, where we arrived to the great joy of all our dear brothers and sisters. Soon after we made a journey to all the town and country congregations after the decree of the Synod was pub-lished here and in Nazareth and Lititz, to do the same with them with what was appropriate for them. And we were finished with this only at the end of October.

In 1771, my dear husband began to sicken greatly, but in 1774 we still made a trip to all town and country congregations. And soon thereafter the unfortunate war broke out that caused much concern and grief due to the conditions that were associated with it.

In March 1779, our dear Brother and Sister Reichel [Bishop Johann Friedrich Reichel] came here to our true comfort, and my good husband seemed to come to life again, but this changed again greatly the year after when the Reichels were in the Wachovia tract [North Carolina] and after Christmas he got about eighty such attacks that cast me into such great despair and worry. That which I had feared became only too true, for on May 17, 1782, he went home very quickly to my indescribable pain. Oh, if only I could have gone with him straight away, how good that would have been for me. For almost a year and a half, I had foreseen nothing except that I would lose him and imagined how heavy this would lie on me, but no imaginings sufficed to express what one experienced at the dissolution of *this* brother.

Now I had lost every dear thing that I had possessed in this world, and often thought that it would not be possible for me to survive this. But my best Friend's close concern for me, His poor child, helped me through this hard trial, and He promised to be my comfort and my one and all in my present solitude.

I often thought about the twenty-one-and-a-half years that I spent in my marriage and found innumerable reasons to become a sinner before the dear Saviour, but still I could say thanks to Him a thousand times for His being with us, for His pledge to us in so many hard things that happened in the fulfilment of our office. Through all mistakes and shortcomings our hearts did remain faithful in intent. We had no other goal or purpose other than the Saviour and His business. Through this we loved each other tenderly and shared joy and pain together. And because he was weak and frail for almost ten years, it was a true blessing for me to serve him day and night and to take care of him as well as possible. I would also have gladly continued to do it for many years, if the dear Saviour had wanted me to do so.

With all my heart I am glad for my dear husband that he is at peace, although often many a tear is still shed by me for him, for I know best of all how much he desired it. The dear Saviour will still aid me His poor sinner in His own time and hour. In the meantime He is my comfort, I know of no other.

Rosina Stoll, née Rohledern
1727–1811

Rosina Stoll came from one of the original Moravian families from what is now Suchdol nad Odron in the Czech Republic. At the age of fifteen she ran away from home to join the Moravians in Herrnhut. From there she went to America at the age of twenty-one, married and worked her whole life as a teacher.

Our late Sister Rosina Stoll, née Rohledern, has dictated to her children
the following brief account for us about her course through life.

I was born on December 4, 1727, in Zauchenthal in Moravia. My dear
parents were descended from the old Brethren and attempted to raise
their children in the fear of God. In my 16th year, because I was anxious
about my salvation and did not think that I heard the Good News of the
Gospel properly in my native land, I left my mother's house secretly, without telling her (my father had already passed away) for I was afraid that
my mother would try to prevent me. But she later had to suffer a hard
imprisonment because she could not say where her daughter had gone. I
left my belongings behind with other people, and these were later confis-
cated by the authorities. Because my departure had to be very hurried, I
took only what I really needed with me, and arrived safely in Herrnhut in
1742 on Good Friday with two of my friends (almost without shoes). Here
I lived quite happily in great poverty and, in 1744, I was received into
the Congregation. And in the same year in December I enjoyed Holy
Communion for the first time with the same Congregation.

In 1748, I received a call to America, and I arrived in Bethlehem in the
same year in Br. Johann Nitschmann's company, and in 1749 I received a
call to serve with the children in Nazareth, where I stayed for eight years
until in 1757 I returned to Bethlehem—again to the same type of service. And here, in 1768, on August 25, I was married to the widower Br.
Johannes Stoll. This marriage was blessed with a son and a daughter, of
whom the daughter is still living and married to Br. Abraham Hübner and
from whom I have had nine grandchildren of whom seven have preceded
me into eternity.

This far the late sister herself.

Her choir sisters add the following:

On March 10, 1801, she became a widow, and because she was already
living with her dear children so the same kept her, and she served them as
long as her strength allowed her to with earnest loyalty wherever she could.
One could clearly feel her quiet and continual conversation with the invisible Friend of her heart, although she never used to say much about this.
In all her difficult trials, of which she had her generous portion in this
dying life, she learned to turn to the Saviour like a child and in faith and
to call on Him for advice and support. He never (according to her own
statement) left her, and stood by her mercifully in all circumstances. That

proved itself to be true especially in her last illness (which was painful and difficult). As she had to endure many years of rheumatic pains, she learned much patience. Last year in the spring her rheumatic pains appeared all the stronger, and other attacks joined in with these so that she was no longer capable of enjoying Holy Communion with the congregation in the Hall but rather had to have it brought to her at home. That was truly painful for her but the proximity of the dear Saviour (which she felt each time during her enjoyment) comforted her richly in this.

At the beginning of this year it seemed as though she would not be here below much longer, and when her illness, which developed into a dropsy, worsened noticeably, she wished in February to be blessed for her homegoing, and her desire was fulfilled. The blessing of the Congregation and her choir was bestowed upon her with a blessed feeling of the presence of God. But she became better and had to endure another school of patience. Whenever it seemed as though she would lose courage, the comfort brought her by visitors was very encouraging, and she expressed her thanks for it every time and was grateful for every service done for her. She acknowledged with special humility the fact that her dear children served her with such earnest loyalty and care and wished for them the rich blessing of the Saviour for it. Her sufferings often pressed from her the sigh, "Oh, how much longer will it take with me . . . dear Saviour, come and fetch me to you out of my misery!" This wish was fulfilled on June 27 in the evening when she went over to the arms of her Redeemer gently and happily at an age of 83 years, 7 months, 23 days.

Her children add the following: "She was a good and loyal mother to our late father and showed much love and patience with him, cared tirelessly for him for seven years when he was blind. Just as tenderly she cared for her own children and step-children. The death of her daughter (Sr. Krause) pained her greatly and she desired greatly that she were in her place. She sent many a sigh to the dear Saviour for the well-being of her grandchildren. The memory of her will remain unforgettable and a blessing to us.

NOTES
GLOSSARY
WORKS CITED
INDEX

NOTES

Introduction

1. For a fuller treatment of the Unity of the Brethren, see Rudolph Řičan, *The History of the Unity of the Brethren: A Protestant Hussite Church in Bohemia and Moravia*, C. Daniel Crews, trans. (Moravian Church in America, 1992). For a history of the Renewed Unitas Fratrum or Moravian Church, see J. Taylor Hamilton and Kenneth G. Hamilton, *History of the Moravian Church: The Renewed Unitas Fratrum 1722–1957* (Bethlehem, Pa.: Interprovincial Board of Christian Education, Moravian Church of America, 1967); for a more specific examination of Herrnhut and Bethlehem in the eighteenth century, see Gillian Gollin, *Moravians in Two Worlds: A Study of Changing Communities* (New York: Columbia Univ. Press, 1967), and most recently, Beverly Prior Smaby, *The Transformation of Moravian Bethlehem: From Communal Mission to Family Economy* (Philadelphia: Univ. of Pennsylvania Press, 1988). An extremely useful collection of original materials can be found in Hans-Christoph Hahn and Hellmut Reichel, eds. *Zinzendorf und die Herrnhuter Brüder: Quellen zur Geschichte der Brüder-Unität von 1722 bis 1760,* (Hamburg: Wittig, 1977). For a complete bibliography of Zinzendorf's works, see Dietrich Meyer, *Bibliographisches Handbuch zur Zinzendorf-Forschung* (Dusseldorf: C. Blech, 1987)

2. Hamilton, 17.

3. Hamilton, 17–18. For a good overview of Zinzendorf's relation to German Pietism, see Ernst Stoeffler, "Zinzendorf and the Renewed Moravian Church," in *German Pietism During the Eighteenth Century* (Leiden: Brill, 1973), 131–67.

4. See Nicholas Ludwig von Zinzendorf, *Texte zur Mission*, ed. Helmut Bintz (Hamburg: Friedrich Wittig, 1979), 37.

5. Stoeffler, 139.

6. Heinz Renkewitz, *Im Gespräch mit Zinzendorfs Theologie: Vorträge aus dem Nachlaß* (Hamburg: Wittig, 1980), 1.

7. Bernhard Becker, *Zinzendorf im Verhältnis zu Philosophie und Kirchentum seiner Zeit* (Leipzig: Hinrich, 1886), 59.

8. See Stoeffler, 146–47.

9. See, for example, Otto Uttendörfer, *Zinzendorfs christliches Lebensideal* (Gnadau: Verlag der Unitätsbuchhandlung, 1940); Wilhelm Bettermann, *Theologie und Sprache bei Zinzendorf* (Gotha: Klotz, 1935).

10. See Erich Beyreuther, "Theologia Crucis: Zinzendorf und Luther," in *Studien zur Theologie Zinzendorfs* (Neukirchen: Neukirchener Verlag, 1962), 236.

11. In his work on Zinzendorf and mysticism, Otto Uttendörfer argues that it was from these sources that Zinzendorf found the justification for the vivid and overly realistic imagery

of the "Sifting Period." See Otto Uttendörfer, *Zinzendorf und die Mystik* (Berlin: Christlicher Zeitschriften Verlag, 1952). For an extended investigation of the vocabulary of the Sifting Period, see Katherine M. Faull, "Faith and Imagination: Nikolaus Ludwig von Zinzendorf's Anti-Enlightenment Philosophy of Self," *Bucknell Review* 38, no. 2 (1995): 23–56;

12. Zinzendorf in *Jüngerhausdiarium*, September 27, 1754, ms, R2A, 35b. p. 314, Moravian Archives, Herrnhut, Germany, henceforth cited as MAH. All translations are my own unless otherwise stated.

13. Uttendörfer *Zinzendorfs christliches Lebensideal*, 71.

14. Ibid., 81f.

15. See present volume, 13.

16. See present volume, 34.

17. See present volume, 20.

18. See present volume, 20.

19. See present volume, 37.

20. Zinzendorf, *32 Homilien*, January 16, 1746, 15–16, as quoted in Uttendörfer, *Zinzendorf und die Mystik*, 211. The notion of Christ as "Eternal Bridegroom" is also part of Zinzendorf's *Ehe-Religion* according to which all souls are feminine and thus can be united with Christ as the husband after death. Manhood is conceived of as a merely earthly contrivance to allow mortal men to act as the substitutes of Christ for women until death. For an extended analysis of this see Erich Beyreuther, "Ehe-Religion und Eschaton" in *Studien zur Theologie Zinzendorfs* (Neukirchen: Neukirchener Verlag, 1962), 35–73.

21. Renkewitz, 9.

22. Uttendörfer, *Zinzendorfs christliches Lebensideal*, 16.

23. See A. J. Lewis, *Zinzendorf the Ecumenical Pioneer: A Study in the Moravian Contribution to Christian Mission and Unity* (Philadelphia: Westminster Press, 1962), 121–22.

24. Uttendörfer, *Zinzendorfs christliches Lebensideal*, 271.

25. For a full description of Bethlehem during this period, see Helmut Erbe, *Bethlehem, Pa: Eine kommunistische Herrnhuter-Kolonie des achtzehnten Jahrhunderts* (Stuttgart: Ausland und Heimat Verlags-Aktiengesellschaft, 1929).

26. August Gottlieb Spangenberg, Spangenberg folder 1, 1-a, ms, Moravian Archives, Bethlehem, Pa., henceforth referred to as MAB.

27. "Nachricht von der gemeinschaftlichen Haushaltung in Bethlehem, Zusammengeschriebene kurze Erklärungen von Zahlreichen Brüdern und Schwestern," R.14 A 41a, MAH.

28. "You are more delicate than the brothers, because your tabernacles are not formed from a lump of earth but rather of flesh and blood. Also the sisters usually have something more cheerful and light in their natures than the brothers. Already in earliest youth something harder reveals itself in the boys than in the girls. The body of Jesus has far less to kill in you than in us." Speech, 26 October, 1750. As quoted in Otto Uttendörfer, *Zinzendorf und die Frauen* (Herrnhut: Missionsbuchhandlung, 1919), 9.

29. Ibid., 9.

30. Speech 19 April, 1756. Uttendörfer, *Zinzendorf und die Frauen*, 14.

31. Ibid., 28.

32. In her examination of the demographic changes in Bethlehem from the period of the General Economy until the 1820s when the community was no longer exclusive, Beverly Smaby discusses at some length the effect the communal structure had on the women. She writes, "The eradication of nuclear family life and the separation of the sexes had an enormous effect on the lives of the Moravian women. Male and female roles were much more

symmetrical than in any other colonial society, including the Quakers," Smaby, 13. For an examination of the importance of women to the Pietist movement, see Richard Critchfield, "Prophetin, Führerin, Organisatorin: Zur Rolle der Frau im Pietismus," in *Die Frauen von der Reformation zur Romantik*, ed. Bärbel Becker-Cantarino (Bonn: Bouvier, 1980), 112–37.

33. See, for example, Zinzendorf's speech of February 24, 1757, in which he states, "It is impossible that in a congregation of the Saviour that the sisters be served only by the brothers. The reason is this. The two sexes are of quite different types. Regarding their external condition there is no question about this; but the true difference lies not only in the quite unique constitution of the passivity of the female form which is in strict opposition to the activity of the male body, but also in their differing humour" (Uttendörfer, *Zinzendorf und die Frauen*, 62).

34. On this see Erbe, "All posts are filled twice. In regard to pastoral care, the woman has equal rights with the man and is also a member of the Conferences. And, second, one is not married in Bethlehem because of personal inclination, rather the deciding factor in everything is whether both partners possess the necessary capabilities to fulfill the calling of pilgrim" (Erbe, 36).

35. Zinzendorf's speech to the Gotha Synod, 17 June 1740 (Uttendörfer, *Zinzendorf und die Frauen*, 24).

36. "Ordinationsrede Nathaniel Seidel zu Bischof," ms, Zinzendorf Box D German Discourses, 1755–60, MAB.

37. Uttendörfer, *Zinzendorf und die Frauen*, 29. One of the first women to be ordained as priest was his daughter, Agnes von Zinzendorf.

38. Anna Johanna (Piesch) Seidel, "Memoir," ms, MAB. See present volume, 126.

39. Anna Seidel, "Memoir," ms, MAB. See present volume, 126.

40. Anna Seidel, "Memoir," ms, MAB. See present volume, 127.

41. Zinzendorf's speech to the married women, 19 July, 1744 (Uttendörfer, *Zinzendorf und die Frauen*, 39). This notion that the ideal relationship between women and Christ should be one of female passivity to male action is actually paralleled in other Protestant churches in Early America. The Quakers, for example, led by Mother Ann Lee, developed a feminine spirituality that also gave supervisory and spiritual responsibility to women. See Laurel Thatcher Ulrich, "Vertuous Women Found" *American Quarterly* 28 (Spring 1976): 20–40; and Mary Maples Dunn, "Saints and Sisters: Congregational and Quaker Women in the early Colonial Period," *American Quarterly* 30 (Winter 1978): 583–95.

42. For an overview, see Katherine M. Faull, "The American *Lebenslauf*: Women's Autobiography from eighteenth-Century Moravian Bethlehem, Pennsylvania," *Yearbook of the Society for German-American Studies* 27 (1992): 23–48. For an investigation of Pietist women's memoirs in Germany, see Jeannine Blackwell, "Herzensgespräche mit Gott: Bekenntnisse deutscher Pietistinnen im siebzehnten und achtzehnten Jahrhundert," in *Deutsche Literatur von Frauen: Vom Mittelalter bis zum Ende des achtzehnten Jahrhunderts*, ed. Gisela Brinker-Gabler (Beck: München, 1988), vol. 1, 265–89. In this article, Blackwell draws on the published collections of narratives in volumes such as Johann Reitz' *Historie der Wiedergeborenen* (1717) to come to the conclusion that the imposed form of the memoir actually limits women's self-scrutiny and self-expression. Of significance here is, of course, the editorial policy exercised by Reitz, that is, his purpose in the *publication* of these particular personal documents. Blackwell recognizes this limitation in her statement, "The potential power of these confessions is actually dissipated by the fact that they are framed by the warning and explication, the 'sermon' of the male editor or narrator" (Blackwell, 268).

43. Rosemary Radford Ruether and Catherine Prelinger, "Women in Sectarian and Utopian Groups," in *Women and Religion in America*, ed. Rosemary Ruether and Rosemary Keller (New York: Harper and Row, 1983), vol. 2, 298.

44. Ibid. In their latest volume, *In Our Own Voices: Four Centuries of American Women's Religious Writing* (San Francisco: Harper, 1995) Ruether and Keller mention Moravian women only briefly and include none of their writings.

45. As Shea has pointed out in reference to the New England religious communities' writings, the author's form of expression can be somewhat repetitive in her choice of language. See Daniel B. Shea, Jr., *Spiritual Autobiography in Early America* (Princeton: Princeton University Press, 1988), 40. I would, however, agree with Mary Anne Schofield that beyond the prescribed narrative shape and language of the spiritual narrative, women find a voice not usually granted them within their society. See Mary Anne Schofield, " 'Womens Speaking Justified': The Feminine Quaker Voice, 1662–1797," *Tulsa Studies in Women's Literature* 6 (1987): 61–77.

46. For example, Bernd Neumann, *Identität und Rollenzwang: Zur Theorie der Autobiographie* (Frankfurt: Athenäum, 1970), considers the narratives to be devoid of personal comment and to be written only to serve the interests of the increasing imperialism of Protestantism.

47. Smaby analyses the Moravian memoirs by constructing a flow diagram of the major decisions and stages in life cycles in the period of the General Economy and then seventy years later. Based on examination she makes the interesting claim, "Gender distinctions, though less important than age, had also become more important for the later biographies than for the earlier ones. Gender distinctions govern only four per cent of the topic boxes on the earlier flow chart and fifty per cent of those on the later one" (Smaby, 142).

48. *Jüngerhausdiarium* 1747, 22. Juni, as quoted in Hellmut Reichel, "Ein Spiegel der Frömmigkeit und des geistlichen Lebens: Zur Geschichte des brüderischen Lebenslaufes," *Brüderbote* 464 (März 1988): 4–7, at 4. Unfortunately, the practice of writing a memoir has all but died out in the modern-day Moravian Church in America and Great Britain but attempts are being made to revive the custom. However, only a small number of Moravians write their own memoirs, most being written by the congregation's minister. In Germany it is still customary to write one's memoir.

49. See present volume, 40.

50. The memoirs were considered to be so important by one Moravian church historian, Johannes Plitt, that he suggested compiling a collection of them for each epoch of the church. During the nineteenth century a bimonthly publication of the Moravian church did print the memoirs of some of its members. See *Nachrichten aus der Brudergemeine* (Gnadau: Verlag der Unitäts-Buchhandlung, 1819–94).

51. See present volume, 32.

52. See Rahel Edmonds, memoir, ms, MAB.

53. Oskar Pfister, *Die Frömmigkeit des Grafen Ludwig von Zinzendorf. Eine psychoanalytische Studie* (Neudeln, Liechtenstein: 1925; rpt. 1970).

54. For a detailed discussion of the uses of the Blood and Wounds theology in the Moravian Church, see my essay, "Faith and Imagination," *Bucknell Review* 38, no. 2: 23–56.

55. For further discussion of the language of the Sifting Period, see Jörn Reichel, *Dichtungstheorie und Sprache bei Zinzendorf: Der 12. Anhang zum Herrnhuter Gesangbuch* (Bad Homburg: Gehlen, 1969).

56. See present volume, 58.

57. Interestingly enough, this intersubjective and dependent self is the narrative voice

also found in the Moravian men's memoirs. There the men use the same vocabulary as the women to speak of their faith and dependence on Christ, of their passivity in the shaping of their lives. The major difference between the men's and women's memoirs in the eighteenth century lies in the men's greater emphasis on their professional lives. This insight leads one then to ask whether the model of the intersubjective, dependent narrator is gender-specific or rather the product of Zinzendorf's Christocentric theology.

58. Mary Mason, "The Other Voice: Autobiography of Women Writers," in *Autobiography: Essays Theoretical and Critical,* ed. James Olney (Princeton: Princeton Univ. Press, 1980), 207–35, specifically, 210.

59. Hellmut Reichel, "Ein Spiegel der Frömmigkeit und des geistlichen Lebens: Zur Geschichte des brüderishen Lebenslaufes." *Brüderbote* 464 (Mar. 1988): 4–7.

60. Speech to the Synod, 2 July 1756, as quoted in Otto Uttendörfer, *Zinzendorfs christliches Lebensideal,* 8.

61. Zinzendorf apparently insisted upon this fact: "The memoirs must relate nothing but the complete truth. Otherwise the Disciple (Zinzendorf) is horrified and then it does not smell good." (*Extract von den Ratskonferenzen von 1753,* as quoted in Hellmut Reichel, 6).

62. Shea, 91

63. Samuel J. Preus, "Secularizing Divination: Spiritual Biography and the Invention of the Novel," *Journal of the American Academy of Religion* 59 (1991): 454.

64. Ibid.

65. Ian Watt, *The Rise of the Novel* (Berkeley: Univ. of California Press, 1966).

66. Günter Niggl, *Geschichte der deutschen Autobiographie im achtzehnten Jahrhundert* (Stuttgart: Klett, 1977). Niggl dates the earliest occurrence of a first-person-singular Moravian narrative in 1752. He claims that early memoirs consisted of only a list of dates (62–63). Niggl also claims that the shift in narrator is accompanied by an increased secularization of the originally spiritual narrative, a process traced from a sociological perspective by Smaby.

67. "From the very beginning the pietistic autobiography has had the tendency of seeing the external facts of life not only as an indispensable (chronological-topographical) framework, but has granted secular life space with and alongside the religious narrative, or, speaking in terms of genre, the traditional models of religious confessional and the career autobiography are linked hypotactically, that is arranged equally." Günter Niggl, "Zur Säkularisation der pietistischen Autobiographie im achtzehnten Jahrhundert," in *Prismata,* ed. Dieter Grimm et al. (Pullach bei München: Verlag Dokumentation, 1974), 155–72; specifically, 166.

68. According to Becker, Zinzendorf refused to recognize a separation between the secular and religious and rather considered that the secular had to be interfused with the religious: "In this regard he [Zinzendorf] claims that religion does not consist in words but in being and possessing, it is nothing thought up but rather something given, nothing learned but rather something essential, a nature. [R]eligion must control the practical lived life of the human being" (Becker, 57–58).

69. Smaby makes precisely this claim in her analysis of the early memoirs. See Smaby, 138.

Memoirs of the Single Sisters

1. May 4, 1750. *Diarium der ledigen Schwestern angefangen den 14. November 1748,* ms, MAB.

2. "The actual profession of a Single Sister when she is in the Congregation is to enter into marriage." Zinzendorf's address to the Single Sisters, June 25, 1747, *ZudF,* 38. "We see

you as the model from which we can learn simplicity, a childlike essence, and Hagneia (chastity), a childlike and yet also staid behavior: for they (the women) must leave their chaste state when they are a certain age but then they find it again and keep it for their whole life." (Zinzendorf's Speech, June 23, 1755, *ZudF,* 16).

3. Deleted in ms: "to whom I also gave my heart".

4. Deleted in ms: "my cousin".

5. Deleted in ms: "with whom I had lived for seven years and had been very comfortable in material things".

6. Deleted in ms: "the Congregation in".

7. Deleted in ms: "on 15th April, that is, on the great Sabbath".

8. Deleted in ms: "On the 15th, on the Great Sabbath, in the evening".

9. Peter Boehler (1712–1775) was one of the most influential leaders of the Moravian Church on both the European and North American continents. Born in Frankfurt am Main, he came into contact with the Moravians through his lecturer at the University of Jena, August Gottlieb Spangenberg, and joined with early Moravian missionary efforts in Georgia. On his way to America he stayed in England and met with the Charles and John Wesley at Oxford. Although the mission in Georgia failed, Boehler continued his work with the Moravians in the 1740s in the fledgling congregation of Bethlehem and also preached in New York City. At the time Benigna Zahm heard him preach, he had been in Bethlehem for seven years. He continued to work as a leader in the Moravian Church until his death in England in 1775. For further details of his life, see Edmund de Schweinitz, *Some Fathers of the American Moravian Church* (Bethlehem, 1881) and J. P. Lockwood, *Memorials of the Life of Peter Boehler* (London, 1868).

10. Amadeus Paulinus Thrane (1718–1776) served as principal preacher (*Ordinarius*) in Bethlehem from 1761 until his death.

11. Isaiah 50:6.

Memoirs of the Married Sisters

1. For a discussion of the dispute between the leaders of the Ephrata Cloister and Zinzendorf, see Jobie E. Riley, "An Analysis of the Debate Between Johann Conrad Beissel and Various Eighteenth Century Contemporaries Concerning the Importance of Celibacy" (Ph.D. diss., Temple Univ., 1974). For a more general overview of Zinzendorf's position among the Pennsylvania Lutherans, see Peter Vogt, "Zinzendorf und die Pennsylvanischen Synoden 1742," *Unitas Fratrum* 36 (1994), 5–62.

2. *Ehechorreden,* as quoted in Beyreuther, *Studien zur Theologie Zinzendorfs,* 166.

3. *Instructionen für die Chorhelferinnen der ledigen Schwestern . . .* (1785), para. 29, ms, MAB.

4. Ibid.

5. On September 13, 1744, "An Act for Securing His Majesty's Government of New York" was passed by the General Assembly of New York, which expelled Moravians from the state for practising or proselytizing their faith. They were under suspicion of being in league with the French.

6. The Single Sisters Choir was originally housed in Bethlehem and then moved to Nazareth in 1746.

7. Eva Maria Spangenberg, first wife of August Gottlieb Spangenberg, bishop of the church and leader of Bethlehem at that time.

8. Br. James Greening and his wife, Elizabeth, arrived in New York City in 1743 as part of the Second Sea Congregation. They were both from England and remained in New York to serve the English-speaking members of the Moravian Society there.

9. Hector and Eleanor Gambold came to New York City to serve the Society from June 1746 to February 1747. Hector Gambold (1714–1788) was originally from Wales and was the brother of John Gambold, the English Moravian bishop. His wife, Eleanor, née Gregg, was from New York. He was ordained in 1755, labored in the ministry in Pennsylvania, New York, and New Jersey. He was the first permanent Moravian minister on Staten Island. He died in Bethlehem in 1788. Their son, John, was one of the pioneers of the mission to the Cherokees. See John Mortimer Levering, *A History of Bethlehem Pennsylvania 1741–1892 with Some Account of its Founders and Their Early Activity in America* (1903; rpt, New York: AMS, 1971), 123.

10. Anna Ramsberg arrived with the Third Sea Congregation in May 1749.

11. Deleted in the text: "I also had the intention."

12. Deleted in the text: "father's sister".

13. The first Store was built as an addition to Timothy Horsfield's house in 1753. It was entrusted to William Edmonds in 1754.

14. This sentence would appear to refer to the time at which the scribe's additions were written, namely early March 1773.

15. Plainfield was a township in Northampton County, north of present-day Easton.

16. Inserted in the original.

17. Inserted in original: "in writing and orally."

18. Deleted in ms: "And we would prefer to refer to this version."

19. The version of Johanette's memoir in the *Bethlehem Diary* adds the place of birth as Hachenburg. See *Bethlehem Diary*, 36, 499–504.

20. Marienborn in Wetteravia is two hours' walk from Herrnhaag. Here the Moravians founded schools. The "Economy" was the term used to describe the Congregational settlement there. Inserted in ms: "In the following year I was received into the Congregation and also went to holy communion. How I felt then I cannot express in words."

21. Wealthy Dutch merchants, Cornelius and Jacob Schellinger, lent Zinzendorf large amounts of money at a low interest in the 1750s. Which of these merchants is meant here is unclear.

22. Moravian Congregation settled in 1746 in the Netherlands.

23. Johannes de Watteville and his wife, Benigna, née von Zinzendorf.

24. Lindheim was a manor house near Marienborn, the seat of the von Schrautenbach family. The children were in Herrnhut at the time and the son was the later biographer of Zinzendorf.

25. Inserted in margin: "Two of her children, namely a son Jakob and a daughter Magdalena, were born in Carolina. Her son Johannes born in Pennsylvania and her daughter Johanna went to the Saviour before her. From her children she has had seven grandchildren."

26. Inserted in ms: "She revealed herself in all suffering to be very patient and her cheerful spirit and childlike happy mood was a comfort to us all."

27. Domine (for Dominie) was a title commonly used for Dutch Calvinist ministers. There was probably a Calvinist minister in New York named Ritzema.

28. Reference to Zinzendorf's hymn "Christi Blut und Gerechtigkeit" (The Saviour's Blood and Righteousness).

29. The author's mother, Sarah Chase, was born in Staffordshire on December 22, 1713. She was received into the Congregation on July 1, 1751, received Holy Communion on October 27, 1751, and died in 1794, that is, after her daughter, the author.

30. John Ockershausen (note correct spelling) was the Moravian preacher at Mirfield in Yorkshire in 1743. In 1745, he was arrested and imprisoned in York Castle as a suspected "papist."

31. Ann (1723–1783) and William (?-1777) Mail, members of the Fetter Lane Congregation.

32. Location of the Moravian Chapel until 1941.

33. John Gambold was the Moravian minister at Fetter Lane from 1744–1763.

34. According to the minutes of the Elders Conference in London, Anna Chase was first refused admission on Saturday, March 21, 1761, but then was admitted on Saturday, July 4 of the same year. She was then received into the Congregation on July 6, 1761, and received her first Holy Communion with the Congregation on February 12, 1764, and not 1763 as she claims.

35. The Moravian Church's central governing body at this time (1769–1899). It was based in Größhennersdorf (1769–71) and then Barby (1771–84).

36. The author is probably referring to the Brothers Christian Gregor, Johannes Loretz, and Hans Christian von Schweinitz.

37. The following is a translation of Margarethe Jungmann's memoir in her own hand as found in the Moravian Archives in Bethlehem, ms Memoirs Box 5. There also exists an edited version in English in the Moravian Archives in London.

38. In German *gesetzlich*. The Moravians called the unawakened "under the Law," i.e., trying to achieve salvation by strict adherence to the moral law rather than by faith alone.

39. Separatists (also known as Independents) were English Christians from the sixteenth and seventeenth centuries who wished to separate from the Church of England. They later became known as the Congregationalists. The Inspired was an itinerant religious group with its origins in the Protestant resistance in the Cévannes to Louis XIV. Manifestations of faith among the Inspired included visions, trances, speaking in tongues, and second sight. Followers of the Inspired could be found in France, Germany, and Great Britain in the eighteenth century.

40. The necessity for this school was determined at a conference held on April 17, 1742, at the house of Johannes Bechtel (Margarethe's father). See Levering, 104. According to Hamilton, "This boarding school for girls was established in the Ashmead house on May 4, 1742. It opened with twenty-five pupils and a staff of six: the young Countess Benigna von Zinzendorf, Sisters Magdalene Müller and Anna Desmond, Brethren Anthony Seifferth, J. William Zander, and Georg Neisser. On June 28 of the same year the school was transferred to Bethlehem" (Hamilton, 657).

41. Count Nicholas Ludwig von Zinzendorf.

42. Schekomeko, in Duchess County, upstate New York, was the first Moravian mission among the Mohicans, led by Christian David Rauch.

43. According to John Heckewelder, *Narrative of the Mission of the United Brethren among the Delaware and Mohigan Indians from Its Commencement in the Year 1740 to the Close of the Year 1873* (Philadelphia, 1823) after Büttner's death at the age of 29 the missionaries set off back to Bethlehem and were arrested at Sopus (Esopus) under suspicion of treason. Here a mob gathered and, although prevented from committing bodily harm to the Moravians, spat on them and hurled abuse (see Heckewelder, 29).

44. One of the neighboring villages to Schekomeko, it flourished until the 1770s.

45. Seven Years War, 1756–63.

46. John Jacob Schmick and his wife were Moravian missionaries who served at various stations.

47. Also known as Wyalusing, a village belonging to the Muncy Indians on the east side of the Susquehanna, opposite the mouth of Sugar Run. After its establishment as a Moravian mission in 1763, it was named Friedenshütten.

48. Festival Day of the Married People's Choir was on September 7.

49. Moravian Indian village on the east bank of Beaver River between Shenango River and Slippery Rock Creek in Lawrence County, also known as Friedensstadt.

50. David Zeisberger (1721–1808) was one of the most famous Moravian missionaries to the Delaware Indians. He worked in Pennsylvania and Ohio, translated Moravian hymns, litanies, and liturgies into the Delaware language, and kept a voluminous diary of his experiences in his mission work. See *David Zeisberger, Herrenhuter Indianermission in der Amerikanischen Revolution: Die Tagebücher von David Zeisberger, 1772–1781* ed. Hermann Wellenreuther and Carola Wessel, (Berlin; Akademie Verlag, 1995).

51. The settlement on the Muskingum river had already been set up in the 1760s by the Delawares wishing to escape their troublesome Iroquois neighbors and also the threats of the white settlers.

52. "Meadow of Light", according to Wallace, "a Moravian town in Ohio, established 1776, at the request of Netawatwees. It was situated on the east side of the Muskingum, two miles below Goschochking (Coshocton), the new Delaware [nation] capital. When Gnadenhütten was abandoned in 1778, Lichtenau received its members. Lichtenau itself was evacuated, 1780." Paul Wallace, *The Travels of John Heckewelder in Frontier America* (Pittsburgh: Pittsburgh Univ. Press, 1958; rpt. 1985), 421.

53. The American War of Independence caught the Delaware between the opposing British and American armies. Whereas other Indian nations such as the Huron and the Shawnees sided with the British, the Delawares (and for that matter the Moravians) attempted to remain neutral.

54. Wheeling, W. Va.

55. Township in Lancaster County, five miles south of Lancaster.

56. Anton and Elisabeth Wagner, members of the Second Sea Congregation, arrived in Bethlehem in 1742 and were dispatched to Heidelberg in January 1744.

57. Deleted in ms: "At Easter."

58. Inserted in margin: "They lived together in Friedensthal, then in Nazareth, and lastly in Gnadenthal".

59. Inserted in margin: "which happened blessedly yesterday morning at 6 o'clock with the blessing of her husband".

60. For confirmation.

61. Levering lists John Michael and Gertrude Graf and Joachim and Elizabeth Busse as being on the *Irene* with Nathaniel Seidel, David Zeisberger, Schlosser and his two children from Pforzheim, Durlach, and his maid, Schaemel. She was released from service to the Schlossers and employed by the Single Sisters as a maid (see Levering, 261).

Memoirs of the Widowed Sisters

1. See Felix Moeschler, *Alte Herrnhuter Familien* (Herrnhut: Missionsbuchhandlung, 1922), 115. Rose was married to Catharina Riedler (a widow) in Georgia and had two

children: Maria (later Bader) who died in Jamaica, and Anna (later Unger, then Boehler) the author of this memoir.

2. For an account of the settlement, see "Annals of Early Moravian Settlement in Georgia and Pennsylvania," *Memorials of the Moravian Church*, vol. 1, ed. William Reichel (Philadelphia: Lippincott, 1870), 155–87.

3. See Levering, 166. See also *The Bethlehem Diary*, 1742–1744. Vol. 1 trans. and edited by Kenneth G. Hamilton (Bethlehem, Pa.: Archives of the Moravian Church, 1971), 155: "The girls similarly are to be taken care of in Bethlehem, so soon as their rooms are ready, until such time as Brother Spangenberg will arrive; then all will be properly arranged."

4. A Moravian village community in Lehigh county at the foot of the South Mountain. One of the most important deliberations of the Synod held in Bethlehem in 1748 was the development of the work among the children. For a summary of this period see Levering, 230–33.

5. *Versammlung* refers to a religious meeting or service.

6. Deleted in text: "since the Home increased greatly in size".

7. "Prayer Day" refers to a day of intercession for Moravian work throughout the world, during which letters from Moravians in the other congregations, especially overseas, were read.

8. The Children's House in Germantown was closed for financial reasons, and the girls were brought to Bethlehem and placed in the Ysselstein House on the south side of the Lehigh river. This house was only maintained until a house was vacated in Bethlehem.

9. "Hall" refers to the large room used for worship.

10. A candidate for Holy Communion was allowed to observe the service, either from a gallery, or, in the *Gemeinhaus* in Bethlehem, from an adjoining room.

11. The Hourly Intercessions were one of the first features of the daily order to be established. Their origin stems from the revival of the Church at Herrnhut on August 13, 1727. "Prayer bands" took their turns to pray for an hour from 5 A.M. to midnight. The intention was that there should be continual prayer for the Congregation and its members. This custom exists in modified form today.

12. The sisters slept in one large dormitory but had their own shared sitting rooms.

13. Ps. 51:10 (AV).

14. A verse from Zinzendorf's version of Paul Gerhardt's hymn "O Haupt voll Blut und Wunden," *Londoner Gesangbuch: alt und neuer Brüder-Gesang.* (1753; reprint, Hildesheim: G. Olms, 1980), vol. 2, no. 1095.

15. This is the leading Single Sister assigned to Sister Boehler, with whom she had her "conversations" about the condition of her heart, especially before communion.

16. Township in Lehigh county.

17. War of Independence.

18. Oath of allegiance to the British Crown. Most Moravians in America, especially those actually born in Moravia of Moravian descent, refused to swear oaths on religious grounds.

19. She probably means that the *Gemeinnachrichten* and *Bethlehem Diary* could not get through as well as the regular letters of encouragement.

20. "Plan" refers to an agreed role or set of instructions (in accordance with the Saviour's intentions) and the place or area where it is to be carried out.

21. This was one of the thirty-one preaching places of the Moravian Church which had sprung up between 1742 and 1748. Francis Boehler, the brother of the famous Peter Boehler, ran the school there.

22. Important Moravian congregation founded in 1754 in Lancaster County.

23. The expression "went near to her" means "touched her deeply."

24. For the life story of Magdalene's husband, see the memoir of Ofodobendo Wooma (Andrew), translated in Daniel B. Thorp, "Chattel with a Soul: The Autobiography of a Moravian Slave," *Pennsylvania Magazine of History and Biography* 112 (1988): 433–51. For an extended treatment of Zinzendorf's theory of race and missions as it relates to the writing of spiritual memoirs, see Katherine M. Faull, "Self Encounters: Two Eighteenth-Century African Memoirs from Moravian Bethlehem," in *Cross-Currents: Germany, Africa, and America, in the Modern World;* ed. C. Aisha Blackshire-Belay, Leroy Hopkins and David MacBride (New York: Camden House, forthcoming).

25. Acts 16, v. 14. "One who listened was a woman named Lydia, a dealer in purple goods from the town of Thyatira. She already reverenced God, and the Lord opened her heart to accept what Paul was saying."

26. The chapter in the Book of Isaiah that describes the punishment of Edom and includes the prayers of the people of Israel—that the Lord might once again come to their aid.

27. New Brunswick, New Jersey.

28. At this time in Germany, a burgher of the city was an inhabitant who enjoyed its rights and freedoms and might also able to be chosen as a city councilor.

29. *Die Brüdergemeine.* A literal translation is used here rather than the modern English term, "the Moravian Church."

30. Rhymes in the original.

31. Member of the aristocratic von Schweinitz family from Upper Lusatia who were early supporters of Zinzendorf.

32. Zinzendorf's headquarters, which from 1749–55 were in London, were from 1749–51 in Northumberland House, Bloomsbury Square.

33. Granddaughter (1726–1788) of Father Nitschmann (David), the daughter of Georg Piesch, conductor of the Sea Congregation, Anna Johanna Piesch was one of the leaders of the Congregation from her very youth. She was Eldress of the Single Sisters, niece of Anna Nitschmann, and later wife of Bishop Nathaniel Seidel. See her memoir in the present volume, p. 121–29.

34. Ferdinand Philip Jacob Detmers was for many years the warden of the congregations at Bethlehem, Lititz, and Nazareth.

35. Original German: "kam ich zu fremden leuten."

36. Inserted in the margin: "of these she has had 35 grandchildren and 20 greatgrandchildren; three sons are still living".

37. Inserted in the margin: "Philadelphia".

38. See memoir in this volume.

39. Inserted in the margin: "She was always very patient".

40. Inserted as a footnote: "Of her children three sons are still alive, Peter, Georg, and Martin—the former in Germantown and the two others in the Congregation in Emaus".

41. This is in what is known today as the Saarland.

42. The Moravian mission at Gnadenhuetten on Mahony Creek.

43. Fort Duquesne.

44. Goshgoshing, (or Goschgoschünk) a former Muncee and Delaware village at the mouth of Tionesta Creek, Forest County, settled around 1765. The area is depicted in Christian Schuessele's famous painting of Zeisberger preaching to the Indians.

45. For the sin against the Holy Spirit, see Mark 3:29 and parallels.

46. Township in Lebanon County, bounded in the North by Dauphin County, in the East by Bethel Township, in the south by Lebanon, and the west by Annville.

47. "She had often thought fondly maternal love of her son Thomas, who had been away from her for many years, and although she wished to see him again in this life, she comforted herself with the hope that, if it no longer happened here, she would see him again before the throne of God one day." Inserted in manuscript as footnote.

48. Chief sidesman in the Anglican Church.

49. Moravian farming settlement founded in 1745 on the Nazareth tract. See Levering, 190.

50. Deleted in ms:"my dear mother".

51. Matthew 5:20 (AV).

52. Deleted in ms: "I cannot express the faithfulness of my dear Saviour in words".

53. Deleted in ms: "on November 24".

54. These were a militant band of Huguenots who refused to succumb to the religious tyranny of the Catholic French King, Louis XIV, after the Edict of Nantes in 1675. The sect was best known for the physical manifestations of their inspiration which included speaking in tongues, shaking, convulsions, and prophecy. Their most famous convert was perhaps Mother Ann Lee from Manchester, England, who went on to America to found the Shakers. Zinzendorf disagreed with their teachings vehemently and refused French Prophets entry to Herrnhut when they sought refuge there.

55. The Ronneburg was the castle, a few kilometers from Herrnhaag in which Zinzendorf initially lived before moving to Marienborn and Herrnhaag.

56. A misspelling of Joseph Sturgis, the other man to escape from the attack. See Levering, 311 *passim.*

57. Today known as Lebanon, also on the Swatara, this Moravian settlement was built on the site of the major Indian crossing points of the Swatara, the Quitapahilla. This area was settled by Germans from the Palatinate during 1723–29.

58. A Moravian village near Nazareth.

59. Lehigh Mountain—South Mountain.

60. Johann Christopher Pyrlaeus (1713–1785) was appointed Zinzendorf's "Adjunctant Assistant" in Philadelphia while Zinzendorf was working there as a Lutheran minister in 1742. In his own memoir, Pyrlaeus recounts how while preaching he was "violently drawn from the Pulpit" by a drunken mob on July 29, 1742. After Zinzendorf left Philadelphia in 1743, Pyrlaeus went to Conrad Weiser to learn the Indian languages in order to work as a missionary among them. This he did until 1751 when he was called back to Europe and worked as a minister in England.

61. A Moravian village, better known as Friedensstadt (the German translation of the Indian name), was situated on the west bank of the Beaver River near Slippery Rock Creek, and the Indian village was on the east bank.

62. The Moravian mission settlement of Schoenbrunn (today New Philadelphia in Ohio) was built on the Muskingum River, now known as the Tuscarawas River.

63. This Gnadenhuetten, named after the destroyed Indian village in Pennsylvania, was situated ten miles down the valley from Schoenbrunn. In 1782 almost all the Indian inhabitants of Gnadenhuetten were murdered by European Americans as an act of revenge for the murder of European settlers on the Monongahela by American Indians.

64. According to A. J. Lewis, the Berlin clergy was so opposed to Zinzendorf that no

church was open to him and he therefore preached in his own house. Women were invited on Tuesdays and Thursdays, men on Sundays and Wednesdays. See A. J. Lewis, *Zinzendorf, the Ecumenical Pioneer: A Study in the Moravian Contribution to Christian Mission and Unity* (Philadelphia: Westminster Press, 1962), 124.

65. Livonia is the same as Livland, a Baltic territory which from 1721 belonged to Russia. Zinzendorf enjoyed the hospitality of one of his mother's friends there, Frau von Hallert. For a discussion of pietism in the Baltic States which includes the influence of Zinzendorf and the Moravians there, see W. R. Ward, *The Protestant Evangelical Awakening* (Cambridge: Cambridge Univ. Press, 1992), 144–55.

66. That is, on the day of the Choir Festival of the Single Sisters.

67. Zinzendorf's son, Christian Renatus.

68. At the 1769 Synod in Marienborn the necessity for a readjustment was discussed. The Church was felt to be moving away from its initial enthusiasm and faith, and it was at this Synod that the Church was reorganized. Its new governing body was the Unity Elders Conference, which was composed of three separate departments: the Board of Supervisors who liased with states and outside society; the Board of Helpers or Elders, which had charge over the inner life of the Church; and the Board of Servants which dealt with the financial matters of the Church. The reason for Anna's tears possibly lay in the reading of the farewell letter from the dying Frederick von Watteville, which outlined the ways in which the present day Church had moved away from its honest faith and consciousness of sin.

GLOSSARY

Acolyte (*Acoluth*): A member of the Moravian Church who has been formally marked for lifetime service within the Church but who is not ordained. An acolyte can assist the ordained minister in the distribution of the elements of Holy Communion but cannot administer the sacrament independently.

August 13: One of two chief festival days of the Moravian Church. It was at a communion service in the parish church of Berthelsdorf on August 13, 1727, that the residents of Herrnhut experienced the unity in the spirit that formed than into the community that became the Moravian Church.

Bethlehem Diary: The Bethlehem congregation, like every other Moravian congregation, had the duty to keep a diary that recorded all the important events, actions, and experiences on a daily basis. Copies of these congregational diaries were forwarded to the Church headquarters in Europe. From there a summary account was made up and circulated to all other Moravian congregations around the world in the *Gemeinnachrichten*.

Blessed (*selig*): Term frequently used to denote feelings accompanying intimate association with Jesus the Saviour (*Heiland*). It is also used to refer to a member of the congregation who has died and is now "blessed" in heaven. In this context it is translated as "departed".

Brother (*Bruder*): Term applied to a male communicant member of the Moravian Church. The term is not applied to nonmembers of the Church.

Brother Joseph: Bishop Spangenberg.

Brothers and Sisters (*Geschwister*): Term used when both male and female communicant members of the Moravian Church are being referred to.

Choir: Term used to designate a segment of the congregation constituted of all the individuals of a similar age group and who share the same sex or marital status. In the eighteenth century the system included Choirs of Children, Little Boys, Little Girls, Greater Boys, Greater Girls, Single Brethren, Single Sisters, Married People, Widowers, and Widows. In Bethehem, the Single Brethren, Single Sisters, and Widows lived, labored, and worshipped in close fellowship within their respective Choir Houses.

Choir Festival (*Chorfest*): A special day of prayer and reconsecration put aside for each of the Choirs of the Congregation. March 25—Festival of all the Choirs; April 30—Widows' Choir Festival; May 4—Single Sisters Festival; June 4—

Greater Girls Festival; July 9—Greater Boys Festival; August 17—Children's Choir; August 29—Single Brothers Festival; August 31—Widowers' Choir Festival; September 7—Married People's Festival.

Choir Helper (*Chorpfleger/in*): Person in a Choir to whom the spiritual life of the Choir is entrusted.

Choir Labourer/ess (*Chorarbeiter/in*): An individual appointed to spiritual leadership within a Choir. The term could also be applied to a Choir warden or business manager as well.

Congregation (*Gemeine*): Term commonly used to designate either the Moravian Church as a whole or a single congregation within it. It often is not easy to determine which meaning the word may have in a given case. In this volume "Congregation" denotes the Moravian Church as a whole and "congregation" refers to a single congregation within it.

Congregation Council (*Gemeinrat*): A gathering of the members, which was held weekly during the early period and provided them with an opportunity to consider all matters affecting the life of the congregation. Regulations regarding membership in the body and the degree of authority that it possessed were frequently modified throughout the following years.

Congregation Day (*Gemeintag*): In the eighteenth century this was a monthly congregational festival dedicated to prayer, discussion of matters of moment to the congregation, the reading of letters and reports from other congregations and the mission field, the receiving of members, etc.

Congregation Hour (*Gemeinstunde*): A service attended by the members of the congregation and designed to minister to their spiritual needs. Held usually on a Sunday evening.

Congregational Settlements: Exclusive communities established by the Moravians in various parts of the world. In them only members of the Church could own property (but no land) or carry on business, and only very few friends of the Church were allowed to reside who would agree to observe its regulations. Segregation from the world without was intended to strengthen the members' faith, deepen their convictions, and develop the qualifications they would need when engaging in evangelistic activity among persons indifferent or hostile to the Christian faith. Such settlements, it was also hoped, would be shining examples of Christian piety for the encouragement of earnest believers within other denominations. See also **place congregation.**

Daily Texts: A manual meant to assist congregations or individual members in their daily devotions. The Moravian Church has published it annually since 1731. In the earliest years its format varied considerably. From 1760 on, the watchwords (*Losungen*) and the doctrinal texts (*Lehrtexte*) have been distinguished by the way in which they were selected. Since 1788, the watchword has been drawn by lot from the Old Testament. The Doctrinal Text is not drawn by lot but rather is selected from the New Testament to underscore or expand the thought contained in the watchword. Moravians early came to trust in the spiritual guidance afforded them by the texts for each day. The Daily Texts are now distributed throughout the world and translated into forty-one languages and dialects. It has been described as "probably the most widely read daily devotional guide in the world, next to the Bible."

Deacon/ess (*Diakon/in*): First order of the Moravian ordained ministry. A Moravian deacon can administer the sacraments and rites of the Church and serve as pastor of a congregation. The feminine term was applied sometimes to the wife of a minister, who was also ordained and assisted in the spiritual work among the women of a congregation, and, during Zinzendorf's life, it could also be applied to unmarried women selected for service in the Church.

Diaconie (*Diakonie*): From the Greek *diakoni* meaning "service." The financial organization of the Church as a whole, or of a congregation or a Choir, with special reference to any business carried on in that name.

Disciple's House: See **Pilgrim's House.**

Disciple (*Jünger/Jüngerin*): Zinzendorf or Anna Nitschmann.

Economy/Oeconomie: An extended household that consisted of all the brothers and sisters working and living at a settlement or Indian mission, which included the Indian Moravians.

Elder's Festival (November 13)(*Ältestenfest*): On November 13, 1741, it was announced in the Moravian congregations in Europe that the office of Chief Elder was no longer held by any individual among them. Rather, the Church would look solely to Jesus Christ to guide it as its Chief Elder. This was decided at a conference in London on September 16, 1741. However, until 1748, Bishop Spangenberg was Chief Elder in America. He resigned from that post in November 1748, and on November 13, 1748, the extension of Christ's Chief Eldership to America was proclaimed there.

God's Acre (*Gottesacker*): Term based on St. Paul's figure of speech in I Corinthians 15:42–44 and often used throughout Germany for a graveyard.

Going Home (*Heimgang*): Term applied to the death of a Moravian. It was not used for non-Moravians.

Great Sabbath (*Große Sabbath*): The day before Easter. Moravian congregations frequently held services on the Great Sabbath to commemorate Jesus' day of rest in the tomb before Easter Sunday.

Großhennersdorf: The large country house near Herrnhut belonging to Zinzendorf's grandmother, Henriette Catharine von Gersdorf, in which Zinzendorf grew up and which later served as the Children's House.

Hall (*Saal*): The term was used by the Moravians to designate the place in which the congregation or one of its Choirs met for worship. Even when separate buildings were set apart for worship, the use of this term persisted. Originally, the word resulted from a conscious effort of theirs to distinguish their meetinghouses from the "churches" of other ecclesiastical bodies, the State Churches in particular.

House Congregation (*Hausgemeine*): The members constituting the local resident congregation, who by labor and prayer sustained the nonresident members, or "pilgrims," active in evangelistic or educational work.

Helper (*Helfer/in* or *Pfleger/in*): A church official, usually responsible for the spiritual life of the congregation or one of its Choirs, often the ordained pastor or one of his assistants. When the Helpers meet as a deliberative body it is termed the *Helfer Conferenz*, the head pastor presided as primus inter pares.

Herrnhaag: Founded in 1738, Herrnhaag, built in Wetteravia, was destined to become the second Herrnhut during the 1740s. It was gradually disbanded between 1748–50 after the "excesses" of the previous decade had caused the Congregation to come into disrepute and debt. From it many of the early settlers of Bethlehem had come to America.

Herrnhut: The "mother church" of the renewed Unitas Fratrum, a community founded by Moravian refugees in 1722 on the Berthelsdorf estate of Count Zinzendorf in Saxony.

Hourly Intercessions (*Stundengebet*): This institution grew out of the deep-going revival at Herrnhut on August 13, 1727, and the opposition widely experienced by Moravians around the middle of the eighteenth century. The intercessors were pledged to spend an hour a day in prayer, stated periods being assigned to them so that continuous prayer would be offered by the Church, night and day. This intercession continued unbroken for approximately a century.

Hutberg: The name of the hill on the outskirts of the town of Herrnhut. The "God's Acre" of that community is located on its slopes. In the eighteenth century this name was often substituted by Moravians for the graveyard of their settlement.

Kiss of Peace: See I Peter 5:14. In the apostolic Church the kiss of peace or kiss of love appears to have had a recognized place in its ritual as an expression of brotherly affection and trust. The Moravian custom was a conscious effort to restore this ancient rite. It was most frequently referred to by them as the kiss of peace. In time, the giving of the right hand of fellowship was substituted for this symbol.

Labourer/Labouress (*Arbeiter/in*): A member of the Moravian Church employed full-time to take care of the spiritual well-being of the members of a particular Choir. Term also used to describe ministers of a congregation and their wives, wardens and their wives, and directors of schools and their wives.

Litany of the Wounds (*Wundenlitaney*): Composed by Zinzendorf, his son, Christian Renatus, and Zinzendorf's future son-in-law, Johannes Langguth (later von Watteville) in 1744, the *Wundenlitaney* contains some of the most pervasive and realistic images of Christ's life and Passion. Among Moravians it was a particularly popular and frequently sung litany that, through its drastic representation of Christ's Wounds, enabled the individual to establish a more intimate relationship with the Savior. Despite being the subject of some of the heaviest criticism of the Moravian Church from its opponents, its influence stretches far beyond the 1740s, with images occurring well into the 1770s and 1780s. For the full text, see *12. Anhang zum Herrnhuter Gesangbuch*, No. 1949.

Lot: In the eighteenth century Moravians made frequent use of the lot in an effort to determine the will of the Lord in any situation in which their right course of action was not clear to them. They were convinced that they could in this way rely on Christ's guidance because of their acknowledgment of Him as the Chief Elder of their Church. After a prayer, the Elders would draw one of three lots—there were usually three possibilities, positive, negative, and blank. A blank was interpreted to mean "wait."

Lovefeast (*Liebesmahl*): A service instituted by the Moravian Church in 1727. It has come to represent the New Testament *agape*. In the middle of the eighteenth century it served both as a social gathering and as a happy religious service, offering the members of the Bethlehem congregation one of the few opportunities for relaxation. A Lovefeast could be observed by groups within the church fellowship or by Choirs or by the entire congregation.

Mama: Anna Nitschmann.

Marienborn: A castle in Wetteravia, Germany, leased by Count Zinzendorf as a residence during his banishment from Saxony.

Memoir (*Lebenslauf*): An (auto)biographical account of the life of a member of the Congregation, which was supposed to give special attention to spiritual struggle and progress. The final illness and deathbed scene were described by the Choir Helper. The memoir was preserved and read at the departed's funeral.

Mile End: In the eighteenth century, an English Moravian Girls' School at Mile End, then on the outskirts of London.

November 13th: One of the Moravian Church's two chief festivals or "Memorial Days." It was on November 13, 1741, that Christ was proclaimed as Chief Elder of the European Moravian congregations. On this day in 1741 the Moravian congregations in Europe were officially notified of the decision reached on September 16 that year (see **September 16**). All church members were urged to pledge allegiance and loyalty to their divine Head.

Old style (o.s.)(Julian) calendar; new style (n.s.)(Gregorian) calendar: As the calendar reform of 1582 had decreed that the year should begin on January 1, rather than March 25, 10 days were eliminated from the calendar in 1582. Thus, new style dates were ten days ahead of old style dates until 1700. However, in order that the new calendar was in step with the solar calendar, three leap years were also eliminated from every four centuries. This was done by making each century year which was divisible by 400 a leap year. Thus, 1700 was a leap year according to the old style but not according to the new style, thereby making the difference in the 1700s eleven days. Most European countries accepted the new style; however, until 1752 England did not. Many immigrants to the American colonies used a double calendar system, written in the form of fractions; e.g. 5/16 October where the first date is the old style and the second the new style.

Opportunities: Services.

Ordinary/Ordinarius: Term sometimes applied specifically to Zinzendorf or to the presbyter or priest (second rank of ordained ministry) and hence usually the leading minister of a congregation.

Papa: Zinzendorf.

Pilgrim Congregation (*Pilgergemeine*): In America this term designated those brethren and sisters used by the Church as its missionaries to evangelize all who were willing to hear them, whites, Indians, and Negroes alike, or to preach to those members of other denominations who were without pastoral care, or to teach children who had no opportunity for schooling. In Europe, centering at Marienborn in Wetteravia, the *Pilgergemeine* designated a group of dedicated men and women who were closely associated with Count Zinzendorf and ready at shortest notice to travel from place to place in the service of their Savior.

Pilgrim's House (*Pilgerhaus*): A pilgrim's house was a building in which a pilgrim congregation—or *the* Pilgrim Congregation—lived. The Pilgrim Congregation stood at the head of affairs during the years of Zinzendorf's banishment from Saxony. It consisted of a group of men and women (Zinzendorf and his family and the most prominent menbers of the Moravian Church at that time) which moved from place to place, London, Berlin, Zeist, as was needed to spread the message of Moravianism.

Place Congregation (*Ortsgemeine*): The official term for a congregation settlement, as distinct from a congregation whose members lived in a town that already existed. The **Ortsgemeine** was established by the Moravian Church, and its civic and eccleciastical life was regulated by the Church authorities. In an **Ortsgemeine** an individual had to obtain permission from these authorities to reside in the settlement, to lease land, or trade in it.

Plan: An agreed role or set of instructions (in accordance with the Saviour's intentions) and the place or area where it is to be carried out.

Reception: Men and women were received into a congregation sometimes quite a long time before they became communicant members. The decision whether or not to receive a petitioner into the Congregation was made through use of the lot. See also **Lot.**

Sea Congregation: In the eighteenth century, when a group of Moravians traveled together on shipboard, they permitted their usual activities to be interrupted as little as possible. Thus they organized themselves as a congregation, maintaining services, discipline, physical care of the individual travelers, etc.

September 16: On that day in 1741, during a synodical conference in London, leading Moravians became convinced that it was their Lord's will for them no longer to fill the office of Chief Elder of their denomination but to let their Saviour Himself be their Head and Elder. This day thereafter was observed as a covenanting day for the ministers of the Church.

Servant (*Diener*): In its broader sense this term was used to designate a church official, including an ordained minister in pastoral service. In the 1740s, however, it more frequently signified individuals in charge of temporal affairs, the wardens or supervisors of the congregation or of a Choir. But in a more restricted sense it could also apply to a sacristan. At times it is difficult to be certain which meaning it carries in given cases in the Diary. The official board of Diener, the Diener Collegium, was as a rule presided over by the warden of the congregation.

Sickroom (*Krankenstube*): A room specifically set aside for the care of the sick.

Sickwaitress (*Krankenwärterin*): Nurse.

Singing Hour (*Singstunde*): A service devoted to singing. The congregation would join in a series of hymn stanzas, which the brother or sister in charge of the service had carefully selected to develop some specific devotional theme, thus making the service resemble a sermon in song. Ordinarily no address would be delivered in it, although the service would be opened with prayer.

Sinner (*Sünder*): Term used to denote someone who has acknowledged sinfulness in a given situation, assumed full responsibility for it, and has humbly repented. The adjective form "*sinnerlike*" (*sünderhaft*) is frequently used in the memoirs and has a positive connotation, suggesting humble reliance on the Savior's mercy.

Sister (*Schwester*): Term used to refer to a female communicant member of the Moravian Church. Not used for nonmembers of the Church.

Society (*Societät*): An association of people affiliated with the Moravian church and served by a Moravian minister but not fully organized as a Moravian congregation. Members of a Society usually lived in towns, cities, or surrounding country areas, too far away to allow them to attend services regularly. Membership requirements were less stringent than those for a *Gemeine*.

Speaking (*Sprechen*): On stated occasions, especially prior to Communion, every communicant belonging to a congregation was expected to have a private interview with the pastor or choir helper. In this interview the individual's spiritual life and preparedness to partake of the sacrament was discussed. Speakings sometimes also took place when there were particularly pressing circumstances.

Synod: Highest legislative body in the Moravian Church, composed of clergy and lay delegates from the congregations. In the eighteenth century the administration of the worldwide church was done from Germany, with delegates from other areas participating in the deliberations.

Texts: See **Daily Texts.**

Watchword: See **Daily Texts.**

WORKS CITED

Archival Sources

Archives of the British Province of the Moravian Church, London, Great Britain.
Moravian Archives, Bethlehem, Pa.
Archiv der Brüder-Unität, Herrenhut, Germany.

Primary Sources

Bethlehem Diary, 1742–1744, The. Vol. 1. Translated and edited by Kenneth G.
  Hamilton. Bethlehem, Pa.: Archives of the Moravian Church, 1971.
Londoner Gesangbuch: Alt und neuer Brüder-Gesang. 3 vols. 1753. Reprint. Hildesheim:
  G. Olms, 1980.
Nachrichten aus der Brüdergemeine. Gnadau, Verlag der Unitäts-Buchhandlung,
  1819–94.
Zinzendorf, Nicolaus Ludwig. *Ergänzungsbände zu den Hauptschriften.* Edited by
  Erich Beyreuther and Gerhard Meyer. Hildesheim: G. Olms, 1966.
———. *Hauptschriften in sechs Bänden.* Edited by Erich Beyreuther and Gerhard
  Meyer. Hildesheim: G. Olms, 1965.
———. *Materialien und Dokumente.* Hildesheim: Georg Olms, 1971.

Secondary Sources

Becker, Bernhard. *Zinzendorf im Verhältnis zu Philosophie und Kirchentum seiner Zeit.*
  Leipzig: Hinrich, 1886.
Bettermann, Wilhelm. *Theologie und Sprache bei Zinzendorf.* Gotha: Klotz, 1935.
Beyreuther, Erich. *Studien zur Theologie Zinzendorfs.* Neukirchen: Neukirchener Ver-
  lag, 1962.
Blackwell, Jeannine. "Herzensgespräche mit Gott: Bekenntnisse deutscher
  Pietistinnen im siebzehnten und achtzehnten Jahrhundert." In *Deutsche Literatur
  von Frauen: Vom Mittelalter bis zum Ende des achtzehnten Jahrhunderts,* edited by
  Gisela Brinker-Gabler, vol. 1, 265–89. Beck: München, 1988.
Critchfield, Richard. "Prophetin, Führerin, Organisatorin: Zur Rolle der Frau im

Pietismus." In *Die Frauen von der Reformation zur Romantik,* edited by Bärbel Becker-Cantarino, 112–37. Bonn: Bouvier, 1980.

Dunn, Mary Maples. "Saints and Sisters: Congregational and Quaker Women in the Early Colonial Period." *American Quarterly* 30 (Winter, 1978), 583–95.

Erbe, Helmut. *Bethlehem, Pa: Eine kommunistische Herrnhuter-Kolonie des achtzehnten Jahrhunderts.* Stuttgart: Ausland und Heimat Verlags-Aktiengesellschaft, 1929.

Faull, Katherine M. "The American *Lebenslauf:* Women's Autobiography from Eighteenth-Century Moravian Bethlehem, Pennsylvania." *Yearbook of the Society for German-American Studies* 27 (1992): 23–48.

———. "Faith and Imagination: Nikolaus Ludwig von Zinzendorf's Anti-Enlightenment Philosophy of Self." *Bucknell Review* 38, no. 2 (1995): 23–56.

———. "Self Encounters: Two Eighteenth-Century African Memoirs from Moravian Bethlehem." In *Cross-Currents: Germany, Africa, and America, in the Modern World,* edited by C. Aisha Blackshire-Belay, Leroy Hopkins, and David MacBride. New York: Camden House, forthcoming.

Gollin, Gillian. *Moravians in Two Worlds: A Study of Changing Communities.* New York: Columbia Univ. Press, 1967.

Goodman, Katherine. *Dis/Closures: Women's Autobiography in Germany Between 1790 and 1914.* New York: Lang, 1986.

Hahn, Hans-Christoph, and Hellmut Reichel, eds. *Zinzendorf und die Herrnhuter Brüder: Quellen zur Geschichte der Brüder-Unität von 1722 bis 1760.* Hamburg: Wittig, 1977.

Hamilton, J. Taylor, and Kenneth G. Hamilton. *History of the Moravian Church: The Renewed Unitas Fratrum 1722–1957.* Bethlehem, Pa.: Interprovincial Board of Christian Education, Moravian Church of America, 1967.

Heckewelder, John. *Narrative of the Mission of the United Brethren among the Delaware and Mohigan Indians from Its Commencement in the Year 1740 to the Close of the Year 1873.* Philadelphia: n.p., 1823.

Levering, Joseph Mortimer. *A History of Bethlehem Pennsylvania 1741–1892 with Some Account of Its Founders and Their Early Activity in America.* 1903. Reprint. New York: AMS, 1971.

Lewis, A. J. *Zinzendorf the Ecumenical Pioneer: A Study in the Moravian Contribution to Christian Mission and Unity.* Philadelphia: Westminster Press, 1962.

Lockwood, J. P. *Memorials of the Life of Peter Boehler.* London: n. p., 1868.

Mason, Mary. "The Other Voice: Autobiography of Women Writers." In *Autobiography: Essays Theoretical and Critical,* edited by James Olney, 207–35. Princeton: Princeton University Press, 1980.

Meyer, Dietrich. *Bibliographisches Handbuch zur Zinzendorf-Forschung.* Dusseldorf: C. Blech, 1987.

Moeschler, Felix. *Alte Herrnhuter Familien.* Herrnhut: Missionsbuchhandlung, 1922.

Neumann, Bernd. *Identität und Rollenzwang: Zur Theorie der Autobiographie.* Frankfurt: Athenäum, 1970.

Niggl, Günter. *Geschichte der deutschen Autobiographie im achtzehnten Jahrhundert.* Stuttgart: Klett, 1977.

———. "Zur Säkularisation der pietistischen Autobiographie im achtzehnten Jahrhundert." In *Prismata,* edited by Dieter Grimm et al, 155–72. Pullach bei München: Verlag Dokumentation, 1974.

Pfister, Oskar. *Die Frömmigkeit des Grafen Ludwig von Zinzendorf. Eine psychoanalytische Studie.* 1925. Reprint. Neudeln, Liechtenstein, 1970.

Preus, Samuel J. "Secularizing Divination: Spiritual Biography and the Invention of the Novel." *Journal of the American Academy of Religion* 59 (1991): 441–66.

Reichel, Hellmut. "Ein Spiegel der Frömmigkeit und des geistlichen Lebens: Zur Geschichte des brüderischen Lebenslaufes." *Brüderbote* 464 (March 1988): 4–7.

Reichel, Jörn. *Dichtungstheorie und Sprache bei Zinzendorf: Der 12. Anhang zum Herrnhuter Gesangbuch.* Bad Homburg: Gehlen, 1969.

Reichel, William, ed. "Annals of Early Moravian Settlement in Georgia and Pennsylvania." *Memorials of the Moravian Church.* Vol. 1, 155–87. Philadelphia: Lippincott, 1870.

Renkewitz, Heinz. *Im Gespräch mit Zinzendorfs Theologie: Vorträge aus dem Nachlaß.* Hamburg: Wittig, 1980.

Řičan, Rudolph. *The History of the Unity of the Brethren: A Protestant Hussite Church in Bohemia and Moravia.* Translated by C. Daniel Crews. Bethlehem, Pa.: Moravian Church in America, 1992.

Riley, Jobie E. "An Analysis of the Debate Between Johann Conrad Beissel and Various Eighteenth Century Contemporaries Concerning the Importance of Celibacy." Ph.D. diss., Temple Univ., 1974.

Ruether, Rosemary, and Rosemary Keller. *In Our Own Voices: Four Centuries of American Women's Religious Writing.* San Francisco: Harper and Row, 1995.

Ruether, Rosemary Radford, and Catherine Prelinger. "Women in Sectarian and Utopian Groups." In *Women and Religion in America,* edited by Rosemary Ruether and Rosemary Keller, vol. 2, 260–315. San Francisco: Harper and Row, 1983.

Schofield, Mary Anne. " 'Womens Speaking Justified': The Feminine Quaker Voice, 1662–1797." *Tulsa Studies in Women's Literature* 6 (1987): 61–77.

Schweinitz, Edmund de. *Some Fathers of the American Moravian Church.* Bethlehem: n.p., 1881.

Shea, Daniel B., Jr. *Spiritual Autobiography in Early America.* 1968. Reprint. Princeton: Princeton University Press, 1988.

Smaby, Beverly Prior. *The Transformation of Moravian Bethlehem: From Communal Mission to Family Economy.* Philadelphia: Univ. of Pennsylvania Press, 1988.

Stoeffler, Ernst. *German Pietism During the Eighteenth Century.* Leiden: Brill, 1973.

Thorp, Daniel B. "Chattel with a Soul: The Autobiography of a Moravian Slave." *Pennsylvania Magazine of History and Biography* 112 (1988): 433–51.

Ulrich, Laurel Thatcher. "Vertuous Women Found." *American Quarterly* 28 (Spring 1976): 20–40.

Uttendörfer, Otto. *Zinzendorf christliches Lebensideal.* Gnadau: Verlag der Unitätsbuchhandlung, 1940.

———. *Zinzendorf und die Frauen.* Herrnhut: Missionsbuchhandlung, 1919.

———. *Zinzendorf und die Mystik.* Berlin: Christlicher Zeitschriften Verlag, 1952.

Vogt, Peter. "Zinzendorf und die Pennsylvanischen Synoden 1742." *Unitas Fratrum* 36 (1994): 5–62.

Wallace, Paul. *The Travels of John Heckewelder in Frontier America.* 1958. Reprint. Pittsburgh: Pittsburgh Univ. Press, 1985.

Ward, W.R. *The Protestant Evangelical Awakening.* Cambridge: Cambridge Univ. Press, 1992.

Watt, Ian. *The Rise of the Novel.* Berkeley: Univ. of California Press, 1966.

Zeisberger, David. *Herrnhuter Indianermission in der Amerikanischen Revolution: Die Tagebücher von David Zeisberger, 1772–1781.* Ed. Hermann Wellenreuther aud Carda Wessel. Berlin: Akademie Verlag, 1995.

Zinzendorf, Nicholas Ludwig von. *Texte zur Mission,* edited by Helmut Bintz. Hamburg: Friedrich Wittig, 1979.

INDEX